Healthcare Fraud

Healthcare Fraud

Auditing and Detection Guide

REBECCA S. BUSCH

BICENTENNIAL
1807
WILEY
2007
BICENTENNIAL

John Wiley & Sons, Inc.

Library of Congress Cataloging-in-Publication Data:
Busch, Rebecca S.
  Healthcare fraud: auditing and detection guide / Rebecca S. Busch.
    p. ; cm.
  Includes index.
  ISBN 978-0-470-12710-0 (cloth: alk. paper)
1. Medicare fraud.   2. Medicaid fraud   3. Medical care—Law and legislation—United States–Criminal provision.   I. Title.
[DNLM: 1. Fraud—prevention & control.   2. Computer Security.
3. confidentiality.   4. Fraud—economics.   5. Medical Records—standards. W 32.1 B977h 2008]
  KF3608.A4B87 2008
  345.73′0263—dc22

                                           2007028028

Printed in the United States of America

10 9 8 7 6 5 4 3 2

In dedication to my grandmothers, Rebecca and Gregoria, and my mother, Francisca, who have modeled perseverance; and to my father, Alberto, who has modeled incontrovertible truth.

Contents

Preface

Before reading this book, recall an experience in your personal or professional life, preferably both, in which you have been told a lie, believed it, and acted on it. Hold onto that thought and then ask yourself, "Why? What gut reaction did I ignore? What clues did I miss? What evidence walked by me?" Follow those questions with, "What price did I pay personally or professionally?"

That is the frame of reference required to appreciate the behind-the-scenes look that the charts, tables, diagrams, rules, and audit to-do lists used throughout this book give you. In the course of all life experiences—and in particular audit, detection, and investigation—seeking 20/20 vision is the objective. This vision is further enhanced by the ability to see what no one else has seen. Each chapter begins with a reflective quote that has inspired the work contained within. The book progresses by providing the building blocks for understanding the entire healthcare market and its respective players. Intertwined throughout this book is subject matter and skill set expertise. The cases and methodologies presented provide actual audit and investigative tools. Theoretical applications are identified and include those from various studies and established organizations. The case studies are actual public cases in addition to cases on which I have worked personally. Some of them are modified in detail, location, and names to avoid identification.

I believe the greatest masters of innovation are failure, fear, and survival. The methodologies and tools that I use in my practice are explained in this book, with the goal being to answer any question presented at any point in the healthcare continuum. Keep in mind that it is a process of learning. By no means is this book represented to cover all possible scenarios. It is presented from lessons learned with the expectation that it will complement your own evolving experiences. Further, methods and checklists should evolve with ongoing regulatory changes and emerging market tools. New questions that cannot be answered within the current models will generate new algorithms within the audit checklists noted in this book. The concepts of theft, waste, and abuse, of course, remain the same.

The school of hard knocks has resulted in my drive to share and teach all I have learned about audit and detection of healthcare fraud. I write this book to share with others processes that I have developed to reach a state of incontrovertible truth. As new challenges and unique behaviors of the ethically challenged enter the market, updates on concepts will be provided. That aside, the tools provided in this book are structured to move with market changes.

My background gives me a number of different perspectives. I started off as a nurse and evolved into the role of a medical auditor for a hospital. Internal audit expertise now complements my clinical background. This role involved setting up internal controls for documentation and reimbursement-related issues. Finance was required to move to the next level. My career progressed to setting up audit programs for insurance carriers. In 1991, I started my own company, Medical Business Associates, with the idea of taking clinical folks and training them on audit and finance. During this time period, my audit experience led me into employer advocacy of healthcare benefits, and thus into more audit programs for controlling employee healthcare expenses. All roles involved data analytics and research. The introduction of investigation and fraud was a natural evolution. In between I have audited on behalf of patients and other ancillary market players. In each context, scenarios involving ethically challenged behavior have presented themselves, leading me to get involved with forensics and disputes. The legal world often requires experts to "answer that question" or "contribute to the tier of facts." Finally, the detailed avenues of this process have been filed in a patent referred to as an *anomaly tracking system* that integrates some of the concepts in this book. Thus, this book is written from a number of perspectives—clinical, research, internal audit, investigative, data intelligence, and forensic.

Why is healthcare so complex? The healthcare market is fragmented, layered, and segmented. Why is it so difficult to manage? We have too many current and changing rules, too many relationships, and too many old dynamics whose historical and political roots are often lost or forgotten.

What have we created in healthcare? A Tower of Babel! While the market attempts to correct itself and U.S. legislative and executive branch politicians most likely pursue their sixth attempt since 1927 for national healthcare reform, use this book as a navigation guide to break apart and discover all the relationships involved and to answer whatever questions are at hand. The goal is to create a common language to understand the events in question.

A general comment on fraud: Outside of the legal context of its definition, simply view it as individuals or entities taking things that do not belong to them. Do not bury yourself in one particular market player such as "provider" fraud. The ethically challenged can look like providers, but also like payers, employers, plan sponsors, patients, and vendors. This guidebook is structured to identify what is normal at any point in the healthcare continuum on both individual and aggregate scales, the assumption being that everything else is *abnormal*. The building blocks contained within this book will help you whether you are just beginning your career or are an experienced professional looking for an out-of-the-box perspective or a new set of application skills.

The world of healthcare fraud is my passion. It is much more than just stealing money or a corporate asset. Healthcare fraud steals the very essence of human life. Stories include false claims by perpetrators who perform needless procedures that disable or kill, fake insurance broker or inappropriate payer denials that leave a patient disabled or with an untimely death, and fake drugs that hit a 16-year-old liver transplant survivor who almost loses his life while taking a counterfeit adulterated drug critical to his survival. The list of examples is shocking and demoralizing, and generates a sense of hopelessness and a book in and of itself. More disturbing is that the world of healthcare fraud has become one of high-tech, highly skilled, educated, and professional perpetrators.

When was the last time you witnessed a consumer walking into a used car dealership with his guard up? Always! Unlike buying cars, healthcare is a personal, intimate experience with a high level of trust from a patient who most likely is in a compromised physical and emotional state. In other words, the guard is naturally down. With this in mind, if anything I have written and shared within this book helps any party prevent, detect, and shut down a perpetrator, then I will consider that my greatest accomplishment. Thank you for taking the time to learn and participate in this very important subject.

Acknowledgments

Personal acknowledgments cannot go without thanking my whole family for support and for instilling a fountain of youth for learning. I especially want to acknowledge my children, Samantha, Andy, and Albert. They have taught me more about life than any degree or credential.

Professionally as of this writing, I have over 100 combined articles and presentations. A special thank-you to all the students and professionals who have participated in my classes, read my articles, e-mailed responses to my questions, and shared their experiences. These experiences have generated insight and thought-provoking conversations, all of which have contributed to the writing of this book. Finally, in my own professional development, a thank-you to all professors and academic organizations that continue to educate and refine my understanding of this subject.

CHAPTER 1

Introduction to Healthcare Fraud

Truth is often eclipsed but never extinguished.

—LIVY, HISTORIAN (59 B.C.–A.D. 17)

When Willie Sutton, an infamous twentieth-century bank robber, was asked why he robbed banks, he replied, "Because that's where the money is." The healthcare industry, too, has lots of money. Long considered a recession-proof industry, healthcare continues to grow. Statistics from the Centers for Medicare and Medicaid Services (CMS), formally known as the Healthcare Financing Administration, show that, in 1965, U.S. healthcare consumers spent close to $42 billion. In 1991, that number grew in excess of $738 billion, an increase of 1,657 percent. In 1994, U.S. healthcare consumers spent $1 trillion. That number climbed to $1.6 trillion in 2004, which amounted to $6,280 per healthcare consumer. The figure is expected to hit over $2.2 trillion by 2008, which translates to about $250 million per hour.

How many of these annual healthcare dollars are spent wastefully? Based on current operational statistics, we will need to budget $550 billion for waste. A trillion-dollar market has about $329.2 billion of fat, or about 25 percent of the annual spending figure. The following statistics are staggering in their implications:

- $108 billion (16 percent) of the above is paid improperly due to billing errors. (Centers for Medicare and Medicaid Services, www.cms.gov)

- $33 billion of Medicare dollars (7 percent) are illegitimate claims billed to the government. (National Center for Policy Analysis, www.ncpa.org)

- $100 billion private-pay dollars (20 percent) are estimated to be paid improperly. (www.mbanews.com)

- $50 billion (10 percent) of private-payer claims are paid out fraudulently. (Blue Cross/Blue Shield, www.bcbs.com)

- $37.6 billion is spent annually for medical errors. (Agency for Healthcare Research and Quality, www.ahrq.gov)

- Ten percent of drugs sold worldwide are counterfeit (up to 50 percent in some countries) (www.fda.gov). The prescription drug market is $121.8 billion annually (www.cms.gov), making the annual counterfeit price tag approximately $12.2 billion.

What do these statistics mean? About $25 million per hour is stolen in healthcare in the United States alone. Healthcare expenditures are on the rise and at a pace faster than inflation. The fight against bankruptcy in our public and privately managed health programs is in full gear.

Use this how-to book as a guide to walk through a highly segmented market with high-dollar cash transactions. This book describes what is normal so that abnormal becomes apparent. Healthcare fraud prevention, detection, and investigation methods are outlined, as are internal controls and anomaly tracking systems for ongoing monitoring and surveillance. The ultimate goal of this book is to help you see beyond the eclipse created by healthcare fraud and sharpen your skills as an auditor or investigator to identify incontrovertible truth.

WHAT IS HEALTHCARE FRAUD?

The *Merriam-Webster Dictionary of Law* defines fraud as

> any act, expression, omission, or concealment calculated to deceive another to his or her disadvantage; specifically: a misrepresentation or concealment with reference to some fact material to a transaction that is made with knowledge of its falsity or in reckless disregard of its truth or

falsity and with the intent to deceive another and that is reasonably relied on by the other who is injured thereby.

The legal elements of fraud, according to this definition, are

- Misrepresentation of a material fact
- Knowledge of the falsity of the misrepresentation or ignorance of its truth
- Intent
- A victim acting on the misrepresentation
- Damage to the victim

Definitions of healthcare fraud contain similar elements. The CMS website, for example, defines fraud as the

> Intentional deception or misrepresentation that an individual knows, or should know, to be false, or does not believe to be true, and makes, knowing the deception could result in some unauthorized benefit to himself or some other person(s).

The Health Insurance Portability and Accountability Act (HIPAA) of 1996 is more specific, defining the term *federal health care offense* as "a violation of, or a criminal conspiracy to violate" specific provisions of the U.S. Code, "if the violation or conspiracy relates to a health care benefit program" 18 U.S.C. § 24(a).

The statute next defines *health care benefit program* as "any public or private plan or contract, affecting commerce, under which any medical benefit, item, or service is provided to any individual, and includes any individual or entity who is providing a medical benefit, item, or service for which payment may be made under the plan or contract" 18 U.S.C. § 24(b).

Finally, *health care fraud* is defined as knowingly and willfully executing a scheme to defraud a healthcare benefit program or obtaining, "by means of false or fraudulent pretenses, representations, or promises, any of the money or property owned by . . . any health care benefit program" 18 U.S.C. § 1347.

HIPAA establishes specific criminal sanctions for offenses against both private and public health insurance programs. These offenses are consistent with our earlier definitions of fraud in that they involve false statements, misrepresentations, or deliberate omissions that are critical to the determination of benefits payable and may obstruct fraud investigations.

Healthcare fraud differs from healthcare abuse. *Abuse* refers to

- Incidents or practices that are not consistent with the standard of care (substandard care)
- Unnecessary costs to a program, caused either directly or indirectly
- Improper payment or payment for services that fail to meet professional standards
- Medically unnecessary services
- Substandard quality of care (e.g., in nursing homes)
- Failure to meet coverage requirements

Healthcare fraud, in comparison, typically takes one or more of these forms:

- False statements or claims
- Elaborate schemes
- Cover-up strategies
- Misrepresentations of value
- Misrepresentations of service

What Does Healthcare Fraud Look Like?

It is important to appreciate that healthcare is a dynamic and segmented market among parties that deliver or facilitate the delivery of health information, healthcare resources, and the financial transactions that move along all components. To fully appreciate what healthcare fraud looks like, it is important to understand traditional and nontraditional players. The patient is the individual who actually receives a healthcare service. The provider is an individual or entity that delivers or executes the healthcare service. The payer is the entity that processes the financial transaction. The plan sponsor is the party that funds the transaction. Plan sponsors include private self-insurance programs, employer-based premium programs, and government programs such as Medicare and Medicaid. A vendor is any entity that provides a professional service or materials used in the delivery of patient care.

What does healthcare fraud look like from the patient's perspective? The patient may submit a false claim with no participation from any other party. The patient may exaggerate a workers' compensation claim or allege that an injury took place at work when in fact it occurred outside of work. The patient may participate in collusive fraudulent behavior with other parties. A second party may be a physician who fabricates a service for liability compensation. The patient may be involved in an established crime ring that involves extensive collusive behavior, such as staging an auto accident. The schemes repeat themselves as well as evolve in their creativity.

SAMPLE PATIENT FRAUD CASE

At an insurance company, all payments of foreign claims are made to insured's and not to foreign medical providers. An insured patient submitted fictitious foreign claims ($90,000) from a clinic in South America, indicating that the entire family was in a car accident. A fictitious police report accompanied the medical claims. A telephone call to the clinic revealed that the insured and the dependents were never treated in the clinic.

What does healthcare fraud look like from the provider's perspective? The fraud schemes can vary from simple false claims to complex financial arrangements. The traditional scheme of submitting false claims for services not rendered continues to be a problem. Other activities, such as submitting duplicate claims or not acknowledging duplicate payments, are issues as well.

Some schemes demonstrate great complexity and sophistication in their understanding of payer systems. One example is the rent-a-patient scheme where criminals pay "recruiters" to organize and recruit beneficiaries to visit clinics owned or operated by the criminals. For a fee, recruiters "rent," or "broker," the beneficiaries to the criminals. Recruiters often enlist beneficiaries at low-income housing projects, retirement communities, or employment settings of low-income wage earners. Detecting complicated misrepresentations that involve contractual arrangements with third parties or cost report manipulations submitted to government programs requires a niche expertise.

SAMPLE PROVIDER EMPLOYEE FRAUD CASE

A woman who was affiliated with a medical facility had access to claim forms and medical records. She submitted claims for heart surgery, gall bladder surgery, finger amputations, a hysterectomy, and more—27 surgeries in all. The intent was to cash in on the checks for the services. The anomaly was that if a patient has surgery, a corresponding hospital bill should have been submitted and it was not.

What does healthcare fraud look like from the payer's perspective? The fraud schemes in this group tend to be pursued mostly in response to transactions between the payer and a government plan sponsor. They include misrepresentations of performance guarantees, not answering beneficiary questions on claims status, bad-faith claim transactions, and financial transactions that are not contractually based. Other fraudulent activities include altering or reassigning the diagnosis or procedure codes submitted by the provider. Auditing payer activities requires a niche expertise in operational as well as contractual issues.

SAMPLE PAYER FRAUD CASE

A third-party administrator (TPA) processing claims on behalf of Medicare signed a corporate integrity agreement (CIA) with the Department of Justice (CIAs are discussed later in this book) in response to a number of allegations by providers that the TPA (1) failed to process claims according to coverage determinations; (2) failed to process or pay physicians' or other healthcare claims in a timely fashion, or at all; (3) applied incorrect payments for appropriate claims submissions; (4) inaccurately reported claims processing data to the state, including a failure to meet self-reporting requirements and impose self-assessment penalties as required under the managed care contract with the state; (5) failed to provide coverage of home health services to qualified beneficiaries; (6) automatically changed CPT-codes (current procedural terminology codes, used to explain the procedure provided); (7) did not recognize modifiers (modifiers are additional codes that providers submit to explain the service provided); and (8) did not reliably respond to appeals from patients, sometimes not responding at all or waiting over 6 to 12 months to do so.

What does healthcare fraud look like from the employer's perspective? Schemes include underreporting the number of employees, employee classifications, and payroll information; failing to pay insurance premiums, which results in no coverage; creating infrastructures that make employees pay for coverage via payroll deductions; engaging in management activities that discourage employees from seeking medical treatment; and referring employees to a medical facility and in turn receiving compensation for the referrals.

SAMPLE EMPLOYER FRAUD CASE

An employer who colludes with applicants to receive benefits illegally or who commits fraud to avoid taxes will be penalized at least $500, and may also be prosecuted. Collusion is knowingly helping applicants obtain benefits to which they are not entitled, for example, cash wages or other hidden compensation for services performed. In other words, the employer misrepresents the eligibility of the applicant so that he or she can receive benefits not qualified for.

What does healthcare fraud look like from a vendor's perspective? This category has numerous examples that involve a range of participants, from professional healthcare subcontractors to suppliers of equipment, products, services, and pharmaceuticals. These schemes include false claims, claims for altered products, counterfeit medications, and unlicensed professionals. They include collusive behavior among several entities as well as between individual professionals.

A third-party medical billing company, Emergency Physician Billing Services, Inc. (EPBS), provided coding, billing, and collections services for emergency physician groups in over 100 emergency departments in as many as 33 states. Based on allegations presented by a *qui tam relator* (whistleblower reporting a fraud), the United States charged that EPBS and its principal owner, Dr. J. D. McKean, routinely billed federal and state healthcare programs for higher levels of treatment than were provided or supported by medical record documentation. EPBS was paid based on a percentage of revenues either billed or recovered, depending on the client.

In a second case, a supply vendor delivered adult diapers, which are not covered by Medicare, and improperly billed them as expensive prosthetic devices called "female external urinary collection devices."

In a third example of a vendor fraud case, an ambulance company billed ambulance rides for trips to the mall.

Overall, healthcare fraud schemes target one of the following:

- Pursuit of money
- Avoidance of liability
- Malicious harm
- Competitive advantage
- Research and product market advantage
- Addiction
- Theft of personal effects
- Theft of individual and/or corporate identity

HEALTHCARE FRAUD IN THE UNITED STATES

Healthcare fraud is growing at an accelerated rate in the United States. Traditional schemes include false claim submissions, care that lacks medical necessity, controlled substance abuse, upcoding (billing for more expensive procedures), employee-plan fraud, staged-accident rings, waiver of co-payments and deductibles, billing experimental treatments as nonexperimental ones, agent–broker fraud relationships, premium fraud, bad-faith claim payment activities, quackery, overutilization (rendering more services than are necessary), and kickbacks. Evolved schemes include complex rent-a-patient activities, 340 B program abuse activities (setting aside discounted drugs, making them unavailable to those in need), pill-mill schemes (schemes to falsely bill prescriptions), counterfeit drug activities, and organized criminal schemes.

HEALTHCARE FRAUD IN INTERNATIONAL MARKETS

Healthcare fraud knows no boundaries. The U.S. Medicare and Medicaid programs are equivalent to many government-sponsored programs in other countries. Regardless of country, the existence and roles of players within the healthcare continuum are the same. All healthcare systems have patients, providers, TPAs (third-party administrators) that process reimbursements to third parties, plan sponsors (usually government programs or private-pay activities), and support vendors.

Examples of international healthcare fraud are plentiful. In France, a psychiatric nursing home took advantage of patients to obtain their property. In 2004, a newspaper in South Africa reported that "a man who posed as a homeopathic doctor was this week sentenced to 38 years in jail—the stiffest term ever imposed by a South African court on a person caught stealing from medical aids." An Australian psychiatrist claimed more than $1 million by writing fake referrals of patients to himself; he also charged for the time spent having intimate relations with patients.

In Japan, as in the United States, there are examples of hospitals incarcerating patients, falsifying records, and inflating numbers of doctors and nurses in facilities for profit. A U.K. medical researcher misled his peers and the public by using his own urine sample for 12 research subjects. Switzerland, known for its watches, had providers sanctioned for billing 30-hour days. All of these examples include patterns of behavior consistent with the definitions of healthcare fraud in the United States.

WHO COMMITS HEALTHCARE FRAUD?

Do not limit your imagination or develop tunnel vision when it comes to healthcare fraud. Fraud is committed anywhere and by anyone. The list includes providers; insured patients; individuals, both domestic and foreign; approvers (employees) who pay claims to themselves or friends; rings, or a group of criminals who commit healthcare fraud; nonproviders, or non-medical, nonrelated healthcare players who create fraud schemes; payers, agents, and personnel; and vendors and suppliers providing services within the healthcare industry. They are found as employers providing benefit coverage; personnel employed by providers, payers, employers, or various vendors; and formal organized crime entities. The key element as to who they are is always defined by the defrauder's *action*, not by his or her title or role. The literature focuses heavily on provider fraud. Limiting the focus on a particular player in the market merely creates opportunities for other players to concentrate their efforts on areas not receiving the same attention, thus potentially bleeding the system dry.

Regardless, a key element of healthcare fraud (or of any type of fraud, regardless of industry) is that the individuals who commit these types of frauds tend to have no conscience. For example, consider those who suffer from antisocial personality disorder (APD). This disorder affects about 4 percent of the population. That number represents about 11,840,512 individuals in the United States. Worldwide, 4 percent represents about 257,553,015 individuals. In essence, then, there are potentially 269 million people with the perfect psychological profile to commit fraud.

APD should be considered when an individual possesses at least three of the following seven characteristics: (1) failure to conform to social norms; (2) deceitfulness, manipulativeness; (3) impulsivity, failure to plan ahead; (4) irritability, aggressiveness; (5) reckless disregard for the safety of self or others; (6) consistent irresponsibility; (7) lack of remorse after having hurt, mistreated, or stolen from another person. How do you look for clues of APD? First, note examples of outrageous logic—for example, this statement from Al Capone:

> "I am going to St. Petersburg, Florida, tomorrow; let the worthy citizens of Chicago get their liquor the best they can. I am sick of the job—it's a thankless one and full of grief. I have been spending the best years of my life as a public benefactor."

Another clear sign is direct denial of an event, "I never did that," regardless of any incontrovertible evidence. In addition, look for statements that are inconsistent with known events. Follow this by noting examples of inconsistent emotional responses under similar circumstances within the subject's life, lack of any emotional responses at all, or inconsistent emotional responses in comparison to social norms. Finally, another hallmark sign is a series of failures due to lack of planning and consistent irresponsibility in various walks of life.

WHAT IS HEALTHCARE FRAUD EXAMINATION?

Auditing and investigating healthcare fraud is about seeing beyond the eclipse created by defrauders and deciphering *who, what, where, when, why,* and *how.* It is about creating an archaeological road map into the discovery of truth. Audit and investigative techniques excavate information that appears to have been extinguished.

To *examine* means "to observe carefully or critically; inspect" or "to study or analyze" an issue (*American Heritage Dictionary,* 4th ed.). Fraud examination, then, is the thorough inspection, study, or analysis of an issue relating to fraud. The Association of Certified Fraud Examiners (ACFE) is an organization dedicated to the study of fraud across all industry sectors. It is a global professional association providing antifraud information and education to help members fight fraud effectively. As of this writing, the ACFE has 40,000 members in 125 countries; its 103 local chapters provide education, outreach, and networking opportunities. In its coursework, the ACFE provides the figure describing fraud examination shown in Exhibit 1.1.

One common type of fraud examination is forensic analysis, which reconstructs a past event using the health data transactions made by some or all of the parties shown in Exhibit 1.2; that reconstruction is often used in some judicial proceeding (e.g., criminal court, civil court, deposition, mediation, arbitration, settlement negotiation, plea bargaining) (www.acfe .com).

The blend of both figures illustrates the cyclical and often contemporaneous nature of forensic healthcare analysis. In Exhibit 1.3, note that five major players use recognized operational structures, or business functions.

| Fraud Prevention |
| Fraud Deterrence |
| Fraud Detection |
| Fraud Investigation |
| Fraud Loss and Costs Recovery |
| Antifraud Controls Remediation |
| Antifraud Education and Training |

EXHIBIT 1.1   **ACFE Fraud Examination**

Source: Association of Certified Fraud Examiners (www.acfe.com).

These structures include the patient, the provider, the payer, the employer, and the vendor. Healthcare as an industry is unique in that one episode of care at some given time will hit three or more operational systems. This understanding is critical from a forensic perspective because your ability to conduct a forensic analysis of one entity often requires an understanding of at least one other entity in this continuum. Due to the increasing amount of

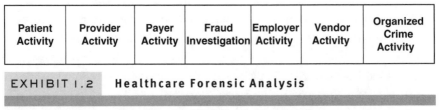

Patient Activity	Provider Activity	Payer Activity	Fraud Investigation	Employer Activity	Vendor Activity	Organized Crime Activity

EXHIBIT 1.2   **Healthcare Forensic Analysis**

Source: Medical Business Associates, Inc. (MBA) (www.mbanews.com).

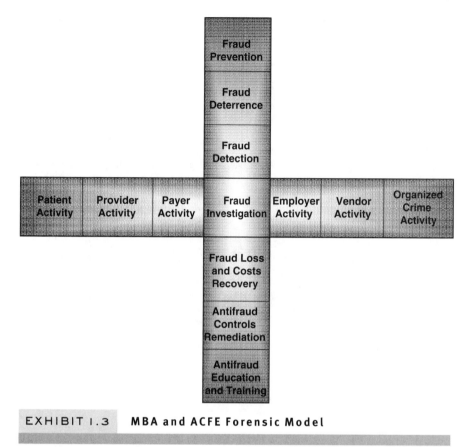

EXHIBIT 1.3   MBA and ACFE Forensic Model

Source: Association of Certified Fraud Examiners (www.acfe.com) and Medical Business Associates, Inc. (www.mbanews.com).

fraud by outside parties, organized crime is given its own designation within this continuum.

THE HEALTHCARE CONTINUUM: AN OVERVIEW

The healthcare continuum (HCC) is shown in Exhibit 1.4 as a diagram representing entities that can and will most likely impact an episode of care. The chapters that follow this one break down the components of this diagram and introduce new terms. The HCC includes health information pipelines (HIPs) for each market player. In addition, this book will guide you through the monetary transactions referred to as *accounts receivable pipelines*

Health Care Continuum (HCC): Follow the $ and PHI

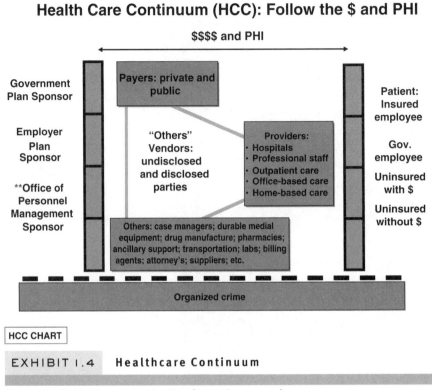

HCC CHART

EXHIBIT 1.4   Healthcare Continuum

Source: Medical Business Associates, Inc. (www.mbanews.com).

(ARPs), which are monetary transactions as well as audit trails of protected health information (PHI). In the HCC model, money is viewed as equivalent to PHI. Note in Exhibit 1.4 that each entity has PHI generated or processed. At each transfer point, money is generated or processed at the same time. Exhibit 1.4 shows organized crime as a disconnected illegitimate third party. It is given its own designation as an entity because of the growing number of complex organized crime schemes integrated into the normal flow of business.

HEALTHCARE FRAUD OVERVIEW: IMPLICATIONS FOR PREVENTION, DETECTION, AND INVESTIGATION

Job security for fraud auditors and investigators remains strong: The healthcare industry continues to have large amounts of cash running through it. It continues to attract the ethically challenged, whose stealing from the system shows no sign of stopping. Implications are many, particularly in the areas of prevention, detection, and investigation. These three areas require a detailed understanding of every legitimate and illegitimate player in the HCC, an ability to identify HIPs and ARPs, and an understanding of how PHI is utilized among all of the players.

It is important not only to understand how the HCC works, but also to follow healthcare market trends and how they impact fraud prevention, detection, and investigation. Fraud usually begins with a tip. That tip leads to an investigation. A comprehensive investigation requires you to understand the dynamics of the healthcare business. Healthcare fraud is often buried within the critical business functions. The purpose of the HIP and ARP process is to identify the functions that should be investigated. Detection will follow once an understanding has been achieved. Investigations and detections will identify vulnerabilities that in turn should be used as prevention tools. Prevention requires an understanding of how the healthcare entity functions and the cycle repeats itself.

With all aspects of auditing and investigations, keep current on activities that are initiated by the Department of Health and Human Services (HHS) and its Office of the National Coordinator for Health Information Technology (ONC). For example, in 2006, initiatives were made on the development and nationwide implementation of an interoperable health information technology infrastructure to improve the quality and efficiency of healthcare; one objective is to eventually convert all current health records to electronic versions.

On October 17, 2005, the ONC published two reports: "Report on the Use of Health Information Technology to Enhance and Expand Health Care Anti-fraud Activities" (www.hhs.gov/healthit/documents/ReportOnThe Use.pdf) and "Automated Coding Software: Development and Use to Enhance Anti-fraud Activities" (www.hhs.gov/healthit/documents/Auto maticCodingReport.pdf).

One of the major findings that emerged from the field research done for the "Report on the Use of Health Information Technology" was that fraud in the healthcare context is defined in many different ways by a number of legal authorities, but all definitions have common elements: a false representation of fact or a failure to disclose a fact that is material to a healthcare transaction, along with some damage to another party who reasonably relies on the misrepresentation or failure to disclose. The report identifies healthcare fraud as a serious and growing nationwide crime that is directly linked to the nation's ever-increasing annual healthcare outlay.

The report continues with the reference that in the calendar year 2003, healthcare expenditures amounted to $1.7 trillion (Centers for Medicare and Medicaid Services, www.cms.hhs.gov/TheChartSeries/downloads/us_health_chap1_p.pdf).

In that same year, estimated losses due to fraud were 3 to 10 percent of the total amount of healthcare expenditures, or $51 to $170 billion. Another finding compared the healthcare industry to the financial services industry. The report noted that the healthcare industry is in a strikingly similar position to that of the financial services industry 15 years ago. At that time, the banking industry began its transformation from a paper system to a sophisticated electronic environment. With a well-thought-out vision and strategy, the banking industry addressed the inefficiencies of paper systems and invested heavily in the information technology infrastructure. Credit card fraud, estimated today to be less than 7 cents out of every 100 dollars, is widely perceived as a major problem. However, healthcare fraud is 100 times more costly.

The report focuses also on the role of technology. Its authors believe that technology can play a critical role in detecting fraud and abuse and can help to pave the way toward prevention. Although technology cannot eliminate the fraud problem, it can significantly minimize fraud and abuse and ultimately reduce healthcare fraud losses. The use of advanced analytics software built into the national health information network (NHIN) is critical to fraud loss reduction.

Information available via the NHIN must comply with all federal and state laws. The federal government continues to expand its initiatives to uncover healthcare fraud, waste, and abuse. It is important that healthcare organizations have an effective compliance program in place. It is particularly important to develop a corporate culture that fosters ethical behavior. Many healthcare organizations are developing such corporate cultures through the adoption of corporate compliance programs.

The ONC is expected to release a second report in 2007. Expect continued follow-up from this office on electronic healthcare record formats that will impact future audits and investigations over the next ten years.

CHAPTER 2

Defining Market Players within the Healthcare Continuum

Since time is a continuum, the moment is always different, so the music is always different.

—HERBIE HANCOCK

To understand, detect, and then prevent healthcare fraud, it is important to understand the concept of the healthcare continuum (HCC), which was introduced in Chapter 1. Although the players in the HCC do not change significantly, the movement within and among each player is always slightly different, creating the same effect as that described by musician Herbie Hancock. Each fraud scheme generated by the ethically challenged is different, too. The individual, professional, or entity involved reacts to the "music" or healthcare event in part using whatever unique experiences, understandings, emotional states, and levels of sophistication are possessed at the time the event is experienced.

THE PATIENT

Who Is the Patient?

A patient is any person who receives medical attention or some type of clinical care or treatment, usually from a physician or other type of medical professional. This type of care is often viewed from the illness model perspective, which emphasizes the illness or health crisis rather than prevention. With evolving wellness models that emphasize illness prevention and maintenance of good health, a more appropriate term may be health consumer, healthcare consumer, or client.

According to *Merriam Webster's Collegiate Dictionary*, the word *patient* is derived from the Latin word *patiens*, the present participle of the verb *pati*, which means "to endure" or "to suffer." *Patient* is also the adjective form of *patience*. Both senses of the word share a common origin.

Traditionally, the term *patient* has implied a parent–child type of relationship between patient and healthcare provider, one that in a sense placed the patient in an inferior position relative to that of the provider. However, the role of the patient is changing. Programs such as consumer-directed health plans rearrange the traditional parent–child-like relationship and place the patient, renamed the consumer, in the driver's-seat role in directing healthcare needs. The term *consumer* also implies a financial relationship as the purchaser of a healthcare service.

A perfect example is from a personal friend who approached me regarding the choice of an obstetrician. "How do I select a doctor who is right for me?" she asked. I gave her the names of three highly recommended physicians and suggested that she schedule three interview appointments and then select a doctor. When she expressed surprise at my suggestion, I asked her, "How much time do you spend researching the purchase of a car? Which decision is more important, the purchase of a car or the delivery of your child?" The wrong time to learn about a physician is when he or she is directing you to "push" or shares during your postoperative recovery that you were the first person he or she has ever performed this type of surgery on. You discover that your doctor is just as excited as you are that you are awake, alert, and on the road to recovery!

With the rise of the electronic world comes the arrival of the e-patient. The e-patient is the evolving patient consumer who uses the Internet to obtain a variety of health information. In addition, this e-patient may use a variety of intranet solutions if offered by his or her doctor, an increasingly common practice among today's healthcare providers. Electronic tools continue to evolve to help healthcare consumers manage their own and their families' health information while also coordinating care among e-caregivers, which provide electronic tools for finding resources and support. (For one example of an e-caregiver, go to the website of the West Central Florida Area Agency on Aging, at www.agingflorida.com.)

In 1998, the President's Advisory Commission on Consumer Protection and Quality in the Health Care Industry drafted a Consumer Bill of Rights and Responsibilities in which it noted several main principles for protecting healthcare consumers. (The Commission's statement is available in full at www.hcqualitycommission.gov/cborr/exsumm.html.) First, on the subject of information disclosure, the Commission stated that consumers have a right to receive information in a timely fashion, as well as receive it in a form that they can easily understand. If information is not easily understood, then assistance should be provided to facilitate that understanding. Information should include

- *Health plans:* Covered benefits, cost-sharing, and procedures for resolving complaints; licensure, certification, and accreditation status; comparable measures of quality and consumer satisfaction; provider network composition; procedures that govern access to specialists and emergency services; and care management information
- *Health professionals:* Education and board certification and recertification; years of practice; experience performing certain procedures; and comparable measures of quality and consumer satisfaction
- *Healthcare facilities:* Experience in performing certain procedures and services; accreditation status; comparable measures of quality and worker and consumer satisfaction; procedures for resolving complaints; and community benefits provided (www.hcqualitycommission.gov/cborr/exsumm.html)

Second, "consumers have the right to a choice of healthcare providers that is sufficient to ensure access to appropriate high-quality health care." This includes a participating network of providers that is sufficient to meet the demands of the group. The network should have access to qualified specialists for women's health services as well as access to specialists in general.

Third, "consumers have the right to access emergency health care services when and where the need arises." Plans should not deny payment for services when consumers seek care at an emergency room for acute symptoms, including severe pain or conditions for which "a 'prudent layperson' could reasonably expect the absence of medical care to result in placing that consumer's health in serious jeopardy, serious impairment to bodily functions, or serious dysfunction of any bodily organ or part."

Fourth, consumers have a right to be involved in the decision-making process. It is expected that "consumers have the right and responsibility to fully participate in all decisions related to their health care. Consumers who are unable to fully participate in treatment decisions have the right to be represented by parents, guardians, family members, or other conservators."

Fifth, "consumers have the right to considerate, respectful care from all members of the health care system at all times and under all circumstances. An environment of mutual respect is essential to maintain a quality healthcare system."

The sixth right involves confidentiality. "Consumers have the right to communicate with health care providers in confidence and to have the confidentiality of their individually identifiable health care information protected." In addition, consumers have the right "to review and copy their own medical records and request amendments to their records." The Health Insurance Portability and Accountability Act (HIPAA) provisions note that providers are obligated to respond to these requests for amendments.

The seventh right involves complaints and appeals. As a consumer of a health plan, the individual has a right to a process in which he or she can communicate disagreements as well as receive a response with a qualified review of the complaint. The appeals process should involve competent staff as well an independent process. For example, notifications by the health plan should be timely with appropriate notification and basis for any denial decision. Resolutions and responses to appeals should also be conducted in a timely fashion. The claim review process should be conducted by professionals with the appropriate credentials and those who were not involved with the initial decision. The follow-up notifications should be in writing and include information on the reason for the determination and instructions on utilizing an external party for further appeals.

The external appeals process should have several characteristics. First, it should be available to the consumer after all internal processes have been exhausted. The only exceptions are with urgent cases of acute care needs. It should "apply to any decision by a health plan to deny, reduce, or terminate coverage or deny payment for services based on a determination that the treatment is either experimental or investigational in nature; apply when such a decision is based on a determination that such services are not medically necessary and the amount exceeds a significant threshold or the patient's life or health is jeopardized." As with the initial appeal process, the professionals involved need to be appropriately credentialed with respect to the subject of the treatment in question. Conflict of interest should be noted, and no part of the appeals process should be conducted by parties who were involved with the initial decision. The decisions should be evidenced based on objective data. Any emergency or acute care issues should utilize the Medicare Standard of 72 hours for a response.

Although the purpose of the Commission's Bill of Rights is to protect the consumer, it also encourages the consumer to accept certain responsibilities:

- Take responsibility for maximizing healthy habits, such as exercising, not smoking, and eating a healthy diet.
- Become involved in specific healthcare decisions.
- Work collaboratively with healthcare providers in developing and carrying out agreed-upon treatment plans.
- Disclose relevant information and clearly communicate wants and needs.
- Use the health plan's internal complaint and appeal processes to address concerns that may arise.
- Avoid knowingly spreading disease.
- Recognize the reality of risks and limits of the science of medical care and the human fallibility of the healthcare professional.
- Be aware of a healthcare provider's obligation to be reasonably efficient and equitable in providing care to other patients and the community.
- Become knowledgeable about his or her health plan coverage and health plan options (when available) including all covered benefits, limitations, and exclusions, rules regarding use of network providers, coverage and referral rules, appropriate processes to secure additional information, and the process to appeal coverage decisions.
- Show respect for other patients and health workers.

- Make a good-faith effort to meet financial obligations.
- Abide by administrative and operational procedures of health plans, healthcare providers, and government health benefit programs.
- Report wrongdoing and fraud to appropriate resources or legal authorities. (www.hcqualitycommission.gov/cborr/exsumm.html)

Further legislation continues to focus on the following issues:

- The right of a patient's medical decision to be made by a doctor
- The right to see a specialist
- The right to go to the closest emergency room
- The right to designate a pediatrician as a primary care doctor for children
- The right to see a medical specialist
- The right to keep the same doctor throughout a patient's medical treatment
- The right to obtain prescription drugs as prescribed by a doctor
- The right to access a fair and independent appeal process if care is denied
- The right to hold a health plan accountable for harm done

What Are Some Examples of Patient Fraud?

When an individual patient perpetuates a fraud scheme against his or her own health plan, it is often called *beneficiary fraud*. Examples of recipient fraud are numerous and include submitting false claims for services never rendered, colluding with doctors to submit multiple claims for services that were provided only once, and working with doctors to make uncovered healthcare services appear to be like ones that are covered by the insurance plan.

Other forms of recipient fraud are submitting claims for multiple office visits to cover noninsured family members or altering claims forms or receipts from providers to receive higher reimbursement for out-of-pocket services. With the increasing issue of prescription abuse, recipients may request excessive drugs, or alter prescriptions, and even create counterfeit prescriptions for reimbursement in addition to access to medications that are not medically necessary. Other areas of abuse include excessive psychotherapy treatments and individuals submitting claims for services allegedly received while traveling abroad.

Finally, the individual patient may participate in a more complex and organized fraud scheme. These examples include crime rings that stage accidents in which individuals falsify injuries and subsequent care. Another complex fraud scheme is called *rent-a-patient*. In this scheme, patients participate in "renting" their bodies to fraudulent providers, who then perform unnecessary procedures to submit to the patients' benefit plans for reimbursement.

How Does the Patient Role Relate to Other Healthcare Continuum Players?

In initiating a fraud scheme, a patient can act independently or collude with any of the other market players in the HCC, for example, by having a provider misrepresent a diagnosis. The patient also could participate in an organized criminal enterprise such as one involved in staging an accident to submit a series of false claims and litigation. Finally, an increasing role for the patient is that of fraud victim. Offenses against patients range from receiving services that are not medically necessary to having their personal information stolen and used to submit claims against their health insurance plans or to create new credit cards in their names. Unfortunately, these victims may not find out until they need to utilize a service and their benefits have run dry or until collection agencies are at the front door.

THE PROVIDER

Who Is the Provider?

The Hospital   The hospital traditionally has been a facility or institution in which healthcare services are provided by physicians, surgeons, nurses, and other healthcare professionals. The hospital provider role has an extensive history that dates centuries back.

Throughout world history, religion and medicine have been linked. In the ancient Greek culture, temples were built for the Greek god of healing, Asclepius. Romans adopted the practice of worshipping sculapius, as they named him, building a temple to him on the island of Tiber in Rome (291 B.C.) (Roderick E. McGrew, *Encyclopedia of Medical History* [New York: Macmillan, 1985], pp. 134–135).

Hospitals in medieval Europe were also based in religious communities. Care was typically provided by monks and nuns, and some hospitals were attached to monasteries. During this time the focus was on managing illnesses or creating hospice-like environments. Many hospitals had a specific purpose such as caring for lepers or providing a refuge for the poor. Within the medieval Islamic world, Muslim hospitals started to focus on standard of care sometime between the eighth and twelfth centuries. Hospitals built in Baghdad in the tenth century actually employed physicians with separate wards for different conditions.

Hospitals in the modern era started sometime in the eighteenth century when institutions began to serve medical needs and create staffs containing physicians and surgeons. In Berlin, for example, the institution Charité was founded in 1710. The theme of treating the poor carried over onto the shores of America. The nation's first hospital was founded by Dr. Thomas Bond and Benjamin Franklin in 1751, "to care for the sick-poor and insane who were wandering the streets of Philadelphia" (www.uphs.upenn.edu/paharc/features/creation.html).

Until this point, these institutions were funded primarily by third parties—that is, by parties other than patients. Third parties also were responsible for the direction and provision of care. Our present-day third-party model, then, is centuries old. Keep this history in mind as you read through this book and appreciate the current market shift of putting the consumer into the driver's seat. The shift of patient from recipient of care directed by another party to consumer who directs his or her own care represents a significant change from approximately 2,500 years of history.

As history moved forward, the public model for the sick evolved into private-model hospitals for patients who were sick and not poor. By the mid-nineteenth century, most European countries and the United States had developed a variety of both public and private hospital systems. Funding of these institutions was generally public. Germany established the first national system of compulsory sickness insurance in 1883. In the United States, mutual benefit societies offered prepaid medical care in the early part of 1900. Third-party relationships with respect to delivery of patient care and its funding have evolved significantly since this time. Today, most hospitals are funded by a blend of public and private funds.

In 1945, Harry S. Truman announced that he wanted compulsory insurance. Within ten years from this announcement, for-profit hospital

EXHIBIT 2.1 Timeline for the Development of For-Profit Hospitals and Other Market Activities

Payer Activity	Growth Rate	National Spending in millions*	Year	Event
			1929	Baylor Hospital contracts with local teachers to pre-pay hospital services
			1930	Blue Cross adopts community-based pricing for health insurance
			1930–1940	Private payers emerge with risk-based models, target low-risk insureds
			1940	Blue Cross joins private risk-based pricing models, targets low-risk insureds
			1945	Truman tells congress he wants a nationalized healthcare plan
$12.90		$117	1950	Payer market; research expenditures $117 million
			1956	Incorporation of MedLabs Inc (later known as AMI—American Medical International)
			1956	Not-for-profit Parkview Hospital built in Nashville, TN, a project led by Dr. Thomas Frist
		$27,534	1960	Partnerships between lawyer Richard Eamer and lawyers Cohen and Bedrosian formed—founders of National Medical Enterprises (NME)
	53%		1960	MedLabs bought its first hospital
			1960	Public outcry on lack of insurance for elderly and other outcast high-risk individuals
$40.70		$42,174	1965	Medicare and Medicaid implemented
			1965	MedLabs changed its name to AME (American Medical Enterprises)
		$1.5	**1965**	Government research expenditures hit $1.5 billion, up 1,824%
		$52,062	1967	AME made a hospital **purchase** in London—first European hospital management company
		$59,012	1968	Dr. Frist and Jack Massey formed a for-profit hospital management company (HCA)
			1968	National Medical Enterprises was incorporated in California
		$66,396	1969	For-profit NME (National Medical Enterprises) **purchases** several not-for-profit hospitals

(Continued)

EXHIBIT 2.1 (Continued)

25%	$83,266	1971	AME **purchased** Chanco Medical Industries (owner of 24 hospitals)
	$92,975	1972	AME changed its name to AMI
	$220,444	1979	HCA **owns** 140 hospitals
	$253,916	1980	AMI **bought** Hyatt Medical Enterprises (owner of 8 hospitals)
253%	$294,182	1981	AMI **purchased** Brookwood Health Services (owner of 11 hospitals)
	$330,736	1982	The Tax Equity and Fiscal Responsibility Act mandates development of inpatient PPS system
	$365,333	**1983**	Medicare Prospective Payment System (DRGs) became effective for 1,500 hospitals
	$402,282	1984	HealthSouth was incorporated in Delaware as Amcare by founder Richard Scrushy
		1984	AMI **purchased** Lifemark Corporation (owner of 25 hospitals)
	$439,876	1985	Amcare changed its name to HealthSouth
	$573,990	1988	AMI sold 104 hospitals in response to declining revenues
	$714,019	1990	AMI merged with AMH (American Medical Holdings)
	$714,019	1990	The Omnibus Budget Reconciliation Acts of 1986 and 1990 mandate an outpatient PPS system
166%	$781,611	1991	NME owned 150 hospitals; they agreed to pay **$1 billion** settlement for fraudulent billing practices, **$132 million** in settlements with patients
	$962,196	1994	NME owned hospitals in Singapore, Australia, Malaysia, Thailand, Indonesia, United Kingdom, Spain, and Switzerland
	$1,016,503	1995	NME merged with America Medical International (AMI) and renamed itself Tenet Healthcare
		1995	Australia restricted NME activities; eventually NME sold international interests
		1997	Tenet Healthcare merged with OrNda for **$3.2 billion**
	$1,125,381	1997	Blue Shield of California paid **$12 million** to settle allegations that it filed false claims for payment under its contract with the government to process and pay Medicare claims

	$1,190,890	1998	Tenet Healthcare paid **$12 million** in fraud settlement charges on behalf of OrNda's past conduct
		1998	The Canadian for-profit LifeMark Health was founded
		1998	BCBSIL pleaded guilty to Medicare fraud charges for the years 1985 through 1994 and agreed to pay $144 million in fines to the federal government, the largest penalty assessed against a Medicare claims processor for fraud
	$1,353,256	2000	HCA pays **$840 million** settlement for Medicare fraud
		2000	APCs take affect
122%	$1,733,436	2003	For-profit HealthSouth was accused of a **$1.4 billion** accounting scandal of value inflation
	$1,987,689	2005	Founder Scrushy of HealthSouth was acquitted
		2005	AmeriChoice of Pennsylvania agreed to settle false claim processing activity for **$1.6 million**
		2006	Founder Scrushy of HealthSouth was convicted of bribery
		2006	Tenet paid **$725 million** settlement for Medicare fraud
		2006	HealthSouth agrees to pay **$445 million** to settle investor lawsuits

*CMS statistics.

Source: Statistics are from the Centers for Medicare and Medicaid Services (CMS) (www.cms.hhs.gov).

chains began to develop. Note in Exhibit 2.1 what happens before Medicare was implemented and the aggressive growth of spending afterward. The government-sponsored programs of Medicare and Medicaid do appear to have impacted corporate medicine.

Providers include an ever-growing list of specialty-type facilities, such as these:

- Acute surgical centers
- Cancer centers
- Children's hospitals
- Clinic facilities
- Emergency medical clinics
- Geriatric hospitals
- Medical research centers
- Psychiatric hospitals
- Trauma centers
- University hospitals

The Professional   The historical focus on the professional provider of care begins with the physician. A physician is a person who practices biological medicine. In the United States, the term *physician* is used to describe a variety of medical professionals. The United States provides licenses for four types of physicians. The first is an *allopathic* physician, who holds an *MD* (Medical Doctor) designation:

> Medicine (or biomedicine) is the science of maintaining or restoring human health through research and the study, diagnosis, treatment, and prevention of disease and injury. Historically an illness-based science, it is now intermingled with both wellness maintenance as well as curative and/or illness management.

The practice of allopathic medicine dates back to the seventh century. Medical doctors are trained in evidence-based schools of medicine and are regulated by the American Association of Medical Colleges. They are licensed to practice in all 50 states, the District of Columbia, and the U.S. territories of Puerto Rico and the Virgin Islands.

The second type of physician is an *osteopathic* physician who holds a *DO* (Doctor of Osteopathy) designation. Osteopathic medicine (formerly known as *osteopathy*) is

> a complete system of medical care with a philosophy that combines the needs of the patient with current practice of medicine, surgery, and obstetrics. The emphasis is on the interrelationship between structure and function, and has an appreciation of the body's ability to heal itself. (www.aacom.org/om/Glossary.pdf)

Osteopathy was founded by Andrew Taylor Still, MD (1828–1917). Osteopathic doctors, like medical doctors, are licensed to practice in all fifty states, the District of Columbia, and the U.S. territories of Puerto Rico and the Virgin Islands.

The third type of physician is a *naturopathic* physician, who holds the designation of *ND* (Doctor of Naturopathy):

> Naturopathic medicine (also known as naturopathy) is a school of medical philosophy and practice that seeks to improve health and treat disease chiefly by assisting the body's innate capacity to recover from illness and injury. Naturopathic care may include treatments such as manual therapy, hydrotherapy, herbalism, acupuncture, counselling, environmental medicine, aromatherapy, wholefoods, and cell salts.

The term *naturopathy* was coined before 1900 by John Scheel. Naturopathic physicians currently are licensed in 15 states—Alaska, Arizona, California, Connecticut, District of Columbia, Hawaii, Idaho, Kansas, Maine, Montana, New Hampshire, Oregon, Utah, Vermont, Washington— and the U.S. territories of Puerto Rico and the Virgin Islands.

The fourth type of physician is a Doctor of *Chiropractic*, designated as *DC*:

> Chiropractic Medicine seeks to diagnose, treat, correct, and prevent neurological, skeletal, or soft tissue dysfunction by employing spinal and other articular adjustments and manipulations.

The chiropractic approach was founded in 1895 by Daniel David Palmer. Other professional health disciplines include podiatry, dentistry, and psychiatry. *Podiatrists* receive a license designation of Doctor of Podiatric Medicine (*DPM*). *Podiatry* is the art and medical science of treating the lower extremity with a focus on the foot and ankle. The professional care of feet dates back to the Egyptians with carvings designating the art in the care of the feet. Hippocrates in his writing noted the treatment regimen for calluses and corns of the feet.

Dentists receive a Doctor of Dental Surgery (*DDS*) degree or Doctor of Dental Medicine (*DMD*) degree. Dentistry is the art and science of prevention, diagnosis, and treatment of conditions, diseases, and disorders of the oral cavity, the maxillofacial region, and its associated structures as it relates to human beings. Dentistry traces its history back 9,000 years, according to a group of anthropologists who in 2006 reported the discovery of sophisticated drilling techniques used to treat dental decay in what is now Pakistan (news.bbc.co.uk/1/hi/sci/tech/4882968.stm). In the United States, the first school of dentistry opened in Maryland in 1840 at the Baltimore College of Dental Surgery.

A *psychiatrist* has the designation of MD and is considered a medical specialist who deals with the prevention, assessment, diagnosis, treatment, and rehabilitation of mental illness. The primary goal of psychiatry is the relief of mental suffering associated with mental disorders such as schizophrenia and improvement of mental well-being. *Psychologists*, on the other hand, are not licensed doctors. They are typically professionals who have doctoral degrees or advanced training in clinical, counseling, industrial, or educational psychology. Psychologists must meet the respective licensing criteria for their state.

Physician specialties continue to evolve. The following is a sample list of those terms:

- Anesthesiology
- Dermatology
- Emergency medicine
- General practice (family medicine)
- Internal medicine
- Neurology
- Nuclear medicine
- Occupational medicine
- Pathology
- Pediatrics

- Physical medicine and rehabilitation
- Preventive medicine
- Radiation oncology
- Radiology
- Surgery

Physician subspecialties also exist, for example:

- Allergy and immunology
- Cardiology
- Endocrinology
- Gastroenterology
- Hematology
- Infectious diseases
- Intensive care medicine (critical care medicine)
- Medical genetics
- Nephrology
- Oncology
- Pulmonology
- Rheumatology

Surgical specialties include

- Andrology
- Cardiac surgery
- Colon and rectal surgery
- General surgery
- Hand surgery
- Interventional neuroradiology
- Neurological surgery
- Obstetrics and gynecology
- Ophthalmology
- Oral and maxillofacial surgery

- Orthopedic surgery
- Otolaryngology (ENT)
- Pediatric surgery
- Plastic surgery
- Surgical oncology
- Thoracic surgery
- Transplant surgery
- Trauma surgery
- Urology
- Vascular surgery

Numerous other healthcare professionals deliver or contribute to patient care. These roles include

- Dietitians
- Emergency room technicians
- Laboratory scientists
- Nurses
- Occupational therapists
- Paramedics
- Pharmacists
- Physiotherapists
- Radiographers
- Respiratory therapists
- Speech therapists

Specialty services provided by these professionals continue to grow as well and include these examples:

- Advance practice nursing
- Audiology
- Dietetics
- Emergency medical services
- Epidemiology

- Medical technology
- Midwifery
- Occupational therapy
- Optometry
- Pharmacy
- Physical therapy (physiotherapy)
- Physician assistant
- Podiatry
- Public health
- Respiratory therapy
- Speech and language pathology

What Are Some Examples of Provider Fraud?

Examples of provider fraud range from submitting claims for services never rendered to misrepresentation of actual services to various accounting irregularities within provider costs reports. Here is a list of examples:

- *Clustering*—used to simplify coding for services where a range of codes may apply, for example, billing for a middle-level code.
- *Controlled-substance abuse*—pharmaceutical diversions (billing for brand-name drugs while dispensing generic drugs, doctor hopping).
- *DRG creep*—assignment of a patient to a higher-paying diagnosis-related group (DRG).
- *Experimental treatment*—submitting a claim for an uncovered experimental treatment under a covered code.
- *Excessive fees*—billing Medicare or Medicaid substantially in excess of usual charges.
- *False cost reports*—cost reports with false or fraudulent information. Examples are incorrect apportionment of costs, inclusion of non-covered services or equipment in allowable costs, claims for bad debts without a genuine attempt to collect payment, depreciation of assets that have already been fully depreciated, and statistic manipulation to obtain additional payment.

- *Hospital gain-sharing arrangements*—an arrangement in which a hospital gives physicians a percentage share of any reduction in the hospital patient care costs attributable in part to the physician's efforts. This arrangement risks limiting services to recipients.

- *Improper modifiers*—codes that alter the basic code. These often result in higher reimbursements.

- *Improper billing for observation patients*—Medicare requirements for billing of observation patients.

- *Kickbacks*—payment to another individual in order to receive a referral or to undergo treatment.

- *Manufacturing: 340 B program abuse*—providers or entities diverting manufactured discounted drugs to unqualified recipients.

- *Medical necessity*—emerging definitions and criteria in the area of abuse. Billing for services and items (durable medical equipment, etc.) not medically necessary.

- *Misrepresentation*—intentionally misrepresenting any of the following for purposes of manipulating the benefits payable:

  - The nature of services, procedures, and/or supplies provided
  - The dates on which the services and/or treatment were provided
  - The medical record of service and/or treatment provided
  - The condition treated or the diagnosis made
  - The charges or reimbursement for services, procedures, and/or supplies provided
  - The identity of the provider or the recipient of services, procedures, and/or supplies

- *Outpatient activity*—billing for "inpatient-only" procedures, violating local medical review policies, incorrect claims for ancillary services, and circumventing multiple procedure discounting rules.

- *Overutilization*—the deliberate performance of unwarranted/non-medically necessary services for the purpose of financial gain.

- *Patient dumping and substandard care*—violating the Social Security Act and Emergency Medical Treatment and Active Labor Act (EMTALA) statutes on properly screening, stabilizing, and treating individuals regardless of ability to pay. Failures include the insufficient operation of the emergency room department in screening and treating; inappropriate transfers.

How Does the Provider Role Relate to Other Healthcare Continuum Players?

The provider is the second key player in the HCC. The relationship between the patient and the provider is contemporaneous, fluid, and fluctuating. With respect to the provider's role, it is important to understand that the provision of care can come from many different types of professionals within many different settings. The history of one patient alone can involve a number of different providers who have treated the patient in various facilities throughout the course of the patient's lifetime. This makes the individual patient's file fragmented. With respect to any general audit or investigation, it is important to understand and appreciate the complexity and fragmentation of just one individual file, let alone a group of patients. With this in mind, the primary reason for committing fraud is money. Therefore, it is important to understand the dynamics of the next player.

THE PAYER

Who Is the Payer?

The payer is literally the one the pays the bill. An interesting quote appeared in a 1919 publication from the *Insurance Monitor* in response to the idea of health insurance:

> the opportunities for fraud [in health insurance] upset all statistical calculations. . . . Health and sickness are vague terms open to endless construction. Death is clearly defined, but to say what shall constitute such loss of health as will justify insurance compensation is no easy task. (July 1919, vol. 67(7), p. 38)

Imagine the insight looking back from 2007. The payer in the HCC is important to understand in terms of its history and its contribution toward the fragmentation in the market today.

With respect to the provision of health insurance, our history timetable takes us to Germany, which in 1883 initiated its compulsory nationalized health insurance program. Many other European countries followed suit. Compulsory nationalized health insurance was attempted in the early part of U.S. history, but it was never successfully passed.

The early part of the 1900s had progressive improvement in the delivery of medicine and treatment of patients. Along with this came increasing demand and costs associated with healthcare services. In 1929, a group of Dallas teachers contracted with Baylor University Hospital to provide 21 days of hospitalization a year for a fixed fee of $6. This model eventually set the stage for health insurance programs in the United States. Blue Cross/Blue Shield emerged from this model. The concept of the prepaid hospital service plan continued to grow. This plan proved effective during the 1930s, when patients and hospitals suffered from falling revenue streams. The physician market eventually was included as part of the reimbursement model.

After the success of the Blue Cross/Blue Shield plan, the market grew at an accelerated rate with commercial companies providing health insurance offerings. According to the *Source Book of Health Insurance Data*, 1965, the number of enrollees in 1940 started under 20 million and rose to 130 million by 1960. By 1952, private commercial carriers were exceeding the enrollment figures of Blue Cross/Blue Shield. At the same time that health insurance plans were becoming more popular, the 1942 Stabilization Act limited wage increases that employers could offer employees. This made the provision of employee insurance plans an especially attractive form of additional compensation. The idea of a benefit package that included healthcare benefits was one form of attracting workers. This remains true today.

The term *third-party administrator* (TPA) is an American business term used in the field of claims processing. A TPA is a contracted agency that processes healthcare claims on behalf of another entity. The risk of any loss remains with the entity that sponsors the benefit plan. In this market, sponsors most typically are self-insured employers. A self-funded healthcare plan involves an employer financing the healthcare costs of its employees by contracting with a TPA to administer the employer's plan. It is not unusual for a self-insured employer to also contract with a reinsurer to pay any amounts in excess of a certain threshold to help minimize or share risk for catastrophic events.

Another typical plan sponsor is a government-funded program such as Medicare, whose monies are sponsored through tax contributions. It is the same concept as a self-insured employer. The government contracts with a TPA to administer the government-sponsored plan on behalf of its qualifying beneficiaries.

Health insurance companies gamble that the prepaid amounts collected will exceed the actual expenditures to treat the patients within their plans. When the employer is self-insured, it in essence is taking on the risk itself. In the marketplace are business entities that work only as TPAs. The marketplace also includes insurance companies that sell risk-based insurance as well as TPA services to self-insured entities.

Remember that a private insurance policy is a contract between the insurance company and the customer. What is important to understand is exactly who the customer is. For example, when an employer contracts with an insurance company, the employer is the customer. It is not the patient or recipient of care. The employer is purchasing a benefit for its employee to receive benefits according to the terms of the contract with the insurance carrier. Typically the only relationship between the insurance company and the patient is that the patient is just a user of the plan. If an individual purchases the insurance product, however, then the relationship changes; the patient becomes the customer. Similarly, in the relationship between the patient and the provider, the patient is the customer. These two sets of relationships provide a sample of market conflict. This is a subtle but very important concept to understand. In the course of any audit or investigation, at some point you are reviewing motivation and drivers among the players. Financial and clinical accountability change depending on exactly who the buyer is and who the customer is in the transaction.

With respect to accountability and complex regulatory environment, one key foundation is important to understand. In any plan that is being administered by a self-insured employer, the employer's plan document is governed and impacted by the Employee Retirement Income Security Act of 1974 (ERISA):

> The Employee Retirement Income Security Act of 1974 (ERISA) is a federal law that sets minimum standards for most voluntarily established pension and health plans in private industry to provide protection for individuals in these plans.
>
> ERISA requires plans to provide participants with plan information including important information about plan features and funding;

provides fiduciary responsibilities for those who manage and control plan assets; requires plans to establish a grievance and appeals process for participants to get benefits from their plans; and gives participants the right to sue for benefits and breaches of fiduciary duty. (www.dol.gov/dol/topic/health-plans/erisa.htm)

If the consumer is purchasing an insurance plan from the carrier, most likely any issues that require resolution will be impacted by the respective state insurance commission.

Medicare and Medicaid started in 1965 as part of the Social Security Act. The Medicare program's initial focus was to provide Americans over the age of 65 with select coverage. It was not intended as a program to provide comprehensive healthcare coverage. In 1977, the Health Care Financing Administration was created under the Department of Health, Education, and Welfare (HEW) to effectively coordinate Medicare and Medicaid. The Health Care Financing Administration is known today as the Centers for Medicare and Medicaid Services. The 1972 Social Security Amendments expanded Medicare to provide coverage for disabled persons receiving cash benefits for 24 months under the Social Security program and persons suffering from end-stage renal disease.

On December 8, 2003, President George W. Bush signed the Medicare Prescription Drug Improvement and Modernization Act into law. Medicare Part D now provides coverage for prescription medications.

Today, according to the Centers for Medicare and Medicaid Services, almost all large U.S. employers offer health insurance to their employees. However, the percentage of large firms offering these benefits to retired employees fell from 66 percent in 1988 to 34 percent in 2002. Rising costs of care and of insurance coverage is leading toward an increase in the number of uninsured.

What Are Some Examples of Payer Fraud?

First, the rise of health insurance coverage opens the door to the first type of vulnerability. The selling of fake insurance is in response to the high cost of coverage and targets those who have limited access to options. These plans are typically initiated by organized crime entities. These entities profit significantly by collecting premiums on fake insurance policies. Fake insurance targets small employers and individual consumers. Nothing can be more devastating than the diagnosis of a terminal illness or a sudden injury, except if you top off such a devastating health outcome with a devastating financial blow: being left with debts of hundreds of thousands of dollars, receiving calls from collection agencies, and, on top of everything, lacking access to severely needed healthcare. Doing your homework upfront can save you the heartache of learning from your provider that the insurance carrier you have been paying premiums to for years really does not provide the coverage it claimed. Expect these types of schemes to evolve.

Established insurance companies are sometimes faced with issues of bad faith. What constitutes bad faith varies by state law. An organization known as Fight Bad-Faith Insurance Companies publishes the following fourteen guidelines:

1. Misrepresentation of pertinent facts of insurance policy provisions relating to coverage at issue

2. Failing to acknowledge and act reasonably and promptly upon communications with respect to claims arising out of insurance policies

3. Failing to adopt and implement reasonable standards for the prompt investigation of claims arising under insurance policies

4. Refusing to pay claims without conducting a reasonable investigation based on all available information

5. Failing to confirm or deny coverage of claims within a reasonable time after proof of loss statement has been completed

6. Not attempting in good faith to effectuate fair and equitable settlements of claims in which liability has become reasonably clear

7. Compelling insureds to institute litigation to recover amounts due under an insurance policy by offering substantially less than the amount ultimately recovered in actions brought by such insureds

8. Attempting to settle a claim for less than the amount to which a reasonable man would have believed he was entitled by reference to written or printed advertising material accompanying or made part of an application

9. Attempting to settle claims on the basis of an application that was altered without notice to, or knowledge or consent of, the insured

10. Making claims payments to insured or beneficiaries not accompanied by a statement setting forth the coverage under which the payments are being made

11. Making known to insureds or claimants a policy of appealing from arbitration awards in favor of insureds or claimants for the purpose of compelling them to accept settlements or compromises less than the amount awarded in arbitration

12. Delaying the investigation or payment of claims by requiring an insured, claimant, or the physician of either to submit a preliminary claim report and then requiring the subsequent submission of formal proof of loss forms, both of which submissions contain substantially the same information

13. Failing to promptly settle claims where liability has become reasonably clear less than one portion of the insurance policy coverage in order to influence settlements under other portions of the insurance policy coverage

14. Failing to promptly provide a reasonable explanation of the basis in the insurance policy in relation to the facts or applicable law for denial of a claim or for the offer of a compromise settlement (www.badfaithinsurance.org)

A recent 2005 case involving a government TPA vendor, AmeriChoice of Pennsylvania, shows one example of payer fraud. This particular TPA was involved in the following activities:

- Several allegations by providers relating to claims processing and coverage determinations

- Failed to process or pay physician or other healthcare claims in a timely fashion, or at all

- Incorrect payment for appropriate claims submissions

- Inaccurate reporting of claims processing data to the state, including a failure to meet self-reporting requirements and impose self-assessment penalties as required under its managed care contract with the state

- Automatically changed CPT codes (*current procedural terminology* codes, used to explain the procedure provided); did not recognize modifiers (additional codes that providers submit to explain the service provided)

- Did not reliably respond to appeals from patients, sometimes not responding at all or waiting over 6 to 12 months to do so

These activities resulted in a negotiated *corporate integrity agreement* (CIA) between the Department of Justice and AmeriChoice of Pennsylvania. A CIA is a negotiated compliance program of the Office of Inspector General (OIG) for the Department of Health and Human Services. CIAs usually last a period of five years and often include the following components:

1. Hire a compliance officer/appoint a compliance committee.
2. Develop written standards and policies.
3. Implement a comprehensive employee training program.
4. Review claims submitted to federal healthcare programs.
5. Establish a confidential disclosure program.
6. Restrict employment of ineligible persons.
7. Submit a variety of reports to the OIG. (http://oig.hhs.gov/fraud/cias.html)

The underlying objective of a CIA is to maintain the integrity of all federal healthcare programs. The majority of CIAs result from violations of the False Claims Act (FCA), which makes it illegal to present a claim on or against the United States that the claimant knows to be "false, fictitious, or fraudulent" (18 U.S.C. § 287). This criminal statute applies to any federal government department or agency. The making of fraudulent claims is a felony, and the 1986 amendments to the FCA mandate both a fine and imprisonment for all convictions. In addition to bringing a criminal action, the government may also bring a parallel civil action seeking relief.

The FCA affords the private citizen new incentives to report suspected frauds. It also gives whistleblowers extensive protection from harassment and retaliation from employers. The law provides "make-whole" relief, including reinstatement with full security, back pay with interest, and compensation for any damages sustained as a result of discrimination.

How Does the Payer Role Relate to Other Healthcare Continuum Players?

The payer handles the cash transaction between the plan sponsor and the provider of care. The risk of those dollars is based on who is funding the plan, and who is reviewing the claims and processing the checks for the services submitted. The involvement of this HCC player introduces another market conflict. Keep in mind that so far we have the relationship between the patient and the provider, the patient and the payer, and the provider and the payer, and only one healthcare episode impacting all these relationships. Considering each one separately, so far we have three market conflicts. Market conflicts can range from opposing influences for profit to unclear and unknown conflicts of interest. For example, payers typically get paid for processing a claim. Holding up a claim for investigation can be costly. However, it is the plan sponsor who gets penalized for paying unsubstantiated or fraudulent claims.

The Employer/Plan Sponsor

Who Is the Employer/Plan Sponsor?

An employer is a person or entity that hires employees. As part of its employment offering, an employer provides wages to the employees in exchange for their labor. In addition to wages, an employer may offer employees healthcare benefits. Our previous discussion included the history of this offering. The specific type of employer in our first example is a self-insured employer. This type of plan sponsor is typically a third party in the process. Historically, a self-insured employer is not directly involved with the claims processing of its employees' healthcare services. It typically contracts with a TPA, which then acts as the conduit for the process. With the rising cost of healthcare, a future market direction would be to watch employers actually take the TPA function in-house.

The second type of plan sponsor is an insurance carrier that sells health insurance directly. When employers purchase health insurance rather than take on the risk by being self-insured, they typically provide demographic information to the insurance company. The carrier determines rates based on this demographic information. The rates reflect the level of risk the insurance company plans to take with respect to that employer's employee population.

Other participants in the development and coordination of a health plan are agents or brokers. They help coordinate relationships or purchase decisions between the employer and the insurance company. It is very important to make sure that during the course of all transactions third parties and their respective fees are fully disclosed.

A final type of plan sponsor is the government-funded plan. The two largest programs are Medicare and Medicaid.

What Are Some Examples of Employer/Plan Sponsor Fraud?

The first type of plan sponsor fraud involves any middlemen in the process of purchasing a health insurance plan—for example, agent brokers. Such a fraud scheme could involve setting up groups that do not qualify for a group rate. Another type of fraud occurs when employers misrepresent their employee populations to obtain more favorable rates. Employers risk liability in fraud schemes that involve contracting with an insurer that does not have adequate reserves to cover healthcare plan payments.

A variety of schemes involve the execution of the plan document—for example, by selling insurance with stated coverage and then not providing that coverage. Another operational type of fraud involves misrepresenting negotiated performance guarantees, especially if they are associated with additional compensation.

How Does the Employer/Plan Sponsor Role Relate to Other Healthcare Continuum Players?

The plan sponsor or private employer in essence foots the bill. The irony for the private employer is that it typically has the least amount of information on direct costs. In 2007, I still encounter employers who have never audited their benefit plans, despite an environment in which double-digit increases occur each year. Prospective employees still target employment with entities that provide coverage. The role of the employer more often than not is that it remains out of the loop, thus adding an additional market conflict and contributing another layer of fragmentation.

Government-sponsored programs are much more actively involved in auditing plans, and require specific reporting structures and right-to-audit clauses. The stronger issue with government programs is the continued access to beneficiary information to submit false claims and/or misrepresent services from a vendor perspective to the government program.

THE VENDOR AND THE SUPPLIER

Who Are the Vendor and the Supplier?

Contributing to the fragmentation of the healthcare industry is another category of HCC players called vendors and suppliers. They are a blend of professional subcontractors. Vendors include healthcare professionals who provide direct patient care, such as nurses, doctors, physical therapists, and home health aides, as well as professional support services, such as billing companies or case management services. Suppliers include companies such as diagnostic laboratories, pharmacies, and medical device manufacturers. Vendors and suppliers are found throughout the HCC as subgroups within each market-player category.

What Are Some Examples of Vendor and Supplier Fraud?

The range of activity is significant and varies by the type of vendor or supplier. A growing area of concern is the pharmaceutical industry. The range of fraud starts with recipient drug abuse. It may involve professional staff drug abuse. The fraud scheme could be finding avenues of drug diversion for illicit use and sale. An egregious scheme involves the introduction of counterfeit drugs into our normal supply chain. The second level is adulterated drugs. This involves actual medications that are altered or diluted. Pharmaceutical issues may also take the form of government-sponsored program abuse. One such example is known as *340 B program abuse*; in this fraud scheme, providers or entities divert manufactured discounted drugs to unqualified recipients.

Supplier schemes often involve durable medical equipment. A false claim submission can occur with more expensive equipment on paper than what was actually provided. In the professional environment, it could include unlicensed personnel providing medical treatments. Professional activity may include misrepresentation of intensity of treatment or the amount of time spent with the patient.

How Do the Vendor and Supplier Roles Relate to Other Healthcare Continuum Players?

So far, we have discussed five sets of relationships between HCC players: the patient and the provider, the patient and the payer, the provider and the payer, the payer and the employer, and the employer and the employee. This represents at least five different market conflicts, and five different transactions, that govern one healthcare episode. In essence you have five different primary market conflicts. Now add vendors and suppliers to each one of these relationships. View this as a second set of five secondary market conflicts. Consider the relationships to also have at least ten layers of fragmentation. Severely fragmented markets invite waste, fraud, and abuse. This is an endless playground for the ethically challenged.

The Government

Who Is the Government?

The prior sections have discussed the government roles with respect to being a plan sponsor for programs such as Medicaid and Medicare. The other major market presence involves ongoing legislative changes and the monitoring of those changes to balance the inequities in the marketplace.

What Are Some Examples of Government Fraud?

Fraud schemes can involve acts committed by government-contracted vendors. Internal issues tend to materialize from a contracting perspective with a particular vendor. If you review the history of indictments of government vendors, you will find examples of TPAs misrepresenting performance guarantees, mishandling claims, and mishandling beneficiary information. The next layer of fraud schemes is the submission of false claims for reimbursement, which can be perpetuated by any player in the HCC.

Organized crime is a growing issue and concern. One example is the case in which the perpetrator did not even set foot on U.S. soil. A Russian obtained the Social Security numbers of a group of deceased Russian American immigrants. He submitted false claims, set up post office boxes in the United States, hired runners to collect the checks mailed to these boxes, and cashed in. With respect to false claims activities, organized crime fraud schemes are similar to those experienced by private insurers and are noted under provider fraud scenarios.

Participating in a government program forms a contractual relationship between the parties. The rule governing the contract may be manipulated, disregarded, or misrepresented. The final category of fraud, then, is contractual in nature. For example, a provider facility could misrepresent its Medicare cost report, not report accurate diagnosis and procedure codes, or submit claims for services that were not provided. It could be the plan sponsor's TPA vendor not processing claims as stipulated within its contract or not adjudicating the claims according to the approved beneficiary benefits.

How Does the Government Role Relate to Other Healthcare Continuum Players?

The government in this analysis is defined in the same manner as the employer. It depends on its contracting TPA to administer the plan as agreed on, in addition to managing the plan beneficiaries. They have the same level of market fragmentations and market conflicts.

ORGANIZED CRIME

This leads us to our final player; organized crime (OC). Fraud can occur in the context previously discussed by non–organized-crime entities among players noted within the healthcare continuum. However, organized crime is attracted to healthcare due to its cash-rich environment and highly fragmented market; the healthcare industry experiences a significant amount of organized criminal activity. OC is presented as a player from the perspective of its design, scope, and organization. OC is viewed as a third-tier market conflict, one that adds another layer of fragmentation. Its designation as an HCC player is not to legitimize its presence but to appreciate its activity and impact. As you read the following section, keep the following categories in mind:

Tier One: Five Market Conflicts/Five Layers of Fragmentation

- The patient and the provider
- The patient and the payer
- The provider and the payer
- The payer and the employer (plan sponsor)
- The employer (plan sponsor) and the employee

Tier Two: Ten Market Conflicts/Ten Layers of Fragmentation

- The patient and the provider + vendors and suppliers
- The patient and the payer + vendors and suppliers
- The provider and the payer + vendors and suppliers
- The payer and the employer (plan sponsor) + vendors and suppliers
- The employer (plan sponsor) and the employee + vendors and suppliers

Tier Three: Fifteen Market Conflicts/Fifteen Layers of Fragmentation

- The patient and the provider + vendors and suppliers + OC
- The patient and the payer + vendors and suppliers + OC
- The provider and the payer + vendors and suppliers + OC
- The payer and the employer (plan sponsor) + vendors and suppliers + OC
- The employer (plan sponsor) and the employee + vendors and suppliers + OC

Who Is Organized Crime?

The *Oxford English Dictionary* defines organized crime as having "a coordinated criminal organization [that directs] operations on a large or widespread scale." The term was first noted in a book called *Organized Crime in Chicago*, published by the Illinois Association for Criminal Justice in 1929: "Organized crime is not as many think a recent phenomenon in Chicago" (p. 25). In essence during the last 80 years, the perception of organized crime has evolved from an integral part of big-city life to an assortment of global criminal players who challenge the most powerful countries in the world.

The introduction of the Internet superhighway, e-commerce, and the globalized economy has taken organized criminal activity and the opportunities for exponential revenue streams to unprecedented levels. We are now far beyond the traditional and nontraditional understandings of the activity called organized crime. Organized crime, as defined by this author, is the opportunity for those ethically challenged entities, regardless of race, color, creed, sex, or religion, to find opportunities to financially exploit and steal the fruits of their neighbor. Organized crime is an industry in and of itself. See Exhibit 2.2.

EXHIBIT 2.2   **Modern Organized Crime Perspective and Technology**

Key Feature	Characterization of Organized Crime	Modern Technology
Activity	Organized crime involves the provision of illegal goods and services	Any demanded commerce or service
Organization	Organized crime involves criminal organizations	Any organized group, both skilled and unskilled professionals
System	Organized crime involves the integration of legal and illegal structures	Banking systems, industry specific systems, electronic media, internet, intranet, laws, and regulations by country

How Does the Organized Crime Role Relate to Other Healthcare Continuum Players?

In essence, organized crime entities attempt to penetrate any established player in the HCC or mimic a particular player in order to perpetuate their schemes. See Exhibit 2.3.

Market Players Overview: Implications for Prevention, Detection, and Investigation

Healthcare is the prevention, treatment, provision, instruction, and management of illness and wellness through services offered by professionals, third-party entities, vendors, and suppliers. Historically, healthcare has been driven by illness models. Not until recently has the focus of wellness been integrated into the overall picture. The market from a clinical perspective is being driven by emerging wellness models. However, the reimbursement side is slowly catching up from a financial perspective. This market conflict impacts how services are generated and represented. As an industry,

EXHIBIT 2.3   **Modern Healthcare Illegal Goods and Services**

Key Feature	Characterization of Organized Crime	Modern Technology
Activity	Organized crime involves the provision of illegal goods and services	Sales of new identities
		Sale of medically unnecessary *legitimate* medications, health products, and procedures
		Sale of *counterfeit* and *adulterated* medications
		Illegal and unethical marketing and recruitment schemes
		Stealing resources and money from government programs, provider delivery systems, payer systems, and vendor systems
		Intrastate or international theft of all of the above activity
		Various schemes include rent-a-patient, pill mill, and drop box
Organization	Organized crime involves criminal organizations	Organization is complex, layered, mulitidisciplined, mutiprofessional, and highly skilled in addition to unskilled labor
System	Organized crime involves the integration of legal and illegal structures	Banking systems, industry specific systems, vendors, payers, providers, employers, and colllusion among parties through the use of electronic media, internet, intranet, laws, and abuse of regulations by country

healthcare has been and will continue to be a demanded service, a high expenditure service, and a continued target for waste, fraud, and abuse. The first step toward initiating or developing an audit program, fraud investigation, and subsequent internal controls is an understanding of this market's history, changes, fragmented relationships, and market conflicts.

Both detection and prevention require a thorough understanding of the HCC, including how health information moves between players, how money moves, and the incentives that drive these relationships. In addition, due to the high volume of transactions, electronic tools are required to sift through large amounts of data.

Ultimately all healthcare fraud investigations build on the ability to detect various fraud schemes. The remainder of this book is structured to help you do this. We focus especially on one common element that each HCC player shares and that is often utilized in fraud schemes: patients' health information. Access to this information is key, both for those who perpetuate fraud schemes and for those who act as gatekeepers or damage-control experts.

Protected Health Information

When it comes to privacy and accountability, people always demand the former for themselves and the latter for everyone else.

—DAVID BRIN, U.S. SCIENCE FICTION WRITER, 1950

One element common among all healthcare continuum (HCC) players is the patient's *protected health information* (PHI) (also called *identifiable protected health information*, or IPHI). PHI is common, too, among many fraud schemes. As the end of Chapter 2 states, access to PHI is key, both for those who perpetuate fraud schemes and for those who act as gatekeepers or damage-control experts. A fine line exists between PHI access and privacy. However, this is a line potential defrauders are eager to cross.

HEALTH INSURANCE PORTABILITY AND ACCOUNTABILITY ACT OF 1996

Privacy of health information is federally protected under the Health Insurance Portability and Accountability Act of 1996 (HIPAA). The HIPAA includes provisions that required the Department of Health and Human Services to create a Privacy Rule to establish "a foundation of federal protections for the privacy of protected health information" (www.hhs.gov/

ocr/hipaa/guidelines/overview.pdf). The Privacy Rule defines PHI as "individually identifiable health information, held or maintained by a covered entity or its business associates acting for the covered entity that is transmitted or maintained in any form or medium (including the individually identifiable health information of non–U.S. citizens)" (http://privacyruleandresearch .nih.gov/pr_07.asp). This includes identifiable demographic information such as the patient's name, account number, and address; information about the past, present, or future medical condition of the patient; and associated payment and payer information that will identify that individual patient.

You should familiarize yourself with the provisions of HIPAA, especially those that protect the release, review, and return of PHI at the conclusion of an audit. It is important to understand that HIPAA is not meant to prevent audits or appropriately initiated fraud investigations. Instead, it is meant to increase accountability by requiring that audits and fraud investigations have procedures in place in case a breach involving PHI occurs.

HIPAA also requires that all covered entities "take reasonable steps to limit the use or disclosure of, and requests for, protected health information to the *minimum necessary* to accomplish the intended purpose" (emphasis added) (www.hhs.gov/ocr/hipaa/privacy.html).

AUDIT GUIDELINES IN USING PHI

During the course of a business audit, it is not unusual for one player in the HCC, even though it has a formal contractual business relationship, to claim that the HIPAA prevents it from conducting due diligence or compliance checks with a vendor. As an auditor, do expect as a third party for one of the covered entities to request your signature on a business associate agreement. It is an agreement that acknowledges your understanding of what PHI is and the limitations of its use. In addition, business associate agreements typically have provisions or procedures to mitigate any unplanned breaches.

Once the formalities of access have been defined, the key issues are the location and use of PHI. The audit may focus on only one or two players within the HCC. Once you have identified these players, use the following key points to guide your analysis of each of them:

- Conduct an operational flowchart of the business functions.
- Conduct an operational flowchart of job titles.

- At each business function, identify all transactions that occur verbally, telephonically, by facsimile, in hardcopy, and electronically.

- At each job title or role, identify all transactions that occur verbally, telephonically, by facsimile, in hardcopy, and electronically.

- Within each of these transactions, identify the data elements that are generated, collected, and accessed.

- Highlight the generation of a patient file and the generation of a cash transaction.

- Highlight the collection of that cash transaction and any amendments to the patient file.

The types of data or documents you collect as part of the audit depend on which HCC players you are examining. Each player in the HCC generates, transfers, or collects PHI. Each one has paper, electronic, and oral sources of PHI information. It is important to understand how your audit of PHI can be impacted by each HCC player. For example, for the collection of patient documents: The employer may have only workers' compensation-related PHI. It may not have nonwork-related information. Other documents may include billing statements or contracts the patient was asked to sign. Oral communications—for instance, queries on what types of instructions the patient received—could be important. Phone logs should list whom the patient communicated with on the phone, when, and why. All relevant e-mail communications should also be included. Review activity prior to receipt of services, during receipt of services, and in follow-up communications.

The provider may include a request for a blank inventory sample of any and all documents that are used in addition to the actual patient record. At times, providers create secondary records to facilitate patient care. A detailed request should be made of all types of documents utilized. Providers who use subcontracted vendors need to make sure that these vendors are not moving documents from the operational or patient care areas. With providers, segment your analysis prior to the service requested, confirm examination of procedures while a service is in progress, and follow up all operational work once a service is completed.

The payer may include documents that are used in precertification, adjudication, post-payment, or post-denial activities. Remember that contracts that govern the relationship between the provider and the payer may differ significantly from contracts that govern the relationship between the payer and the plan sponsor. These considerations should be made as well with the employer, vendor, and supplier.

Within all of these relationships, learn the operational issues that may impact any of these communications. Operational issues include how the business operates. Take, for example, the registration of the patient. What documents are associated with this operational or business function? What documents are associated with the actual delivery of patient care? And what documents are associated with billing and collection? Once again, the critical components of the types of data to collect within each operational function include:

- Electronic
- Paper
- Verbal
- Facsimile
- People
- Systems
- Product or service output

PROTECTED HEALTH INFORMATION OVERVIEW: IMPLICATIONS FOR PREVENTION, DETECTION, AND INVESTIGATION

The use of PHI is the cornerstone to committing fraud in healthcare. With respect to fraud, view PHI as equivalent to money. Inappropriate access to PHI at the registration function in a business can allow the perpetrator to use an existing patient to generate a false claim. Information like a diagnosis or procedure can be valuable in generating a false claim or stealing an insurance check once the claim is paid. A perpetrator can just steal the patient's demographic information to obtain false credit. To perpetuate most healthcare fraud schemes, we need to have a patient—or at least the PHI associated with that patient. Fraud requires information on diagnoses and procedures so they can be mimicked in a false environment. It may be noted that the patient is alive, dead, not alert, or alert and oriented to person, place, and time. Schemes have been perpetuated in all patient-type scenarios.

The audit guidelines set forth in this chapter identify the process of operational flowcharts. Later in this book, we look at the skill of operational flows that define normal business flow. *Normal* is introduced in the context of understanding anomalies. Anomaly detection is critical in the healthcare fraud environment, in particular because the prevalence and evolution of schemes is occurring at an accelerated rate. Fraud is an industry in and of itself. Each new type of possible scheme leaves us in the *pay-and-chase* mode with constant identification of the new fraud scheme methodology. Therefore, a proactive approach requires an anomaly detection methodology. The audit plan that focuses on deviations or patterns outside of the normal course of business provides the optimal environment for both detection and prevention activities.

Once the relevant PHI has been identified, its route along the HCC and its use by the various HCC players should be incorporated into its respective health information pipeline (HIP), the subject of the next chapter.

Health Information Pipelines

Health is not valued till sickness comes.

—DR. THOMAS FULLER (1654–1734), *GNOMOLOGIA* (1732)

Money, like health, often is not valued until it has come and gone. Unfortunately, the pay-and-chase mode still rules in the fraud world. Understanding the operational channels, communication pathways for health information, and money flows is critical in any audit or investigation. This chapter walks you through model audit *health information pipelines* (HIP's). An HIP identifies the route and use of health information. It should include patient information, operational information, and financial information in the delivery of patient services and resources. Use the guidelines in this chapter to help you identify all the appropriate layers for your audit.

THE AUDITOR'S CHECKLIST

We start with a brief explanation of the auditor's checklist. Use this checklist as a guide in collecting appropriate evidence, no matter which player in the healthcare continuum (HCC) you are auditing. Using the auditor's checklist will minimize omissions and subtle forms of evidence that may be easily missed.

Auditor's Checklist

❒   Internal communications

❒   External communications

❒   Critical communication component
  - ❒   Electronic
  - ❒   Paper
  - ❒   Verbal
  - ❒   Facsimile
  - ❒   People
  - ❒   Systems
  - ❒   Product or service output

WHAT ARE THE CHANNELS OF COMMUNICATION IN A HEALTH INFORMATION PIPELINE?

The Patient

Exhibit 4.1 represents a sample operational flow from the patient perspective. The auditor's checklist should be a guide through each activity. The exhibit contains a sample of general activity questions. The auditor should document the communication component of each response. For example, if the patient was referred, was this referral made orally or in writing? Is it documented in a written form, such as a prescription?

Exhibit 4.1 begins with Insurance Plan Status. If the patient has insurance, then you want to collect any information associated with this plan. Ask the patient if he or she had any difficulties with denials for coverage or reimbursement from the insurance company. During the scope of an Illinois-based patient interview, when I presented this question, for example, the patient responded: "They really do not pay much." A few other statements were suspect. A quick Internet search revealed that the Texas-based carrier was being investigated by the attorney general of Massachusetts for selling fraudulent insurance.

The next step involves the patient pursuing a product or service. Sample follow-up questions may include if the patient was sent by referral. If so, you want to collect any associated documents, such as prescriptions. Most

Health Information Pipeline (HIP)

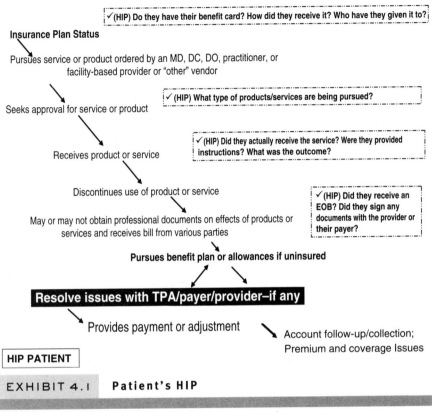

✓ (HIP) Do they have their benefit card? How did they receive it? Who have they given it to?

Insurance Plan Status

Pursues service or product ordered by an MD, DC, DO, practitioner, or facility-based provider or "other" vendor

✓ (HIP) What type of products/services are being pursued?

Seeks approval for service or product

✓ (HIP) Did they actually receive the service? Were they provided instructions? What was the outcome?

Receives product or service

Discontinues use of product or service

✓ (HIP) Did they receive an EOB? Did they sign any documents with the provider or their payer?

May or may not obtain professional documents on effects of products or services and receives bill from various parties

Pursues benefit plan or allowances if uninsured

Resolve issues with TPA/payer/provider–if any

Provides payment or adjustment

Account follow-up/collection; Premium and coverage Issues

HIP PATIENT

EXHIBIT 4.1   **Patient's HIP**

Source: Medical Business Associates, Inc. (www.mbanews.com).

patients who have insurance coverage will seek some type of contact for approval from their carrier. Again, if you follow the auditor's checklist for internal and external communications in addition to the components of communication, you will generate a comprehensive list of evidence to review.

Once the patient receives the services, another layer of documentation is created. Exhibit 4.1 provides an example of questions to ask. Sample documents will include medical records. Typically these records are obtained with appropriate release of information documents via the correspondence clerk within the medical records department. However, what auditors often miss are documents that are generated and remain in the possession of ancillary provider departments. It is important to confirm and verify all sources of documents that reflect the services provided to the patient.

In particular, it is important to ask the patient for any documents he or she received, for example, discharge instructions or product-related information.

Toward the end of the HIP from the patient perspective, the collection of documents from both the provider and payer is important. The patient often receives a document entitled EOB or EOR. An EOB is an "explanation of benefits," and an EOR is an "explanation of review." The information contained is the result of the payer's adjudication activity. Adjudication activity involves the processing of healthcare claims, specifically, the determination of a plan member's (the insured patient's) financial responsibility after a medical claim is compared to the member's insurance benefits or plan rules. A portion of the review process is done manually. When it is done automatically with computer programs, it is referred to as *real-time claims adjudication*. These programs instantaneously adjudicate (*auto-adjudicate*) the claim. A great deal of confidence in program controls is critical. In particular, electronic submissions of false claims can be transmitted to any third-party administrator at a rate of millions per hour.

The Provider

We started off with the patient. The next component is the provider. The auditor's checklist works again in this environment. Exhibit 4.2 shows the typical HIP for a provider. In addition, sample questions are noted. Separate professional office visits from facility-based care from home-health-based care. Each of these areas shares similar HIP flows; however, the actual content of information varies. With providers, it is important to include contractual relationships and their terms, both internal and external contractual relationships. External may include contracts with private payers, contracted professionals, and contracted vendors.

The provider infrastructure is more involved. When you are working with a facility, spend a significant amount of time understanding all the operational components of that facility. If the audit involves the office of professional staff, the same consideration should be made with respect to systems utilized in the delivery of services. Exhibit 4.2 contains sample questions that should be included in the identification of a provider's HIP source.

The HIP for the provider requires more planning and verification. It is not unusual to find different areas within a single facility using different

Health Information Pipeline (HIP)

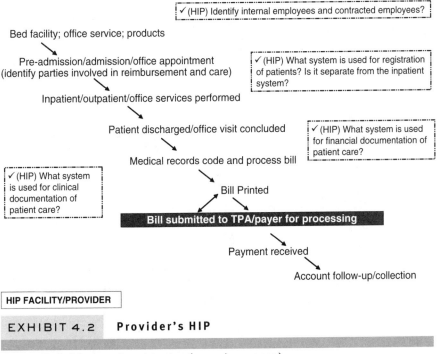

✓ (HIP) Identify internal employees and contracted employees?

Bed facility; office service; products

Pre-admission/admission/office appointment
(identify parties involved in reimbursement and care)

✓ (HIP) What system is used for registration of patients? Is it separate from the inpatient system?

Inpatient/outpatient/office services performed

Patient discharged/office visit concluded

✓ (HIP) What system is used for financial documentation of patient care?

Medical records code and process bill

✓ (HIP) What system is used for clinical documentation of patient care?

Bill Printed

Bill submitted to TPA/payer for processing

Payment received

Account follow-up/collection

HIP FACILITY/PROVIDER

EXHIBIT 4.2   **Provider's HIP**

Source: Medical Business Associates, Inc. (www.mbanews.com).

computer systems for managing patient care. It is important to apply the auditor checklist at each operational component. Do not assume that the same systems are used in all patient care areas.

The Payer

The auditor's checklist may be used for both an insurance agency's claims processing system and one associated with a third-party administrator (TPA). The claims adjudication system has numerous vulnerabilities and constant exposure to false claim submissions.

Exhibit 4.3 provides a sample operational flow. Again, this figure can be used as a guide to confirm the business flow and begin to identify all sources of communications. Use the auditor's checklist as a guide to identify relevant data sources.

Health Information Pipeline (HIP)

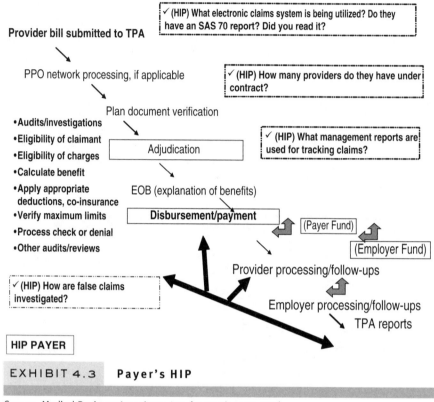

Provider bill submitted to TPA

✓ (HIP) What electronic claims system is being utilized? Do they have an SAS 70 report? Did you read it?

PPO network processing, if applicable

✓ (HIP) How many providers do they have under contract?

Plan document verification

- Audits/investigations
- Eligibility of claimant
- Eligibility of charges

Adjudication

✓ (HIP) What management reports are used for tracking claims?

- Calculate benefit
- Apply appropriate deductions, co-insurance

EOB (explanation of benefits)

- Verify maximum limits
- Process check or denial

Disbursement/payment

(Payer Fund)

- Other audits/reviews

(Employer Fund)

✓ (HIP) How are false claims investigated?

Provider processing/follow-ups

Employer processing/follow-ups

TPA reports

HIP PAYER

EXHIBIT 4.3   Payer's HIP

Source: Medical Business Associates, Inc. (www.mbanews.com).

Exhibit 4.3 lists sample operational questions. The question that asks "How many providers do they have under contract?" would lead to the request of several documents and audit parameters. For example, in the review of the claim file, determine how many claims were actually discounted. Request internal communication routes on how out-of-network claims are handled. The other checklist question is noted. "What internal controls are in place to verify contractual performance guarantees?" If any monetary compensation is associated with these performance guarantees, it is important to understand how the results will be communicated and how verification of those reports can be corroborated. As with any contract, negotiated fee schedules and forms of compensation will place one party at a disadvantage if you cannot verify the monetary transaction against the service provided.

The Employer/Plan Sponsor

The employer or plan sponsor, as of this writing, is considered one of the most vulnerable players within the HCC. (This discussion is limited to self-insured, non-government-sponsored health plans.) With the ever-rising cost and concerns associated with the provision of healthcare benefits to employees, I still find well-established employers who have never conducted a comprehensive healthcare benefit claim and contract audit. Overall, employers will find barriers to conducting the audit of their TPA vendor. These barriers will rear their ugly heads if a clear right-to-audit provision was not negotiated within the original contract terms. That aside, in an environment of publicly traded companies that are subject to the provisions of regulatory requirements such as the Sarbanes-Oxley Act, a regular and accurate account of dollars spent within one's healthcare plan should be on the radar screen for any organization, whether for-profit or not-for-profit.

Within the employer/plan sponsor environment, use the auditor's checklist to initiate general, open-ended questions like these:

- List all sources of internal communications relating to the purchase of a benefit plan.

- List all internal communications with the execution and maintenance of the benefit plan.

- Define these in terms of roles as well as tools utilized.

- What types of documents or reports do you receive from your plan administrator? In what format are they provided (for instance, PDF versus hardcopy document)?

Exhibit 4.4 represents typical operational components that should be identified during the initial audit engagement. Any audit or investigation begins with the review of the contract between the parties. For self-insured employers, it is important to understand whether the TPA is outsourcing the handling of any aspect of the claims information or the employees' health information. These relationships should be identified because the plan sponsor is ultimately responsible for any breaches that result from the handling of the benefit plan information.

The next operational component discusses setting up internal controls for the contracted services and the fees that they represent. Again, a good contract, regardless of terms or rates, is only as good as your ability to

Health Information Pipeline (HIP)

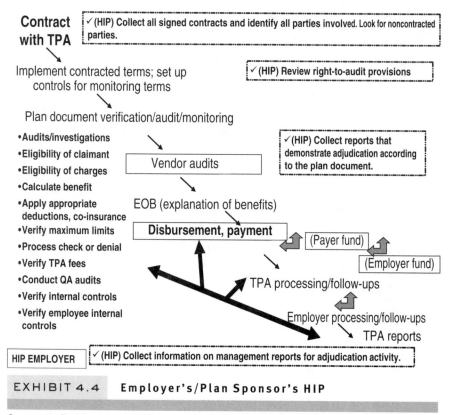

Contract with TPA
✓ (HIP) Collect all signed contracts and identify all parties involved. Look for noncontracted parties.

Implement contracted terms; set up controls for monitoring terms

✓ (HIP) Review right-to-audit provisions

Plan document verification/audit/monitoring

- Audits/investigations
- Eligibility of claimant
- Eligibility of charges
- Calculate benefit
- Apply appropriate deductions, co-insurance
- Verify maximum limits
- Process check or denial
- Verify TPA fees
- Conduct QA audits
- Verify internal controls
- Verify employee internal controls

Vendor audits

✓ (HIP) Collect reports that demonstrate adjudication according to the plan document.

EOB (explanation of benefits)

Disbursement, payment

(Payer fund)

(Employer fund)

TPA processing/follow-ups

Employer processing/follow-ups

TPA reports

HIP EMPLOYER
✓ (HIP) Collect information on management reports for adjudication activity.

EXHIBIT 4.4   Employer's/Plan Sponsor's HIP

Source: Medical Business Associates, Inc. (www.mbanews.com).

corroborate the services rendered along with their respective fees. If you cannot do this, then *buyers beware*. Once you initiate a vendor audit, expect to find that most carriers will request some type of audit agreement with specifications in methodology. Some agreements will insist that the TPA may review and comment on the report prior to any discussion of the employer who hired an independent auditor to review the report findings. Apply your auditor's checklist methodology to all sections that follow: the process, tools, systems, resources, and documents utilized for EOB communications; disbursement and payments; payer fund transactions; TPA processing and employer follow-ups; employer processing and follow-ups; and, finally, TPA reports.

The Vendor/Supplier

The vendors and suppliers category, sometimes termed *Others* in this manual, includes providers of durable medical equipment (DME), pharmaceuticals, ambulance services, case management, litigation, or any other product or service by professionals, nonprofessionals, or facility-based care providers. The audit methodology checklist is helpful in this arena because the list of vendors and suppliers can be very diverse. Focus on identifying any support vendor for another HCC or a party that is acting independently as a supplier of products or services. This particular arena is highly active for fraudulent activity.

Exhibit 4.5 serves as a general guide in auditing any ancillary HCC player, but you should expand on it once you identify a specific service or product. Follow the development of a process flowchart by walking through the auditor methodology checklist for each operational function. In the first stage, the identification of the service or product, note immediately whether you are dealing with an item or service that requires a physician's order.

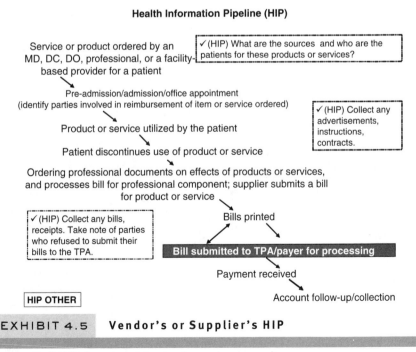

EXHIBIT 4.5   Vendor's or Supplier's HIP

Source: Medical Business Associates, Inc. (www.mbanews.com).

At what type of facility are these services performed? What type of entity distributes the products at a retail level? With respect to products, it is important to understand the market flow from production to packaging to distribution to retail.

The questions presented within Exhibit 4.5 are examples of issues that may be part of your audit at that point in the operational function for your vendor or supplier. Again, each operational function should correspond with each item presented in the auditor methodology checklist. The chapter on operational flow activity will extrapolate two examples: pharmaceuticals and durable medical equipment.

The Government Plan Sponsor

The HIP for a government plan sponsor is very similar to that presented for self-insured employers (see Exhibit 4.6). Government plan sponsors and

Health Information Pipeline (HIP)

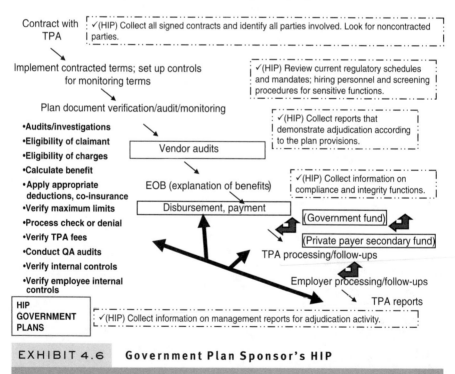

EXHIBIT 4.6   Government Plan Sponsor's HIP

Source: Medical Business Associates, Inc. (www.mbanews.com).

self-insured employers have similar interests in that both entities have contracts with parties to administer or monitor their benefit plans; both are funding a reserve; both have TPAs providing adjudication activity; both have the TPAs pulling from that reserve to meet the cash flow of claims being submitted; and both have reporting requirements to their "client."

Some areas, however, are different. The government-contracted TPA vendor typically has the right to audit provisions without additional audit agreements and minimal barriers, while the self-insured employer typically does not have a strong right—or sometimes any right—to audit provisions and may encounter more barriers. The self-insured employer's plan is subject to ERISA; the government plan is subject to the regulatory requirements of that plan (such as Medicare and Medicaid). Historically, government-contracted TPAs have had corporate integrity agreements for misrepresentations of performance guarantees and false claims activity; the private employer market of sponsored plans has had very little litigation in this arena.

UNAUTHORIZED PARTIES

This chapter introduces the concept of health information pipelines. The purpose is to illustrate all the operational functions in which patient health information can be generated, expanded on, and transferred. When it comes to healthcare fraud, it is important to understand that health information equals money. As a result, significant vulnerabilities exist among all players when it comes to breaches of internal controls. Many fraud schemes are perpetuated by obtaining health information to convert into a financial scheme or initiate identity theft. That theft could result from direct access to specific information or direct access to a product or supply that is associated with a specific patient or operational function.

An unauthorized party is *any* individual or organized entity that penetrates the operational function of one or more market players in the HCC to perpetuate its scheme. With respect to unauthorized parties, the audit methodology checklist applies to the HCC chart presented in Exhibit 4.7, which illustrates each of the market players.

Conceptualize the HIPs of the market players discussed in this chapter. They provide greater details of each component represented in the HCC noted in Exhibit 4.7. Apply the auditor methodology checklist to fully understand security issues as they relate to each operational function within

Health Care Continuum (HCC) Follow the $ and PHI

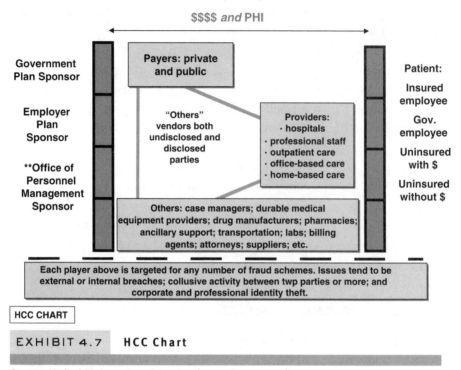

EXHIBIT 4.7   HCC Chart

Source: Medical Business Associates, Inc. (www.mbanews.com).

each market player. The perspective always includes both internal and external access. For example, who has access to the computerized systems? The theft of patient health information can be utilized to submit false claims. This is a common threat. A less common threat would be the intentions of lower-wage unskilled labor. Organized crime entities will plant housekeeping staff or central supply staff within a provider setting just to steal inventory of drugs or supplies. This inventory in turn is resold to the secondary wholesale market—or worse, it is adulterated and then resold to the secondary wholesale market. This market in turn resells the inventory back to the facility. How often are these type of personnel screened for criminal backgrounds? This can also happen with professional staff. A well-known cancer hospital in Texas had a criminal issue with a pharmacist who was stealing hospital inventory and selling cancer drugs to a secondary wholesaler.

HIP Overview: Implications for Prevention, Detection, and Investigation

Health information is the data, the meaning, the everyday usage of any element created throughout the healthcare continuum. It can result from the generation of, processing of, mining of, mapping of, manipulation of, and organization of data in a way that adds diagnostics, knowledge, solutions, and alternatives to the person receiving or sending it. It includes communications, instructions, meanings, patterns, perceptions, and representations of the patient and those involved with and impacted by the patient.

HIPs represent the operational decision trees in which such information is typically channeled. The implications for prevention are primarily focused on internal controls. Do we have the audit log infrastructure and edit controls to flag a transaction before it becomes an issue? If a breach does occur, do we have the controls in place to detect anomalies? Can we trace them to their generation? Can they be traced to the point of processing or to any form of their use? HIPs should serve as a roadmap for detection. Again, if we follow all its possible uses, we should be able to detect the schemes that are perpetuated with health information. Remember, health information is equivalent to money. During all of its normal uses, how can health information be converted toward an illicit monetary gain? Finally, well-developed process flowcharts and electronic systems that include an active audit log within these HIPs will guide a comprehensive discovery process and lead toward a successful investigation.

The next chapter reviews these operational components from the perspective of an accounts receivable pipeline (ARP). The topic of ARPs focuses on the financial aspect of monetary transactions.

CHAPTER 5

Accounts Receivable Pipelines

If money be not thy servant, it will be thy master.
—FRANCIS BACON (1561–1626)

Greed has the infamous ability to degrade the soul and corrupt every established value of an individual. In this, it is little different than the toxic effect of a drug like heroin on the brain and body. It can cause a complete personality change along with the burial of the "conscious" attributes of right and wrong. As auditors and investigators, we need to follow the paths and respect the complexities of those we audit or investigate. Take Dr. Ronald Mikos, a podiatrist from Chicago. A father of five, he lived a $350,000 lifestyle off Medicare by billing surgeries he never performed. On January 27, 2002, Joyce Brannon, a disabled former nurse and patient of Dr. Mikos, was killed gang-style in her home. She refused to lie about the alleged 72 surgeries he billed to Medicare on her behalf and was going to testify against him.

Dr. Mikos was not accustomed to patients who refused to lie on his behalf. The consequence for Brannon was a gang-style shooting of six bullets, two in the back of the head—a strong lesson learned on how a dysfunctional mind responds to the fear of being indicted for Medicare fraud. Mikos's fear was suffering the consequence of a five-year prison term and Medicare fraud fines. His solution was murder. As sound dysfunctional logic would dictate, instead of the five-year prison term, Mikos was indicted and then convicted for first-degree murder, was sentenced to death, and was ordered to pay Medicare $1.8 million for his fraud-related activities. When money becomes thy master, it will defy all the laws of logic.

The *accounts receivable pipeline* (ARP) is all about the money. "Just follow the money," the famous quote from Watergate's journalistic source, Deep Throat, holds true in any audit or investigation. When dealing with the ethically challenged, money will eventually be the master and the fraudster *will* make a mistake. Healthcare reimbursement is complex, segmented, and blended with both private contractual arrangements and those mandated through public government programs. This chapter provides an overview of healthcare reimbursement followed by an understanding of the ARP for each healthcare continuum (HCC) player. Understanding the ARP will further guide you, the auditor or investigator, to generate the appropriate investigative and detection audit trail.

OVERVIEW OF HEALTHCARE REIMBURSEMENT

Reimbursement is driven by rules and contractual arrangements. Understanding this important fact leads an auditor to ask three crucial questions:

1. What are the rules or terms of reimbursement?
2. What is covered and what is not?
3. What is the basis of the contractual arrangements?

Medicare, for example, has three parts: Part A covers inpatient care. Part B covers ambulatory care (most OP Labs Diagnostic) and professional services. Part D provides for prescription drug coverage. Medicare is a federal program. Each state provides a Medicaid program. Each state has its set of rules for what is covered. All public programs have their rules available to the public. In contrast, private-payer offerings and their rules are not publicly available. These policies are typically written based on the customer needs and any legislative mandates. How can this impact an audit?

First let us look at a public program, in particular, the Texas Medicaid program. This program's rules allow for the payment of three prescriptions per month. As an auditor, what would you look for to determine whether a patient was manipulating this limit of three covered prescriptions per month? You could start by looking at whether a family was receiving multiple prescriptions. For example, Mom needs four drugs. Is another family member receiving that fourth prescription to obtain all four drugs for Mom? The art of this detection is discussed in chapter 13 on exploratory data analysis (EDA), or the art of gathering intelligence from data.

In a private plan, the rules may be similar in concept. For example, the rules may dictate that only $1,200 per year will be paid toward chiropractic services. This rule can be manipulated by making a chiropractic service look like physical therapy. A plan sponsor offering dental coverage may have similar provisions regarding the limits of coverage. One way to increase routine dental care is to make the dental problem look like a medical problem so that a group health plan will cover it. Keep in mind from earlier chapters that fraud can occur from any player in the HCC. In the dental coverage example, the opposite could happen as well. A payer may deny a true medical problem that requires dentistry by stating it is not a medical problem when it truly is. This is called *bad faith*, and payers are often exposed to denial liabilities for this type of practice. Recently, some cases have designated this practice as a false claim activity.

Payers face additional liabilities on the concept of denying claims. For example, claims may be denied as "medically unnecessary." From an audit perspective, it is important to understand the internal controls surrounding this practice. Is the decision being based on a clinical review of the patient's condition? Is it being reviewed by competent personnel and processes? In one case, a payer was found to be using a "dentist" for review of all medical cases. The correspondences communicating the results of the review were all being signed by the medical director, who was an MD.

Traditionally, private-payer plans have been driven by illness models. However, the provider market has increasingly focused on wellness programs. While the payer systems adapt to these market changes in providing coverage, an audit check should include wellness activities being presented as illness activities. For example, many plans now include mammogram screenings as part of their wellness initiatives; these screenings used to be covered only when illness was suspected. Expect this wellness model to be a continued focus of future benefit plans.

TYPES OF REIMBURSEMENT MODELS

Another key to understanding healthcare reimbursement is to understand the dynamics of different reimbursement models, which tend to fall into several categories.

Fee-for-Service Model

The fee-for-service reimbursement model is the one traditionally used in healthcare. Volume drives the profit in this model: The greater the number of services provided, the greater the revenue. Many reimbursement models negotiate a percentage of charges as part of the contractual arrangement. The abuse concern results from providing services that are not medically required.

Prospective Model

The prospective model uses predetermined fees. The incentive for profit in this model comes from efficiency. The more efficiently the service is provided, the greater the revenue. An example is Medicare's DRG (diagnosis–related group) prospective payment system. Each hospital has a series of computations that is determined in part by information collected in the annual Medicare cost report. Hospitals receive their lists of DRGs with predetermined amounts for each group. An example includes the heart attack (myocardial infarction) DRG series.

- DRG 121: Circulatory disorders with acute myocardial infarction and cardiovascular complications
- DRG 122: Circulatory disorders with acute myocardial infarction without cardiovascular complications
- DRG 123: Circulatory disorders with acute myocardial infarction expired

A community hospital prospective payment schedule may look like this:

DRG 121: $8,060
DRG 122: $4,923
DRG 123: $7,703

Any time a patient is admitted and discharged at the community hospital with the post-discharge designation of DRG 121, the hospital will receive this flat rate. The hospital will profit if it was able to take care of the patient for less than $8,060 in resources. It is assumed that, on average, the hospital will "win" in some cases and "lose" in others. The DRG is always determined as the condition after study. In other words, the patient may have been admitted for complaints of flu; however, from a reimbursement perspective, it becomes irrelevant if it is determined that the patient did not have the flu. A DRG 121 patient may look like someone who was admitted with congestive heart failure or acute hypertension that leads toward a myocardial infarction. If after all the testing it is determined that the patient had hypertension and congestive heart failure, plus the infarction, it would fall into the group of a patient with a complication.

Likewise, with DRG 122, this patient may look like an individual who was admitted with angina or chest pain. During the hospital stay, these symptoms progressed, and the patient eventually had an infarction. After study, it was determined that the patient did in fact have an infarction; therefore, the hospital would submit reimbursement for DRG 122. The reimbursement for this DRG group is lower because it has been determined from prior studies that the amount of resources required to take care of a patient with DRG 122 versus DRG 121 is less. With this rule in mind, the question presented is: how can this be manipulated? How can abuse or fraud occur?

If a provider truly has a patient that should be designated as DRG 122, it can *interpret* the medical records to appear as if the patient had a cardiovascular complication. Therefore, the provider submits a claim for a DRG 121 patient rather than for a DRG 122 patient. This practice of billing for a service more complicated than it actually was is termed *upcoding*. In our example, upcoding results in an additional reimbursement of $3,137. That is a 39 percent overcharge. Keep this large percentage swing in mind when reviewing studies that appear to be excessive. Depending on the term of the contract, the percentage of overcharges versus undercharges can be a significant swing depending on what type of reimbursement model is being utilized.

The selection of codes is dependent on competent staff trained in two coding systems. The first is the *International Classification of Disease Index* (ICD 9th or 10th edition). This is a numeric listing of all diagnoses. The diagnosis is the assessment.

It is the *why* of treating a patient. The next system is the *Current Procedural Terminology* (CPT) index. This represents procedures that are recognized in treating patients. On a claim form, ICD and CPT codes are submitted for reimbursement. In essence, this communicates the *what* and the *why* for the service provided to the patient. When a healthcare audit or investigation is initiated, understanding how these two data elements are processed is critical because they form the central component of the ARP.

The DRG group is selected by obtaining a list of diagnoses (in particular, the principal diagnoses) plus the procedures and placing the patient into the appropriate group. The determination of the principal versus the secondary diagnoses can impact which DRG group the patient falls into. Therefore, appropriate training is critical. The rules that are applied to determine the correct selection of codes are the same rules that are used in the course of an audit. This is the inpatient side of healthcare.

Coding outpatients is similar, although the terminology is different. Ambulatory patient group (APG) codes are used for outpatients. The professional fees for physicians are also driven by the CPT code. All of these rules for selection of a code to represent the service provided are updated annually. They are driven by rules established in private contractual arrangements as well as those mandated by government-sponsored programs.

The auditor's checklist for the prospective model includes these questions:

- ☐ What type of health plan is involved?
- ☐ What type of facility is involved?
- ☐ What type of provider is involved?
- ☐ What contracts are governing the relationship?
- ☐ Are the terms private or public or a combination of both?

For example, a patient can be Medicare primary plus Blue Cross/Blue Shield (BCBS) secondary. This would be a combination of both public and private coverage. Another type of reimbursement model is the concept of *per diem*. This model means that the patient will be charged a flat rate per day. It is more common in nursing home or extended-care-type facilities. Therefore, the abuse may come into play by keeping the patient in for more days than needed. The claim data may demonstrate this type of anomaly. "All patients from Provider Health are discharged at 20 days. This plan allows coverage for only 20 days. The patients appear to be discharged 100% at 20 days. Therefore, the incentive for profit is to keep the patient until their benefits run out." The quality control or audit determinations here would involve unnecessary length of stay. A later chapter discusses analyzing clinical content for this type of audit.

Capitation-Structured Model

Capitation-structured reimbursement models involve a flat rate per patient per month. The provider receives a flat rate for covered patients regardless of service utilized. The abuse concern results from an underserving of patients' healthcare needs. The incentive for profit is a plan with a significant number of lives and minimal resource expenditure for delivering of care.

The auditor's checklist for this model includes these questions:

❒   What reimbursement model is being used?

❒   What are the incentives for profit?

❒   How can the rules be manipulated?

❒   Is the plan private, public, or both?

Data Contained in Accounts Receivable Pipelines

Where does the data in ARPs come from? It starts with the submission of a claim from the provider of services or products. Form UB-82 was created by the National Uniform Billing Committee, a group sponsored by the American Hospital Association and charged with streamlining the processing of healthcare claims. Amendments to the Health Insurance Portability and Accountability Act of 1996 (HIPAA) introduced a second version, UB-92. The new version included specifications for Medicare, Medicaid, BCBS, the Office of the Civilian Health and Medical Program of the Uniformed Services, and commercial insurance claims. The new UB-04 was implemented in 2007 with updates to facilitate communications and documentation for the submission of claims.

Exhibits 5.1 shows the new UB-04 form (CMS 1450), which replaced the UB-92 form. Effective May 2007, the prior forms will no longer be accepted. Details and current rules in the use of this form are found on the

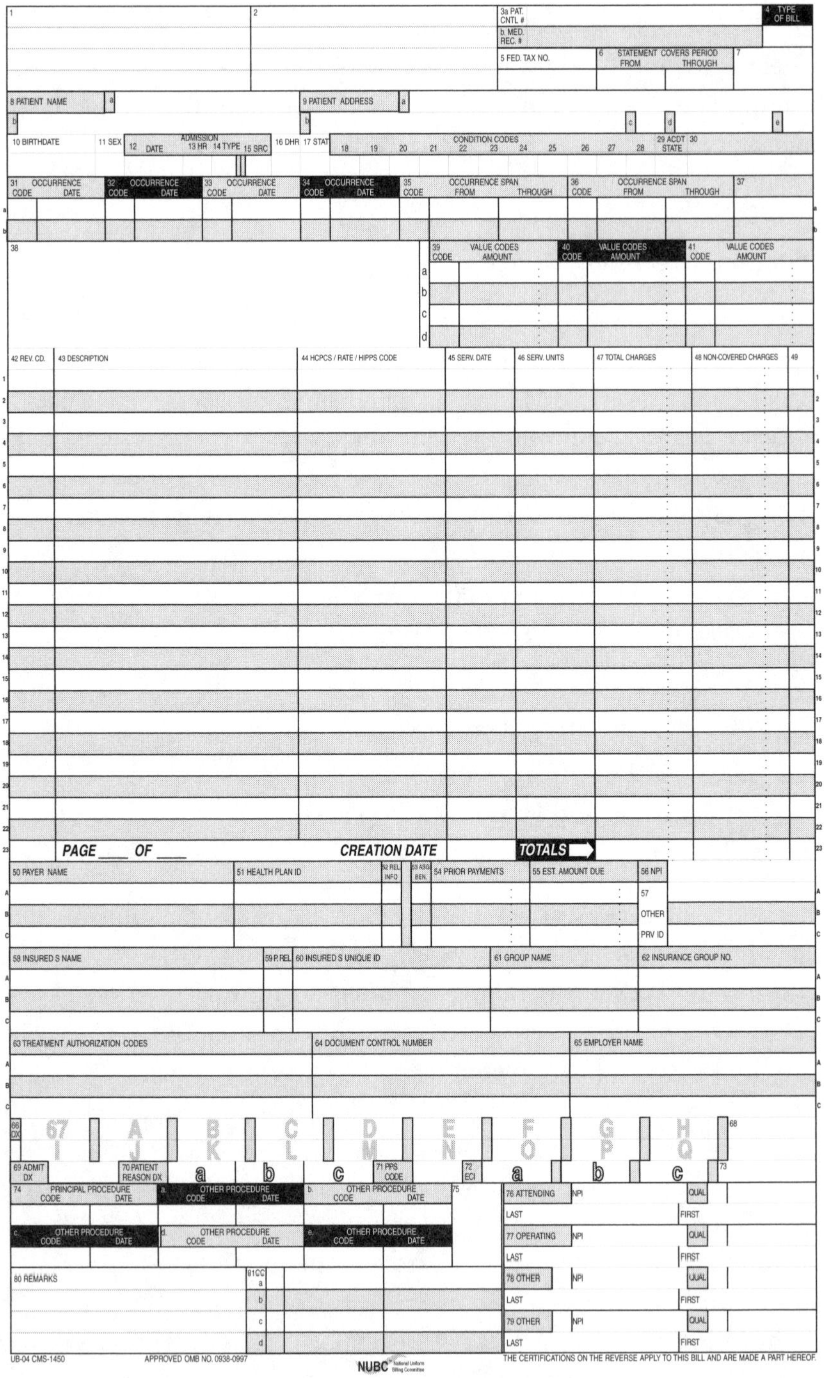

EXHIBIT 5.1   Form UB-04 (Laser Form)

CMS website (www.cms.gov). This form initiates the topic of ARPs, that is, the understanding of how money moves in the HCC and what activities generate the submission of this form.

Note that the forms contain valuable information such as the patient's name, plan sponsor's name, diagnoses codes, and procedures codes. Recall from earlier chapters that in fraudulent activities, personal health information (PHI) equals money. How this fact relates to ARPs and to fraud investigation is discussed in the following sections.

ACCOUNTS RECEIVABLE PIPELINES BY HCC PLAYER

The ARP concept is intended to blend with the prior discussion of health information pipelines (HIPs). Each ARP presents the typical operational flow and introduces its impact on an audit or investigation. The following central auditor checklist applies when auditing any of the ARPs presented in the progression of this chapter:

- ❐ Identify all internal communications that impact
  - ❐ Patient
  - ❐ Provider
  - ❐ Payer
  - ❐ Employer/plan sponsor
  - ❐ Vendor/supplier
  - ❐ Government
  - ❐ Staff
  - ❐ Unauthorized parties
- ❐ Identify all external communications that impact
  - ❐ Patient
  - ❐ Provider
  - ❐ Payer
  - ❐ Employer/plan sponsor
  - ❐ Vendor/supplier
  - ❐ Government
  - ❐ Staff
  - ❐ Unauthorized parties

☐ Define critical components of communications in the form of
  ☐ Electronic
  ☐ Paper
  ☐ Verbal
  ☐ Facsimile
  ☐ People
  ☐ Systems
  ☐ Product or service output

The Patient

Exhibit 5.2 represents the ARP for the patient. In essence, what activities impact a healthcare episode from the patient perspective? How does this tie back to health information and claims submission activity?

The auditor's checklist first defines what type of patient is being reviewed. Exhibit 5.2 indicates the category of "insured employee/patient." The first step is to identify the type of plan: a private employer plan, an independent patient-purchased plan, or a government-sponsored plan. The other types of patients are government employees, individuals who have monetary resources but no insurance, and individuals who have no monetary resources and no insurance.

How does a patient make a healthcare decision? He or she starts by determining insurance status. Regardless of status, the patient then pursues a product or service. Patients who are part of a plan and understand that precertification is required typically contact their plan for approval. (Exceptions, of course, are with emergency care.) This step is followed by seeking approval, receiving the service or product, and discontinuing its use.

At this stage of the ARP pipeline, revenue is generated by an insurance plan's approval for the service. At the front end, what can go wrong? The following is just a sample:

• If the patient seeks precertification for nonemergency services, the service can be denied. This impacts the provider and the patient. If the patient seeks emergency care, he or she will at times receive a denial of services. The audit role includes inappropriate denials for emergency care, working with providers on collection issues with patients who are

Accounts Receivable Pipeline (ARP)

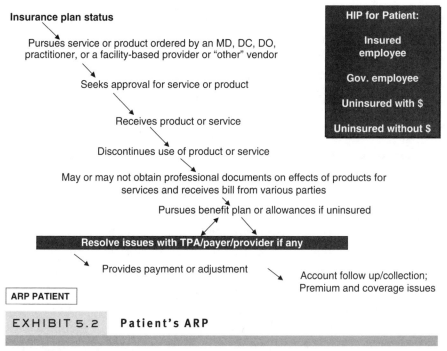

Insurance plan status

Pursues service or product ordered by an MD, DC, DO, practitioner, or a facility-based provider or "other" vendor

Seeks approval for service or product

Receives product or service

Discontinues use of product or service

May or may not obtain professional documents on effects of products for services and receives bill from various parties

Pursues benefit plan or allowances if uninsured

Resolve issues with TPA/payer/provider if any

Provides payment or adjustment

Account follow up/collection; Premium and coverage issues

ARP PATIENT

HIP for Patient:

Insured employee

Gov. employee

Uninsured with $

Uninsured without $

EXHIBIT 5.2   Patient's ARP

Source: Medical Business Associates, Inc. (www.mbanews.com).

denied coverage, and working with payers who have insufficient staff to respond to patient inquiries for certification.

- If the patient seeks precertification for medically necessary treatment that may be viewed as experimental procedures, or noncovered items, the patient may be denied services. What happens to the denial of a stem cell transplant patient? In one case, the patient went through the appeal process; after six months, the treatment was finally certified. The patient received the transplant at seven months and died at twelve months. Would six months have made a difference? Does this raise the issue of liability on the adjudication function of the payer? Does the provider have increased liability for delay in treatment?

- If a patient has no insurance, routine procedures and avoidable complications could land him or her in the emergency department. This has the unfortunate consequence of increasing unreimbursed expenditures. If the provider discharges these patients before they are ready, will they have "patient dumping" liabilities?

The second half of the patient's ARP involves operational processing by the provider of services; this is discussed later in the chapter. With respect to the patient, an area of concern for auditors is "beneficiary" abuse of fraud-related activity. This is seen, for example, when an uninsured friend or family member uses an insured patient's benefit card. The patient instead may sell his or her benefit card to an unsuspecting party. Submitting claims for reimbursement on services never received or paid for is another type of fraud. Finally, you may find patients who participate in fraud schemes such as knowingly receiving services that are not medically necessary or receiving noncovered services and participating in cover-ups to misrepresent the service.

Patients often fall victim to various fraud schemes. Exhibit 5.3 is a sample contract that a patient was requested to sign. The text noted in bold is the consent for treatment. The remaining portion of the text contains contract terms. Note, in particular, this statement: "Insurance and/or Medicare assignment is not accepted as payment." Private payers who sign contracts with providers need to know whether they have their members sign statements that in essence void the contract. In addition, the contract terms are buried in consent for treatment. These two activities should be kept separate.

An increasing concern is access to medications. A common Internet scheme involves an attempt to target patients by advertising certain "FDA approved" medications. The purchase might work like this. The patient calls the agency; he or she speaks to a "doctor," who in turn prescribes a series of medications. The provider does not accept the patient's benefit card, but does accept Visa or Master Card. It mails a receipt with the medications for reimbursement. The patient can submit the claim to his or her benefit plan. Thus the auditor's concern should be twofold. First, the patient buying a bad drug that could be counterfeit and, second, how the payer is going to screen the paper submissions for reimbursement. With respect to the first point it is important to educate the consumer, because this company is off U.S. shores and no opportunity exists to verify whether the medications are real. A significant safety issue occurs. Many of these patients receive counterfeit or adulterated drugs that can actually harm them. They may land in local emergency rooms, treated by unsuspecting doctors who do not immediately discern that the patient was a victim of counterfeit drug ingestion.

Request and consent to perform nuclear medicine study/procedure/ treatment and release of authorization and payment contract.

I request Dr. John Doe to perform the following Nuclear Medicine Study/ Procedure/Treatment: Whole Body Bone Scan & Digital & Spect studies. Please read carefully: I understand and agree to be responsible for full and complete payment of the charges incurred for the above-posted Nuclear Medicine study(ies) including any and all legal and court costs, and any and all discovery matters and deposition, should it become necessary to file a collection action, appear at an arbitration hearing, appear at an adjudication hearing, or file an appeal or appeal answer/defense in an appellate court. This extension or credit with full and complete payment due 30 days from the Date of Service. I understand and agree to the submission, by myself and/or XXXXX Nuclear Medicine Clinic, of a valid, fully executed claim to any and all insurance carriers providing coverage. I understand and agree to pay 1-1/2 percent per month as compound interest on my outstanding balance if I did not pay my bill in 30 days from the Date of Service. Insurance and/or Medicare assignment is not accepted as payment. In Personal Injury cases, in all other types of injury cases, and in Workmen's Compensation cases, neither payment contingent upon the outcome of the case nor a Physician's Lien is accepted as payment. I authorize release of my Nuclear Medicine Consultation Report to any healthcare practitioner(s) who may need it for evaluation and/or treatment purposes, as well as to the person(s)/insurance company(ies)/employer(s)/government agency(ies) responsible for payment of my bill. By signing this, I acknowledge that I have received a copy of this Financial Policy of XXXXXXX Nuclear Medicine and agree with its contents.

Signed_____   Date_____

EXHIBIT 5.3   Sample Contract

From patients' perspective, an auditor's checklist should include the following:

- ☐ Any contracts they were asked to sign by the provider
- ☐ Any online purchases of medications
- ☐ Any written communications from their providers
- ☐ Any written communications from their payers
- ☐ Any written communications from their plan sponsors

The second issue materializes once the "bill" is received by the payer and they have to screen for the authenticity of the claim. Considerations that should be included with this checklist involve examining the circumstances of the service. For example, are the services involved related to

☐ General group health activity (an illness or wellness issue)?

☐ Injuries from an auto accident?

☐ Injuries from a work-related injury?

If the answer to any of the above is *yes*, it is important to understand the implication of "other parties," such as case managers, attorneys, and liability insurers.

Exhibit 5.4 illustrates how the concept of HIP from the previous chapter blends with the current discussion of ARPs.

The Provider

The professional component is shown in Exhibit 5.5, the provider's ARP.

How do providers make healthcare decisions? What impacts an audit or investigation? Exhibit 5.5 illustrates the typical operational flows for professionals providing services and facilities in which these services are rendered. For example, what services are being offered, and what professional staff will be providing the service? The concepts of these functions are the same, but they will look different in a hospital versus a physician's office versus a nursing home or rehabilitation facility. They will vary in support services such as physical therapy centers and diagnostic facilities. Within the patient HIP, the concept of precertification was addressed. Although the health plan is truly a relationship between patients and their employer, providers will assist them in meeting precertification requirements because it will impact reimbursement for the services provided. The process becomes layered in the sense that the provider may provide services to facilitate the relationship between the patient and his or her plan sponsor; however, the provider is also subject to any contractual arrangement it may have with that carrier. This arrangement presents yet another market conflict. The patient hits stage two, which is "Pre-Admission/Admission/Office Appointment (identify parties involved in reimbursement and care)."

Health Information Pipeline (HIP) and Accounts Receivable Pipeline (ARP)

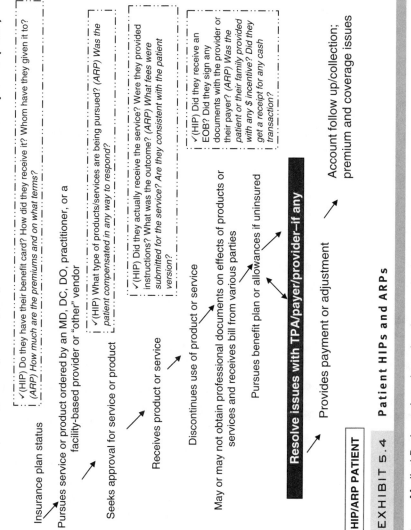

Insurance plan status

✓(HIP) Do they have their benefit card? How did they receive it? Whom have they given it to? (ARP) How much are the premiums and on what terms?

Pursues service or product ordered by an MD, DC, DO, practitioner, or a facility-based provider or "other" vendor

Seeks approval for service or product

✓(HIP) What type of products/services are being pursued? (ARP) Was the patient compensated in any way to respond?

Receives product or service

✓(HIP) Did they actually receive the service? Were they provided instructions? What was the outcome? (ARP) What fees were submitted for the service? Are they consistent with the patient version?

Discontinues use of product or service

May or may not obtain professional documents on effects of products or services and receives bill from various parties

✓(HIP) Did they receive an EOB? Did they sign any documents with the provider or their payer? (ARP) Was the patient or their family provided with any $ incentive? Did they get a receipt for any cash transaction?

Pursues benefit plan or allowances if uninsured

Resolve issues with TPA/payer/provider–if any

Provides payment or adjustment

Account follow up/collection; premium and coverage issues

HIP/ARP PATIENT

EXHIBIT 5.4   Patient HIPs and ARPs

Source: Medical Business Associates, Inc. (www.mbanews.com).

Accounts Receivable Pipeline (ARP)

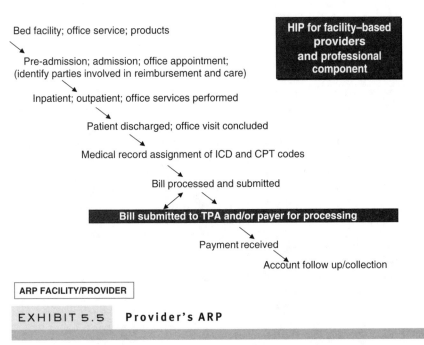

ARP FACILITY/PROVIDER

EXHIBIT 5.5   Provider's ARP

Source: Medical Business Associates, Inc. (www.mbanews.com).

The process at this point can have several operating contracts. (For this discussion, refer back to Exhibit 4.7 in Chapter 4, "HCC Chart.") First is the contract between the plan sponsor and the payer (or third-party administrator [TPA]). The second contract is between the provider and the payer (or TPA). The third possible contract is between the provider and any support vendors. The fourth possible contract is between the payer and any support vendors. The fifth possible contract is a secondary or primary private payer combined with a secondary or primary public sponsored program. Therefore, up to five possible contracts can impact one episode of care. In a typical audit, one party is not privy to all five arrangements. Any HCC player may consider its respective contract as "proprietary," "not-related," "outside the scope of audit," or a perceived "violation of HIPAA." This is the challenge and the complexity of effectively addressing healthcare waste, fraud, and abuse. It is the biggest challenge in maintaining and assessing program integrity. For example, if Medicare conducts an audit of a TPA payer's claims on its beneficiaries, the audit scope will be limited to those direct transactions.

The same is true for a private employer. In fact, self-insured employers at times do not receive a full breakdown of the costs associated with support vendors. A provider may be faced with the receipt of an explanation of benefits (EOB) form that is not consistent with the EOB sent to the patient. How does this get resolved? The answer involves the concept of price transparency. The concept of price transparency is currently being discussed in the market in its relationship between the patient and the provider. However, the substantive definition of price transparency should include the ability to understand what piece of the pie was received by the patient, the provider, the support vendors, the payer/TPA, and the plan sponsor. This fluid communication of transactions is not typically disclosed. The auditor's checklist (in addition to the patient checklist) from the provider perspective should include the following:

- Insured status of the patient
- The dynamic of the plan sponsor; self-insured versus premium-based
- If a government-sponsored plan, which one; confirm eligibility
- Understanding of all possible contracts

Exhibit 5.6 represents the blending of HIP issues with ARP issues.

The Payer

The payer forms two subgroups. The first contains those entities that truly act as TPAs. Their business basically involves self-insured employers or government-sponsored programs. They do not take the risk of insurance products. They do not act in the role of an insurance company. The second class of payers is insurance companies. They sell insurance, collect premiums, and take the risk of providing the health insurance product. Members of this group also serve in the capacity of a TPA. In that role, they have customers such as self-insured employers and government-sponsored programs. In the role of the TPA, they serve to process claims according to the plan document provisions. Exhibit 5.7 represents typical functions in the course of processing a claim.

Health Information Pipeline (HIP) and Accounts Receivable Pipeline (ARP)

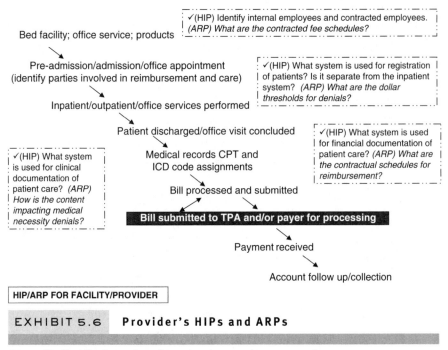

HIP/ARP FOR FACILITY/PROVIDER

EXHIBIT 5.6   Provider's HIPs and ARPs

Source: Medical Business Associates, Inc. (www.mbanews.com).

The payer process is all about the receipt of a claim within the first step. The circle to the left with a list of activities is typically active contemporaneously with the standard pipeline flow. Once the claim is received, the process of plan documentation begins. Several activities can occur during the adjudication process. A certain percentage of claims are *auto-adjudicated*, which means that the electronic system is programmed to provide system checks to verify the appropriateness of the claims. This system avoids human handling. Those that are not auto-adjudicated involve some type of review activity by a claims representative.

The audit process may involve auditing each operational procedure and may include questions such as these:

❑ What internal controls exist when claims are processed through a preferred provider organization?

❑ What assurance is provided that discounts are being applied?

Accounts Receivable Pipeline (ARP)

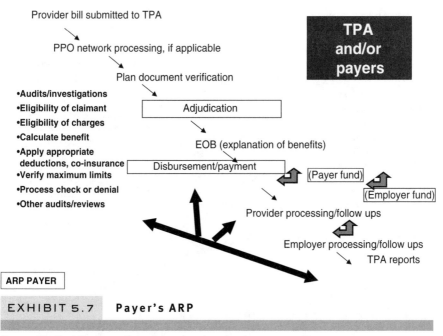

ARP PAYER

EXHIBIT 5.7   Payer's ARP

Source: Medical Business Associates, Inc. (www.mbanews.com).

❐ How is the benefit plan provision verified and tested?

❐ What controls for fraud exist in auto-adjudication activity?

❐ What controls for fraud exist in the claims reviewed by claims staff?

❐ How are the payer and employer fund transaction activities reconciled?

❐ How are denials processed?

❐ What price transparency exists between sponsored plans and provider networks and the patient?

❐ What ongoing training and support is provided to the staff?

Exhibit 5.8 represents a blending of the HIP and ARP for payers.

Overall payer activity has focused on two areas within the marketplace. The first is activity of fraud and abuse within the industry. Payer activity tends to be governed by state laws. However, recent accusations of payers during the adjudication process of altering the codes submitted by the provider and

Health Information Pipeline (HIP) and Accounts Receivable Pipeline (ARP)

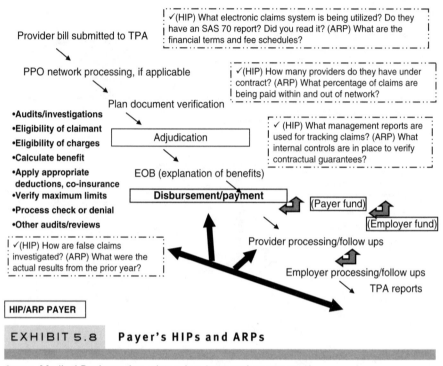

EXHIBIT 5.8   **Payer's HIPs and ARPs**

Source: Medical Business Associates, Inc. (www.mbanews.com).

not responding to beneficiaries have resulted in false claim activity assertions. A review of TPA cases demonstrates this application (see http://oig.hhs .gov/fraud/cia/index.html for a list of CIAs). The second is legislative activity requiring carriers to monitor for fraud and abuse. What is payer fraud and abuse about? It is about *good faith*, which is "willingly" paying claims properly and promptly, and *bad faith*, which is "willingly" not paying, or denying, delaying, or discounting claims.

The False Representation Statute (39 U.S.C. § 3005) is important for all HCC players to know about. This civil law protects the public from aggravated monetary loss where proving fraudulent intent is difficult. Three remedies are available to the Postal Inspection Service under this law in pursuing con artists who use the mail to defraud people. If the Postal Service sues the promoter based on evidence obtained by postal inspectors, it need only prove a particular representation was made, that it is false, and that money or property was sought through the mail.

State laws vary with respect to payer activity. Samples of bad-faith criteria noted by various state insurance commissioners include these:

1. Misrepresenting pertinent facts of insurance policy provisions relating to coverage at issue

2. Failing to acknowledge and act reasonably and promptly upon communications with respect to claims arising out of insurance policies

3. Failing to adopt and implement reasonable standards for the prompt investigation of claims arising under insurance policies

4. Refusing to pay claims without conducting a reasonable investigation based on all available information

5. Failing to confirm or deny coverage of claims within a reasonable time after proof of loss statement has been completed

6. Not attempting in good faith to effectuate fair and equitable settlements of claims in which liability has become reasonably clear

7. Compelling insureds to institute litigation to recover amounts due under an insurance policy by offering substantially less than the amount ultimately recovered in actions brought by such insureds

8. Attempting to settle a claim for less than the amount to which a reasonable man would have believed he was entitled by reference to written or printed advertising material accompanying or made part of an application

9. Attempting to settle claims on the basis of an application that was altered without notice to, or knowledge or consent of, the insured

10. Making claims payments to insured or beneficiaries not accompanied by a statement setting forth the coverage under which the payments are being made

11. Making known to insureds or claimants a policy of appealing from arbitration awards in favor of insureds or claimants for the purpose of compelling them to accept settlements or compromises less than the amount awarded in arbitration

12. Delaying the investigation or payment of claims by requiring an insured, claimant, or the physician of either to submit a preliminary claim report and then requiring the subsequent submission of formal proof of loss forms, both of which submissions contain substantially the same information

13. Failing to promptly settle claims where liability has become reasonably clear less than one portion of the insurance policy coverage in order to influence settlements under other portions of the insurance policy coverage

14. Failing to promptly provide a reasonable explanation of the basis in the insurance policy in relation to the facts or applicable law for denial of a claim or for the offer of a compromise settlement (www.badfaithinsurance.org/definitions.html)

The above noted items can be converted to an auditor's checklist for operational audit activity and internal controls to ensure that the payer does not encounter these issues.

The Employer/Plan Sponsor

Auditing and investigation techniques for the employer or plan sponsor vary, depending on whether the program is a public one, such as Medicare and Medicaid, or one containing self-insured and premium-based employer plans. The government plans have established right-to-audit clauses and mandates for the production of records. Self-insured employers typically learn on their first audit what information and financial transactions they are entitled to review within their benefit plans. They are typically subject to the audit clauses negotiated. Therefore, the first order from the employer perspective is to audit the contract. If it does not contain an audit provision, the payer may still agree to provide access to verify expenditures directly or through an audit agent. When the employer renews the agreement, specific audit provisions should be included. At *minimum*, the auditor's checklist should include these items:

- ☐ A right to audit claims paid
- ☐ The ability to audit TPA fees
- ☐ The ability to audit program guarantees

Many activities are involved in auditing program integrity. However, if the plan sponsor cannot independently corroborate fees and program guarantees, the contract is simply a bad deal. Exhibit 5.9 shows the employer's/plan sponsor's ARP.

Accounts Receivable Pipeline (ARP)

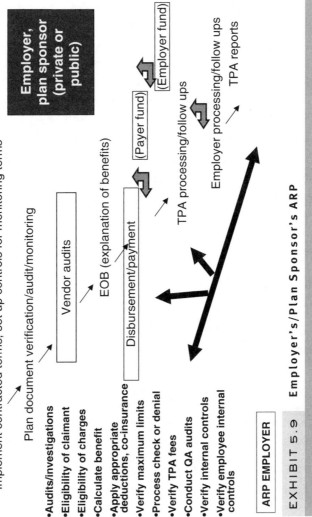

Contract with TPA

Implement contracted terms; set up controls for monitoring terms

Plan document verification/audit/monitoring

Vendor audits

EOB (explanation of benefits)

Disbursement/payment

•Audits/investigations
•Eligibility of claimant
•Eligibility of charges
•Calculate benefit
•Apply appropriate
 deductions, co-insurance
•Verify maximum limits
•Process check or denial
•Verify TPA fees
•Conduct QA audits
•Verify internal controls
•Verify employee internal
 controls

Employer,
plan sponsor
(private or
public)

(Payer fund)

(Employer fund)

TPA processing/follow ups

Employer processing/follow ups

TPA reports

ARP EMPLOYER

EXHIBIT 5.9   Employer's/Plan Sponsor's ARP

Source: Medical Business Associates, Inc. (www.mbanews.com).

93

The pipeline for the plan sponsor begins with the contract. In the private employer market, as an auditor it is important to review the actual signed contract between all parties. Internal controls should be viewed from the perspective of the employer as well. For example, for the audit checklist item below that concerns "eligibility of claimant," the payer is dependent on the employer to provide this information. How often is it updated? What controls are in place that ensure the integrity of the beneficiary and of its qualifications to participate in the plan?

The rapidly rising cost of healthcare has left many without the ability to obtain insurance coverage. Fraud schemes to obtain such coverage have materialized through the generation of *ghost employees*. Look at the scenario for this scheme. A local municipality hires a friend who can't get health insurance. The new hire is placed on the payroll and entered into the benefit plan. The employee does not actually work. The ghost employee receives medical benefits. The ghost employee cashes his payroll check and provides it to the hiring supervisor as compensation for participation in the benefit plan.

The auditor's checklist should include internal controls for the following:

- ☐ How many audits are conducted?
- ☐ How many investigations of suspect claims have been conducted?
- ☐ How is the eligibility of claimant file tested?
- ☐ How is the eligibility of charges tested?
- ☐ How many claims are paid at 100 percent of charges?
- ☐ How are benefits calculated?
- ☐ How are deductions and co-insurance applied and confirmed?
- ☐ How are maximum limits verified?
- ☐ How is a check processed or denied?
- ☐ How are TPA fees verified?
- ☐ Are quality assurance audits conducted, and what are the standards?
- ☐ Does the plan sponsor have an SAS 70 report or equivalent?

Exhibit 5.10 demonstrates the integration of the employer's/plan sponsor's HIPs and ARPs.

Note that the implications for government-sponsored plans are similar in that the program integrity is tested at the same functional levels. However,

Health Information Pipeline (HIP) and Accounts Receivable Pipeline (ARP)

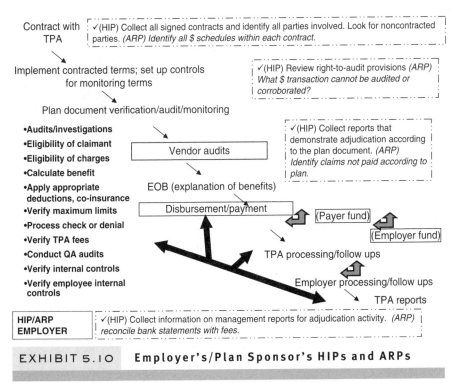

Contract with TPA : ✓(HIP) Collect all signed contracts and identify all parties involved. Look for noncontracted parties. *(ARP) Identify all $ schedules within each contract.*

Implement contracted terms; set up controls for monitoring terms

✓(HIP) Review right-to-audit provisions *(ARP) What $ transaction cannot be audited or corroborated?*

Plan document verification/audit/monitoring

•Audits/investigations
•Eligibility of claimant
•Eligibility of charges
•Calculate benefit
•Apply appropriate deductions, co-insurance
•Verify maximum limits
•Process check or denial
•Verify TPA fees
•Conduct QA audits
•Verify internal controls
•Verify employee internal controls

Vendor audits

✓(HIP) Collect reports that demonstrate adjudication according to the plan document. *(ARP) Identify claims not paid according to plan.*

EOB (explanation of benefits)

Disbursement/payment

(Payer fund)

(Employer fund)

TPA processing/follow ups

Employer processing/follow ups

TPA reports

HIP/ARP EMPLOYER : ✓(HIP) Collect information on management reports for adjudication activity. *(ARP) reconcile bank statements with fees.*

EXHIBIT 5.10   Employer's/Plan Sponsor's HIPs and ARPs

Source: Medical Business Associates, Inc. (www.mbanews.com).

they vary with respect to required reporting functions and specific access to information within each operational function. The auditor's checklist is the same in tracking down the essence of how the program operates and complete identification of the program rules.

Others

The next HCC is the category of "others." Exhibit 5.11 involves a large range of contributors that may present themselves in the course of a healthcare transaction. For example, the patient may receive a service from a provider with subsequent prescriptions for medications or equipment. If it is a workers' compensation event, an "other" may include a case manager. It could be simply the ambulance transport company. It could involve ancillary services such as billing agents. View this category as any

Accounts Receivable Pipeline (ARP)

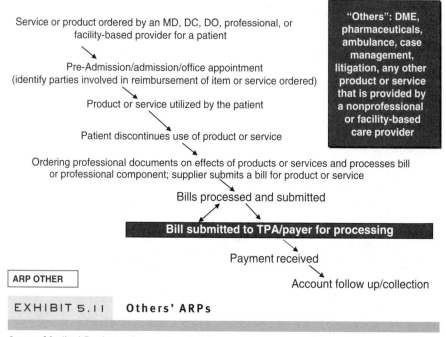

Service or product ordered by an MD, DC, DO, professional, or facility-based provider for a patient

Pre-Admission/admission/office appointment
(identify parties involved in reimbursement of item or service ordered)

Product or service utilized by the patient

Patient discontinues use of product or service

"Others": DME, pharmaceuticals, ambulance, case management, litigation, any other product or service that is provided by a nonprofessional or facility-based care provider

Ordering professional documents on effects of products or services and processes bill or professional component; supplier submits a bill for product or service

Bills processed and submitted

Bill submitted to TPA/payer for processing

Payment received

| ARP OTHER |

Account follow up/collection

EXHIBIT 5.11   Others' ARPs

Source: Medical Business Associates, Inc. (www.mbanews.com).

other product, service, and entity or professional that may be involved in the course of the patient's care.

The auditor process or investigation is similar to the audit checklists provided. As an overview, it is important to understand all parties involved in the transaction from the patient, provider, payer, and employer/plan sponsor perspectives. When you encounter an entity within the category of "other," the relationship back to each one of these parties should be understood. For example, the ambulance company may be contracted by the provider. The case manager may be contracted with the payer. The plan sponsor at some point may fund these transactions, but they may appear to be seamless. As an auditor, it is important to separate the entities that operate behind the scenes.

Exhibit 5.12 represents the integration of HIP and ARP within the general category of "others."

Note that it becomes critical in this general category to identify the basis for relationships identified. Within each relationship, identify *clinical* relationships, which involve only referral of patients for consultations; *financial* relationships, which are those in which some type of financial transaction occurs; and *blended* relationships, which are those that involve both. It is the blended relationships that should be tested for any *Stark*-related issues.

Stark I was enacted as part of the Omnibus Budget Reconciliation Act of 1989 (H.R. 3299 § 6204). The focus was to prevent inappropriate financial influences over physicians' decisions about the best care for their patients. The market problem that evolved was that in practice the prohibitions have caused uncertainty to providers as they struggle to respond to various market forces on cost constraints. The *self-referral law*, as enacted in 1989, prohibited a physician from referring a patient to a clinical laboratory with which he or she (or an immediate family member) has a financial relationship.

- *Stark I* initiated the rule that a physician or immediate family member may not have a financial interest with certain entities providing clinical laboratory services and, in cases in which they did, they may not bill Medicare or Medicaid.
- *Stark II* provided additional amendments expanding the referral and billing prohibitions to additional "designated health services."

The auditor's checklist may include investigation of

☐ A financial relationship between a healthcare entity and physician.
  A financial relationship includes an ownership or investment interest in an entity by a physician or his immediate family member, or a compensation arrangement between a physician or his immediate family member and the entity. The prohibited compensation arrangements include direct or indirect remunerations that are made in cash or kind.

☐ A referral by the physician to the entity for designated health services.
  A referral includes a request for any designated health service payable under Medicare or Medicaid. It is important to note that because Stark II does not have an intent requirement strict liability is imposed for referrals whenever a financial relationship exists.

☐ The submission of a claim for the services.

Health Information Pipeline (HIP) and Accounts Receivable Pipeline (ARP)

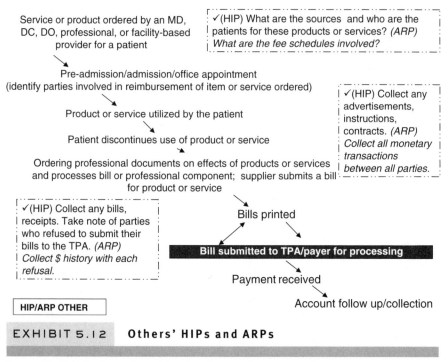

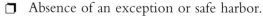

EXHIBIT 5.12   Others' HIPs and ARPs

Source: Medical Business Associates, Inc. (www.mbanews.com).

☐ An entity receiving a prohibited referral may not make a Medicare claim.

Such an entity is also forbidden from billing any individual, third-party payer, or other entity for any designated health services for which the physician made the referral.

☐ Absence of an exception or safe harbor.

The Stark amendments contain several exceptions for certain financial arrangements. These exceptions fall into three categories:

1. Exceptions that are applicable to both physician ownership or investment interests and compensation arrangements

2. Exceptions for ownership or investment interests only

3. Exceptions for compensation arrangements only

Congress extended the law to prohibit a physician from referring patients to providers of ten other categories of healthcare services if the physician (or an immediate family member) has a financial relationship with the service provider. The ten affected services are physical therapy services; occupational therapy services; radiology services and supplies; radiation therapy services and supplies; durable medical equipment and supplies; parenteral and enteral nutrients, equipment, and supplies; prosthetics, orthotics, and prosthetic devices and supplies; home health services; outpatient prescription drugs; and inpatient and outpatient hospital services. The law also prohibits an entity from billing for services provided as the result of a prohibited referral.

ARP Overview: Implications for Prevention, Detection, and Investigation

As discussed earlier in the chapter, reimbursement models are typically negotiated within three general methodologies. Understanding reimbursement models is the cornerstone to successful healthcare fraud investigation. The rules behind reimbursements drive the creativity of the ethically challenged. The goal of the fraudster is to manipulate information, divert funds, and execute various fraud schemes without getting caught. The goal of the auditor or investigator is to understand all the rules so the manipulations can be caught.

The prospective payment system has a specific set of rules. The prospective payment system is a predetermined rate that is calculated for inpatient and outpatient care. A sample prospective payment system includes the current Medicare inpatient model of DRGs. It is not unusual for private payers to negotiate the use of this model for reimbursement of hospitalized care. This model involves listing the diagnosis determined after study, along with the procedures provided to the patient while he or she was hospitalized, in order to determine the appropriate DRG group for billing purposes. Each provider receives a weighted predetermined amount for patients who fall into a particular group. The theory behind a prospective system is that it promotes the provider's effective utilization of services to a patient. Therefore, the motivation for profit is "less is more."

This concept evolved into the outpatient area. Outpatient prospective models include APGs and follow the same model. The professional-based prospective model involved a system called Resource-Based Relative Value Scale (RBRVS). This is a payment model driven by Medicare to establish compensation for physician services. The calculations take into consideration the RBRVS, the geographic practice cost indexes (GPCIs), and the monetary conversion factor. The fee schedule model also referred to is a concurrent fee schedule. These fees include listing of charges, the listing of itemized charges or the à la carte listing or fee for services. Expect continued evolutions and applications of reimbursement models in other patient care settings.

A final note: All models may include a retrospective component. This incorporates some type of contractual retrospective adjustment. Note that one episode of care among all the HCC players may be impacted by as many as five contractual relationships. If one of these contracts has a retrospective adjustment process, it is typically contained within the two parties.

This lengthy chapter introduces the ARP process and blends the ARP concept with that of the HIP process. The players are involved: fragmented and layered operationally, contractually, and financially. Not one entity or player in the normal courses of business has all data elements associated with one entire episode of a healthcare transaction. The market prevents a fluid audit trail from patient to provider to payer to vendor to plan sponsor. In a trillion-dollar market, this is significant when it comes to waste, fraud, and abuse. This is the recipe for any party, entity, or individual to seek the satiation of greed. With this fragmentation in mind, the billion-dollar fraud industry is managed by ethically challenged individuals who have allowed money to be their masters. At every turn, the auditor or investigator is dependent on a number of tools to get at the truth.

The chapter that follows introduces the next requirement in the audit process: blending operational flow activities (OFAs) with ARPs and HIPs.

Operational Flow Activity

> *The Truth is the incontrovertible; malice may attack it, ignorance may deride it, but in the end, there it is.*
>
> —WINSTON CHURCHILL

U p to this point, we have discussed the players within the healthcare continuum (HCC): patient, provider, payer, employer or plan sponsor, and vendor or supplier. The elements of protected health information (PHI) were introduced in Chapter 3, followed by health information pipelines (HIPs) in Chapter 4. Chapter 5 integrated the monetary transactions by auditing the accounts receivable pipeline (ARP). The next step in the pursuit of incontrovertible truth is blending these concepts in an operational flow activity assessment.

OPERATIONAL FLOW ACTIVITY ASSESSMENT

What exactly is operational flow activity (OFA)? Operational flow is the identification and flowcharting of the actual business components. By comparison, HIPs identify the sources and uses of health information. The ARPs identify the monetary implications of the sources and uses of health information. OFAs identify the procedural aspects associated with HIPs and ARPs.

The auditor's checklist includes tracing the operational procedures associated within each market player and creating a process flowchart. At each identified operational function, the following should be identified:

- ☐ Internal communications
- ☐ External communications
- ☐ Critical communication component
  - ☐ Electronic
  - ☐ Paper
  - ☐ Verbal
  - ☐ Facsimile
  - ☐ People
  - ☐ Systems
  - ☐ Product or service output

The Patient

Exhibit 6.1 demonstrates the application of the OFA concept and integrates it into the previous discussion of the patient's HIPs and ARPs.

Note the following flow of audit/investigation preparation:

- ☐ HIP = identification of health information
- ☐ ARP = identification of the monetary aspects of the health information
- ☐ OFA = identification of the procedural aspects of the health information and the monetary transactions

Exhibit 6.1 demonstrates a sample application of the HIP identification. "Did they receive an EOB?" This is the health information associated with the billing of services. The ARP component addresses any financial transaction associated with the information. The OFA addresses the functional aspect of the explanation of benefits (EOB). The OFA is the procedural aspect of the issue at hand. Therefore, the process of HIP identification is to identify the relevant health information within the business flow. Once identified, associate any monetary implication through the process of ARP modeling. Upon completion, add the procedural aspects

Health Information Pipeline (HIP) and Accounts Receivable Pipeline (ARP) and Operational Flow Activity (OFA)

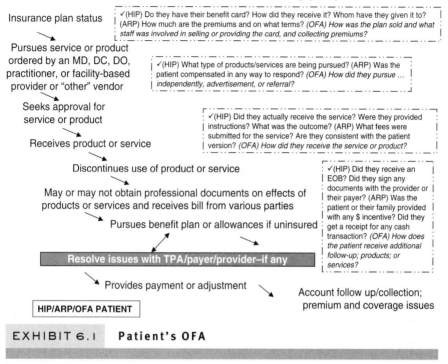

Insurance plan status

> ✓(HIP) Do they have their benefit card? How did they receive it? Whom have they given it to? (ARP) How much are the premiums and on what terms? *(OFA) How was the plan sold and what staff was involved in selling or providing the card, and collecting premiums?*

Pursues service or product ordered by an MD, DC, DO, practitioner, or facility-based provider or "other" vendor

> ✓(HIP) What type of products/services are being pursued? (ARP) Was the patient compensated in any way to respond? *(OFA) How did they pursue ... independently, advertisement, or referral?*

Seeks approval for service or product

> ✓(HIP) Did they actually receive the service? Were they provided instructions? What was the outcome? (ARP) What fees were submitted for the service? Are they consistent with the patient version? *(OFA) How did they receive the service or product?*

Receives product or service

Discontinues use of product or service

May or may not obtain professional documents on effects of products or services and receives bill from various parties

Pursues benefit plan or allowances if uninsured

> ✓(HIP) Did they receive an EOB? Did they sign any documents with the provider or their payer? (ARP) Was the patient or their family provided with any $ incentive? Did they get a receipt for any cash transaction? *(OFA) How does the patient receive additional follow-up; products; or services?*

Resolve issues with TPA/payer/provider–if any

Provides payment or adjustment

Account follow up/collection; premium and coverage issues

HIP/ARP/OFA PATIENT

EXHIBIT 6.1   Patient's OFA

Source: Medical Business Associates, Inc. (www.mbanews.com).

associated with both the information itself and the monetary transactions all into one side-by-side comparison.

The Provider

The provider, as discussed in earlier chapters, is the entity that gives care via a professional or facility-based transaction. Exhibit 6.2 represents the contemporaneous application of the provider's HIPs, ARPs, and OFAs.

The Payer

The payer's role is that of insurance company or third-party administrator (TPA). It is, in essence, the role that processes the actual payment for services rendered. The dynamics of this role involve contractual transactions between

Health Information Pipeline (HIP) and Accounts Receivable Pipeline (ARP) and Operational Flow Activity (OFA)

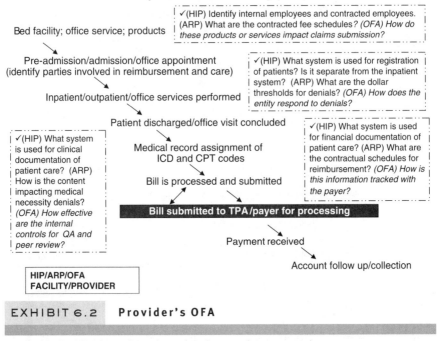

EXHIBIT 6.2   Provider's OFA

Source: Medical Business Associates, Inc. (www.mbanews.com).

the plan sponsor and the provider, in addition to any support- or vendor-type roles. The contractual application and reviews are typically independent of all parties. For example, if an employer is auditing its contractual relationship with the TPA, the information exchange is typically just between the payer and the plan sponsor. Likewise, if an audit is occurring between a provider and a TPA, the review is limited to the transactions between the two parties. Please keep in mind that all relationships can be, and typically are, impacted by the same healthcare episode that was initiated by the patient. Exhibit 6.3 shows the application of the payer's HIPs, ARPs, and OFAs.

The audit and investigative preparation is applied in the payer environment. To illustrate one example, refer to the diagram in Exhibit 6.3. What HIP information is contained within management reports, in particular, for claims that are being processed? This is followed by an understanding of the contractual monetary arrangements that have been agreed on for the handling of these claims. The OFA procedural aspect of this concept is to

Health Information Pipeline (HIP) and Accounts Receivable Pipeline (ARP) and Operation Flow Activity (OFA)

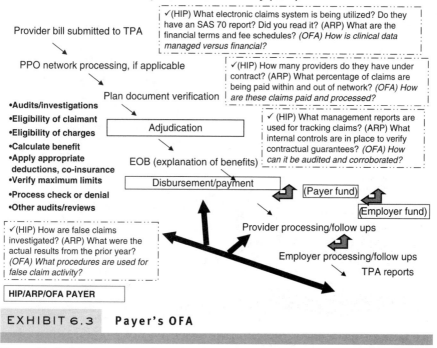

Provider bill submitted to TPA

✓(HIP) What electronic claims system is being utilized? Do they have an SAS 70 report? Did you read it? (ARP) What are the financial terms and fee schedules? *(OFA) How is clinical data managed versus financial?*

PPO network processing, if applicable

✓(HIP) How many providers do they have under contract? (ARP) What percentage of claims are being paid within and out of network? *(OFA) How are these claims paid and processed?*

Plan document verification

•Audits/investigations
•Eligibility of claimant
•Eligibility of charges
•Calculate benefit
•Apply appropriate deductions, co-insurance
•Verify maximum limits
•Process check or denial
•Other audits/reviews

Adjudication

✓ (HIP) What management reports are used for tracking claims? (ARP) What internal controls are in place to verify contractual guarantees? *(OFA) How can it be audited and corroborated?*

EOB (explanation of benefits)

Disbursement/payment

(Payer fund)

(Employer fund)

✓(HIP) How are false claims investigated? (ARP) What were the actual results from the prior year? *(OFA) What procedures are used for false claim activity?*

Provider processing/follow ups

Employer processing/follow ups

TPA reports

HIP/ARP/OFA PAYER

EXHIBIT 6.3   Payer's OFA

Source: Medical Business Associates, Inc. (www.mbanews.com).

determine how management reports and any financial reporting of the claims processing can be audited and corroborated.

The Employer

Many employers provide premium-based coverage to their employees. In essence, the insurance company takes on the risk for coverage by charging a flat rate per employee per month. In this situation, the employer should be concerned about how its "risk" is being measured, for instance, by any utilization reports that are generated on its employee population. They should ask questions like "How does the payer verify and control that fraudulent claims are not being profiled within my organization's utilization report, thus affecting future rate increases?" Exhibit 6.4 highlights typical operational components with the application first of HIP, followed by ARP, and then by OFA sample issues.

Health Information Pipeline (HIP) and Accounts Receivable Pipeline (ARP) and Operational Flow Activity (OFA)

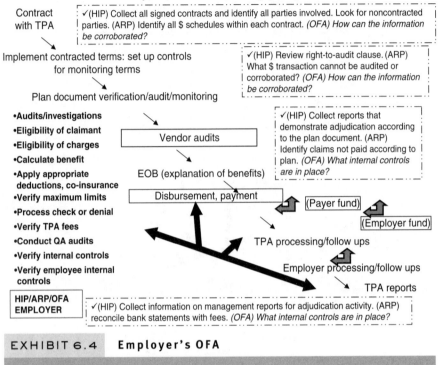

EXHIBIT 6.4   Employer's OFA

Source: Medical Business Associates, Inc. (www.mbanews.com).

The majority of this book focuses on the self-insured employer and the risks that they face. The self-insured employer should be viewed in the same light from a control perspective as is any government-sponsored program such as Medicare and Medicaid. Keep in mind, too, that from a multinational perspective, issues related to government-sponsored programs are similar to any other government-sponsored program in any country. The global similarity in healthcare regardless of country is that we all use a diagnosis coding system for communicating the diagnosis that is being treated by the provider for a particular patient episode. Globally, healthcare delivery is similar from the perspective of the patient receiving services from a provider, a provider submitting claims for payment to a third party, and the plan sponsor being funded by the respective government.

Health Information Pipeline (HIP) and Accounts Receivable Pipeline (ARP) and Operational Flow Activity (OFA)

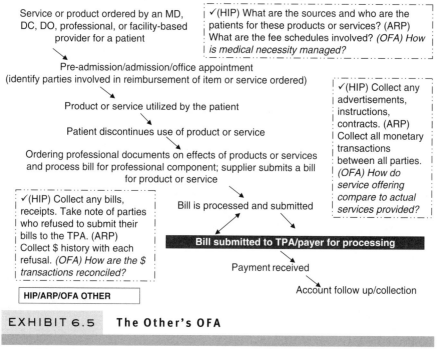

EXHIBIT 6.5   The Other's OFA

Source: Medical Business Associates, Inc. (www.mbanews.com).

The "Other"

This is a major category and, as discussed earlier, can represent any support-type vendor ranging from durable medical equipment to case managers to pharmaceuticals. Exhibit 6.5 shows the OFA concept in relation to the "other."

Conceptually the issues are the same with respect to the process of identifying relevant HIP, ARP, and OFA information. In this scenario, the table provides three different examples at various points in the pipeline of issues that could be addressed. This "other" component can be further broken down. Regardless of what support vendor is being reviewed, the discussion begins with the identification of what is normal in terms of business flow and respective information and money transactions. The process of identifying what is normal will be isolating anything that is outside of this activity. Anomalies will materialize.

OFA Overview: Implications for Prevention, Detection, and Investigation

Incontrovertible truth is obtained by utilizing a methodology that will cut through any blind spots and expunge information in a "pure" form. Purity of evidence is critical for an effective audit and investigation. Malice and ignorance can be mitigated by following the collection guidelines checklist:

- ☐ Internal communications
- ☐ External communications
- ☐ Critical communication component
    - ☐ Electronic
    - ☐ Paper
    - ☐ Verbal
    - ☐ Facsimile
    - ☐ People
    - ☐ Systems
    - ☐ Product or service output

This collection checklist should be followed by the three-layered operational data collection tools of pipelines. The audit and investigation begins by recognizing the layered process of the HIPs. HIP is the process of identifying the health information involved. This is followed by the ARP, collecting the respective monetary transaction. Finally, the next parallel is collecting the OFA, which is the operational flow activity alongside the HIP and the ARP.

When these pipelines are used to identify all normal flows of information, anomalies will then materialize. These anomalies will trigger the appropriate audit and investigation. An effective prevention program will not materialize without this understanding. Detection will certainly be overlooked without this detailed analysis. A comprehensive investigation will not yield sufficient evidence for successful prosecution without the blending of all three functions. Therefore, the key implication for prevention, detection, and investigation is that the OFA concept brings the investor one step closer toward identification of activity that normally would be missed.

The next step is learning to integrate product market activity (PMA) into the audit and investigative process. This is the topic of Chapter 7.

Product, Service, and Consumer Market Activity

We must rapidly begin the shift from a "thing-oriented" society to a "person-oriented" society. When machines and computers, profit motives and property rights are considered more important than people, the giant triplets of racism, materialism, and militarism are incapable of being conquered.

—Martin Luther King, Jr.

Product, service, and consumer market activity is the business side of healthcare. The PMA, SMA, and CMA perspective helps separate the human side of healthcare. How else can the mind rationalize providing invasive procedures to another human being with full knowledge that the service was not necessary? How can a dentist pull healthy teeth from a child? How can a surgeon perform life-threatening surgical procedures with no basis?

Likewise, how can a claims system process deny a procedure that is necessary to sustain the patient's life prior to the completion of the appeals process, therefore making the long-term costs a mute issue? If we walk further down the pipeline of the benefit plan, how can decisions be made on eliminating benefits based on the need for cost savings alone? What if money simply does not exist or the expense of services will not allow for profit shareholder expectations? It is the "thing"-oriented side of healthcare versus the "people" side that often drives the ethically challenged to cross that line in pursuit of profits. Greed has no barriers.

PRODUCT MARKET ACTIVITY

Product market activity (PMA) is identifying the products that are used throughout the healthcare continuum (HCC). Products include software tools to enhance care in addition to tools used during the delivery of care. The major expenditure categories for auditors and investigators include durable medical equipment, supplies, and medications. A classic PMA example is a case involving the use of 340 B drugs. In 1992, the Veterans Health Care Act included a section referred to as "Section 340 B of U.S. Public Law 102–585." In essence, what this does is provide access by covered entities to a significant savings on pharmaceuticals by providers who participate in the program.

Some providers have found an opportunity to exploit this program by obtaining discounted drugs and then reselling them for a profit. A data sample may include a rheumatologist receiving a significant amount of cancer drugs through this program. Exhibit 7.1 incorporates the concept discussed so far in this book. Any audit or investigation will begin by taking the appropriate business flow pipeline. In this case, we are looking at a provider. Since we are talking about a medication, the line begins with the manufacturer. The manufacturer is providing 340 B drugs through the appropriate channels. Parties such as distributors may exist between the manufacturer and the provider. Regardless, the general concepts are covered in Exhibit 7.1.

After the appropriate business pipeline is identified, the first step is the health information pipeline (HIP) process. Within that provider setting, identify the patient profiles associated with the clinic. This is followed by reviewing the appropriate accounts receivable pipeline (ARP) issue, which would include the entities' financial designations and their respective cost reports. Do they meet the standard for appropriate designation to participate in the 340 B program? The third step is the office of fiscal analysis (OFA). What is the business flow and operational flow of the clinic? The PMA activity is simply identifying the 340 B drugs in receipt by the facility. At this point, do

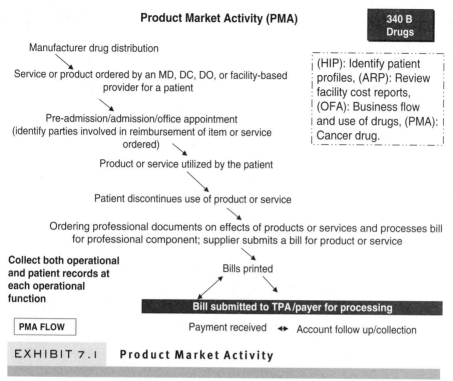

Product Market Activity (PMA)

340 B Drugs

Manufacturer drug distribution

Service or product ordered by an MD, DC, DO, or facility-based provider for a patient

Pre-admission/admission/office appointment (identify parties involved in reimbursement of item or service ordered)

Product or service utilized by the patient

Patient discontinues use of product or service

Ordering professional documents on effects of products or services and processes bill for professional component; supplier submits a bill for product or service

Collect both operational and patient records at each operational function

Bills printed

(HIP): Identify patient profiles, (ARP): Review facility cost reports, (OFA): Business flow and use of drugs, (PMA): Cancer drug.

PMA FLOW

Bill submitted to TPA/payer for processing

Payment received ◄► Account follow up/collection

EXHIBIT 7.1   **Product Market Activity**

Source: Medical Business Associates, Inc. (www.mbanews.com).

they have the facilities to provide the treatment regimen reflective of the drugs that are being received?

SERVICE MARKET ACTIVITY

Service market activity (SMA) is identifying the professional and nonprofessional support services provided to patients and their families. Another perspective in the analytics of a healthcare service is lining up the products that are charged to a patient and the professionals who are providing those services. Does a skill set match? The expectation would be that if the facility is purchasing cancer drugs, the professional staff should include physicians who are trained in oncology. The facility should be structured to treat these patients while receiving the cancer medication. In continuing this example, we progress by adding the SMA component to the audit process (see Exhibit 7.2). In the data set provided for this example, a red flag would be occurring prior to the next step. We have Dr. Rheumatoid receiving 340 B cancer drugs. He

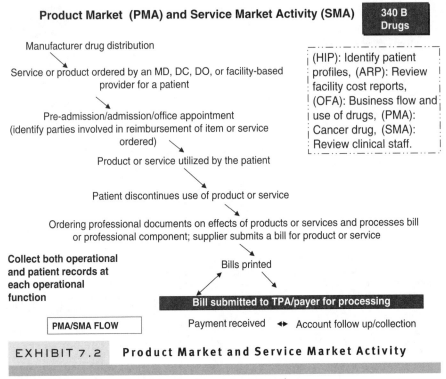

EXHIBIT 7.2   Product Market and Service Market Activity

Source: Medical Business Associates, Inc. (www.mbanews.com).

does not have the patient population or the staff to support the provision of the drugs. This would then lead us to take a closer look at the patients in receipt of the medications. This would require a consumer market activity analysis.

CONSUMER MARKET ACTIVITY

Consumer market activity (CMA) is identifying the behavior patterns of the patient and their families. This includes purchase, choice, and selection decisions by the consumer and the influences driving them. The continued analysis should incorporate lining up how the patient makes the consumer choice along with the product and services being provided by the provider. What was the source of the patients associated with the 340 B drugs? Were they recruited? Were they referred? If referred, does any type of financial relationship exist with the referring party? In continuing this example, we

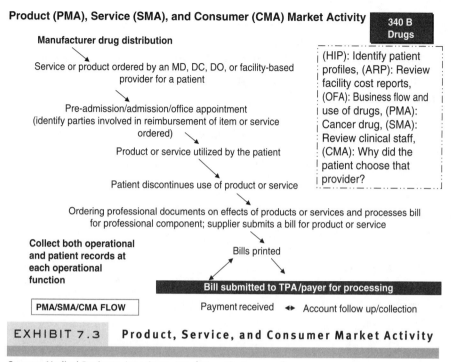

Product (PMA), Service (SMA), and Consumer (CMA) Market Activity

340 B Drugs

Manufacturer drug distribution

Service or product ordered by an MD, DC, DO, or facility-based provider for a patient

Pre-admission/admission/office appointment
(identify parties involved in reimbursement of item or service ordered)

Product or service utilized by the patient

Patient discontinues use of product or service

(HIP): Identify patient profiles, (ARP): Review facility cost reports, (OFA): Business flow and use of drugs, (PMA): Cancer drug, (SMA): Review clinical staff, (CMA): Why did the patient choose that provider?

Ordering professional documents on effects of products or services and processes bill for professional component; supplier submits a bill for product or service

Collect both operational and patient records at each operational function

Bills printed

PMA/SMA/CMA FLOW

Bill submitted to TPA/payer for processing

Payment received   ◂▸   Account follow up/collection

EXHIBIT 7.3   Product, Service, and Consumer Market Activity

Source: Medical Business Associates, Inc. (www.mbanews.com).

progress by adding the CMA component to the audit process (see Exhibit 7.3).

The data sample that initiated this discussion included a provider who was a rheumatologist. In this example, the rheumatologist's clinic was approved by the Department of Health and Human Services to receive 340 B program drugs. Within the list of medications was a series of cancer treatment drugs. The doctor created files on these patients at his clinic to meet the perceived documentation standard of the 340 B program; however, the patients were treated at other clinics in other states by oncologists. The "treatment" is defined as the actual receipt of the 340 B medication at a different facility by a different treating provider. Dr. Rheumatoid sold his supply of 340 B program cancer drugs to the oncology clinics for a fee higher than what he paid and lower than what the manufacturer would normally charge for the medication. Therefore, is this an abuse of a 340 B program medication? Does Dr. Rheumatoid have issues with redistributing medications across state lines? Another question would involve the issue of fee splitting and any inappropriate referrals under the Stark laws (laws that target physician referrals that may result in medically unnecessary services wherein a financial incentive for the referral exists).

This book has presented several specific auditors' checklists for initiating an audit and pursuing an investigation. The following is a summary of these items.

Auditor's Checklist of Communication Activity

- ☐ Internal communications
- ☐ External communications
- ☐ Critical communication component
    - ☐ Electronic
    - ☐ Paper
    - ☐ Verbal
    - ☐ Facsimile
    - ☐ People
    - ☐ Systems
    - ☐ Product or service output

Auditor's Checklist of Operational Activity

- ☐ HCC = identification of the healthcare continuum player involved in the transactions
    - ☐ Patient
    - ☐ Provider
    - ☐ Payer
    - ☐ Employer/plan sponsor
    - ☐ Vendor/supplier
    - ☐ Government
    - ☐ Staff
    - ☐ Unauthorized parties

- ☐ HIP = identification of health information
- ☐ ARP = identification of the monetary aspects of the health information
- ☐ OFA = identification of the procedural aspects of the health information and the monetary transactions

❐ PMA = identification of products involved in the delivery of healthcare services

❐ SMA = identification of the services involved in the delivery of healthcare services

❐ CMA = identification of the consumer selection or choice activity in the delivery of healthcare services

Auditor's Checklist of Rule-Based Activity

❐ What regulatory issues are involved?

❐ What contracts govern the parties?

❐ Are the terms public, private, or both?

❐ Are the public terms subject to state or federal laws?

❐ What reimbursement models are being used?

❐ What is the incentive for profit?

❐ How can the rules be manipulated?

❐ What are the loopholes?

❐ Can the rules be audited and corroborated?

A sample of HCC segment activity may include:

The Patient

❐ Any contracts they were asked to sign by the provider

❐ Any online purchases of medications

❐ Any written communications from their providers

❐ Any written communications from their payers

❐ Any written communications from their plan sponsors

The Provider

❐ Insured status of the patient

❐ The dynamic of the plan sponsor; self-insured versus premium-based

❐ If a government-sponsored plan, which one; confirm eligibility

❐ Understanding of all possible contracts

The Payer

☐ What internal controls exist when claims are processed through a preferred provider organization?

☐ What assurance is provided that discounts are being applied?

☐ How is the benefit plan provision verified and tested?

☐ What controls for fraud exist in auto-adjudication activity?

☐ What controls for fraud exist in the claims reviewed by claims staff?

☐ How are the payer and employer fund transaction activities reconciled?

☐ How are denials processed?

☐ What price transparency exists between sponsored plans and provider networks and the patient?

☐ What ongoing training and support is provided to the staff?

The Employer

☐ A right to audit claims paid.

☐ The ability to audit TPA fees.

☐ The ability to audit program guarantees.

☐ How many audits are conducted?

☐ How many investigations of suspect claims have been conducted?

☐ How is the eligibility of claimant file tested?

☐ How is the eligibility of charges tested?

☐ How many claims are paid at 100 percent of charges?

☐ How are benefits calculated?

☐ How are deductions and co-insurance applied and confirmed?

☐ How are maximum limits verified?

☐ How is a check processed or denied?

☐ How are TPA fees verified?

These checklists have been provided in the pursuit of auditing and investigating healthcare fraud. The focus of healthcare fraud has been the misrepresentation of a healthcare service. The submission of a false claim, the submission for services that are not medically necessary, the submission of claims for services that were never rendered, counterfeit medications—the list is extensive. The 340 B program abuse example presents another complicated type of fraud that is pervasive throughout the healthcare market. This is referred to as *economic structural fraud* (ESF). ESF is the manipulation of the systematic structure of the market players within the HCC and their contractual written and verbal arrangements. The 340 B program requires that the provider must have a patient record. Could 340 B program abuse result if the rules are manipulated? For example, the 340 B program has a criterion that the providers maintain a patient record. However, the 340 B program does not specify, from an audit perspective, exactly what constitutes a patient record. Dr. Rheumatoid created patient records that included basic demographic information and then sold the cancer drug to the clinic that would be providing the clinical treatment. Therefore, could Dr. Rheumatoid feel justified in his actions by creating a physical file with patient demographic information to meet the minimum criteria for receipt of the 340 B cancer drug?

The patients involved are real, have diagnoses of cancer, and are receiving the medications appropriately by the third-party clinics. The issue is not a misrepresentation of the healthcare service but an economic and structural misrepresentation of the financial transactions of a government-initiated program. In keeping with the drug theme of economic structural fraud, the following series is represented as well. The goal when working within a particular HCC player is to identify the normal pattern within the market segment. The added emphasis of *normal* is critical. See Exhibit 7.4. Since patterns for healthcare fraud and economic structural fraud are constantly evolving in theme and methodology, the only constant factor is defining the normal operational flow. Therefore, the premise is if you identify normal, *abnormal* should become apparent to the trained observer.

Exhibit 7.5 demonstrates numerous abnormal activities that can result from this market segment. They involve both healthcare-fraud-related activity and economic structural fraud. The impact of distribution activities can be noted on the retail level. Foreign retail issues may include improper storage, contamination, malfunction, improper construction, product substitution, or counterfeits. Other types of fraud may include websites based outside the United States offering to dispense products without a prescription by a licensed practitioner or a physical examination. Bypassing the traditional doctor–patient relationship may result in patients receiving

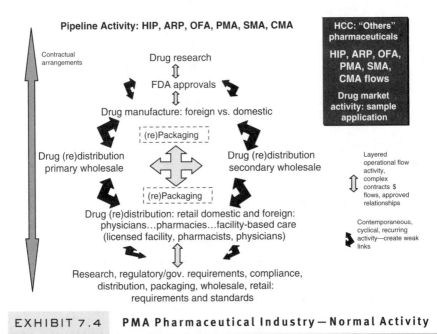

EXHIBIT 7.4   **PMA Pharmaceutical Industry — Normal Activity**

Source: Medical Business Associates, Inc. (www.mbanews.com).

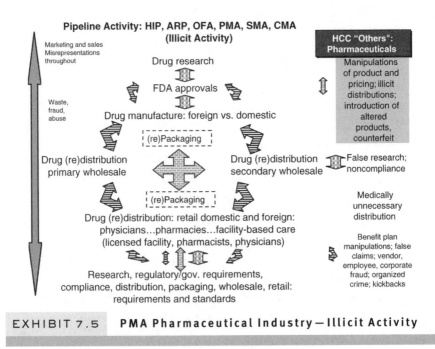

EXHIBIT 7.5   **PMA Pharmaceutical Industry — Illicit Activity**

Source: Medical Business Associates, Inc. (www.mbanews.com).

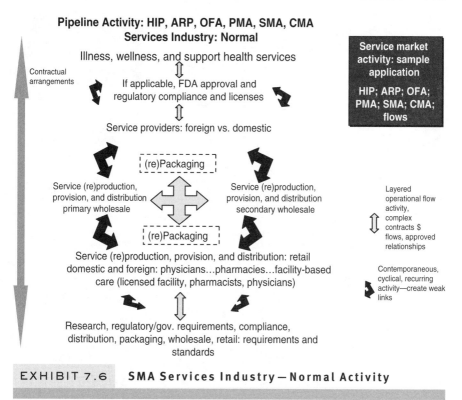

Pipeline Activity: HIP, ARP, OFA, PMA, SMA, CMA
Services Industry: Normal

Illness, wellness, and support health services

Contractual arrangements

If applicable, FDA approval and regulatory compliance and licenses

Service providers: foreign vs. domestic

(re)Packaging

Service (re)production, provision, and distribution primary wholesale

Service (re)production, provision, and distribution secondary wholesale

(re)Packaging

Service (re)production, provision, and distribution: retail domestic and foreign: physicians…pharmacies…facility-based care (licensed facility, pharmacists, physicians)

Research, regulatory/gov. requirements, compliance, distribution, packaging, wholesale, retail: requirements and standards

Service market activity: sample application

HIP; ARP; OFA; PMA; SMA; CMA; flows

Layered operational flow activity, complex contracts $ flows, approved relationships

Contemporaneous, cyclical, recurring activity—create weak links

EXHIBIT 7.6   SMA Services Industry — Normal Activity

Source: Medical Business Associates, Inc. (www.mbanews.com).

inappropriate products due to misdiagnoses, failing to receive appropriate products or other medical care, or using a product that could be harmful, resulting in substandard care, unnecessary care, or a fatality.

Products differ from services in the sense that a physical object that can be seen or measured is involved. At the service level, the combination of healthcare fraud and economic structural fraud will require a different type of assessment. Exhibit 7.6 represents a typical flow of activities for consideration when services are associated with the product.

The auditor's checklist summarized in this chapter is structured to guide the auditor to search for any anomalies or abnormal behavior simply by noting the exception (see Exhibit 7.7).

Service distribution issues may be noted on both a foreign and a domestic level—for example, unlicensed, untrained professionals or services without proper testing or clinical standards. Websites based outside and within the United States offer brokerage or auctioned health services without proper

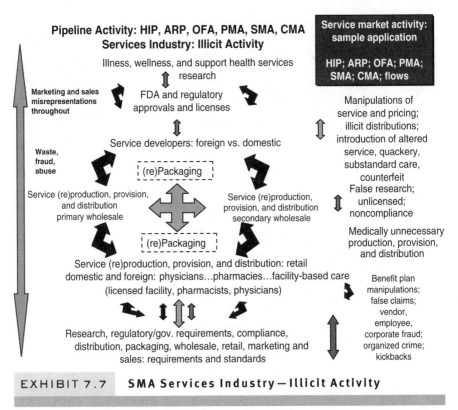

Pipeline Activity: HIP, ARP, OFA, PMA, SMA, CMA
Services Industry: Illicit Activity

Service market activity: sample application

HIP; ARP; OFA; PMA; SMA; CMA; flows

Illness, wellness, and support health services research

Marketing and sales misrepresentations throughout

FDA and regulatory approvals and licenses

Service developers: foreign vs. domestic

Waste, fraud, abuse

(re)Packaging

Service (re)production, provision, and distribution primary wholesale

Service (re)production, provision, and distribution secondary wholesale

(re)Packaging

Service (re)production, provision, and distribution: retail domestic and foreign: physicians...pharmacies...facility-based care (licensed facility, pharmacists, physicians)

Research, regulatory/gov. requirements, compliance, distribution, packaging, wholesale, retail, marketing and sales: requirements and standards

Manipulations of service and pricing; illicit distributions; introduction of altered service, quackery, substandard care, counterfeit

False research; unlicensed; noncompliance

Medically unnecessary production, provision, and distribution

Benefit plan manipulations; false claims; vendor, employee, corporate fraud; organized crime; kickbacks

EXHIBIT 7.7   SMA Services Industry—Illicit Activity

Source: Medical Business Associates, Inc. (www.mbanews.com).

assessments by a licensed practitioner or a physical examination. Bypassing the traditional doctor/patient relationship may result in patients receiving inappropriate services due to misdiagnoses, failing to receive appropriate medical care and support services, receiving medically unnecessary care or substandard care, or suffering the effects from experimental programs that are harmful or even fatal. In the mix of all these activities, remember that the traditional fraud schemes range from identity theft and rent-a-patient to general false claim activity.

PMA, SMA, and CMA Overview: Implications for Prevention, Detection, and Investigation

The PMA and SMA blended with the CMA contribute to the understanding of both healthcare fraud and economic structural fraud. These market activity issues are applicable throughout the HCC. They can be isolated by market player or occur in collusion with one or more continuum players. For example, an accident crime ring can involve the injured patient, the provider treating the patient, and the claims adjustor. The relevant PMA would be manipulation of insurance products. By applying the checklists reviewed in this chapter, internal controls can be initiated to prevent this type of activity.

From a detection and investigation viewpoint, the checklists provided will help present the opportunity to mitigate damage and stop the bleeding as well as collect sufficient evidence for a successful prosecution. That being said, we are not done. We have had extensive discussion in understanding the environment. The fragmented high volume of healthcare comes with a huge price, and that is lots of data. Effective management of data requires an understanding of how to find it. Once it is found, it has to be mapped and mined correctly. Ultimately, preparation is the key to effective prevention, detection, and investigation of healthcare fraud and economic structural fraud.

Data Management

In the fields of observation, chance favors only the prepared mind.

—LOUIS PASTEUR

With the prevalence of healthcare fraud and economical structural fraud, being anything other than thoroughly prepared leaves a gaping gateway of ongoing and new vulnerabilities. According to the Association of Certified Fraud Examiners, the *tip* is still the number-one source of identification of one-time or ongoing frauds (www.acfe.com). Without the development of sophisticated data management models, an effective audit or investigation will never reach the analytics of prevention or detection. The next several chapters are dedicated to the fundamental understanding of data; they serve as building blocks toward effective audits and investigations.

The number of store-shelf computer *data mining* software products is increasing at an accelerated rate, as is the number of software engineers who custom-program business solutions for data analytics. In addition, various professional organizations are dedicated to the subject. A group established in 1839 and known as the American Statistical Association (ASA) (www .amstat.org) is one resource for statistical science in applying analytics to healthcare fraud investigations. Another professional association, founded in the late 1970s, is the Data Management Association (DAMA) (www.dama.org). It is focused on the development and practice of managing data, information, and knowledge.

DATA MANAGEMENT

Data management (DM) is the structured organization of information and resources. DAMA defines DM as "the development and execution of architectures, policies, practices, and procedures that properly manage the full data lifecycle needs of an enterprise" (www.dama.org/public/pages/index .cfm?pageid=71). This group is setting market practice standards. Exhibit 8.1 represents DAMA's framework for best practices in data management. The application in audit and detection could incorporate these components when designing a process to collect and maintain audit data.

The model given in Exhibit 8.1 can be used as a guide in developing data models to be used in the audit and detection of healthcare fraud. The

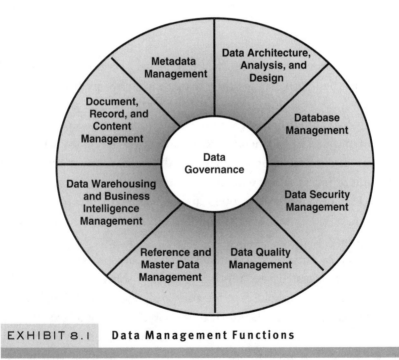

EXHIBIT 8.1   **Data Management Functions**

category of Document, Record, and Content Management is seen as an opportunity to identify your list of data elements to be collected within your audit scope. For example, are you looking only at the internal communications of a provider? Will you be analyzing internal and external data elements between an employer and a payer? Under Data Architecture, Analysis, and Design is, in essence, how your data will be structured, organized, and processed. Database Management involves specific policy and procedure for the application, execution, update, and maintenance of your database. Database Security Management is critical to ensure the integrity of your application. Any breaches or alterations can result in the demise of any audit or investigation. With respect to Metadata Management, as data is collected, the ability and resources to document this information would be invaluable. The next category noted in the DAMA model is Data Warehousing and Business Intelligence Management. In the course of this book, this category has been applied as the opportunity to develop audit intelligence. Audit intelligence in the scope of this book is the learning of and understanding of healthcare waste fraud and abuse.

Audit intelligence can be developed from the use of relational database tools and management. A relational database contains data that corresponds to a data dictionary (header files) within a specified table of information. The database can have a series of tables with header file information and the content data that is attached to each header file. Consider it similar to a dictionary in which all the words are noted in alphabetical order (the header file) and the definitions are noted next to each word (the content data). In a relational database, the content is programmed to relate and be compared within the database, thus generating knowledge that typically confirms existing assumptions or presents new ones.

The term *relational database* was originally coined and defined by E. F. Codd, a pioneer in the development of relational database models. He proposed 13 rules that are required for a database management system to be considered relational. The acronym *RDBMS* (relational database management system) has its history in the works of E. F. Codd.

Keep in mind that what follows represents the ideal format for a RDBMS. Rules 6, 9, 10, 11, and 12 still require a great deal of market development and sophistication. Presented in a theoretical framework, all are from C. J. Date, *An Introduction to Database Systems* (5th ed., 1990), in which the author gives his version of Codd's original 13 rules.

- Rule 0: Qualification rule.

  "The system must qualify as *relational*, as a *database*, and as a *management system*. For a system to qualify as a relational database management system (RDBMS), that system must use its *relational* facilities (exclusively) to *manage* the *database*."

- Rule 1: Information rule.

  "All information in a relational database is represented explicitly at the logical level and in exactly one way—by values in tables." Everything within the database exists in tables and is accessed via table access routines.

- Rule 2: Guaranteed access rule.

  "Each and every datum (atomic value) in a relational database is guaranteed to be logically accessible by resorting to a combination of table name, primary key value and column name." To access any data item, you specify which column within whichever table it exists. There is no reading of characters 10 to 20 of a 255-byte string.

- Rule 3: Systematic treatment of null values.

  "Null values (distinct from the empty character string or a string of blank characters and distinct from zero or any other number) are supported in fully relational DBMS for representing missing information and inapplicable information in a systematic way, independent of data type."

  If data does not exist or does not apply, then a value of NULL is applied. This is understood by the RDBMS as meaning non-applicable data.

- Rule 4: Dynamic online catalog based on the relational model.

  "The database description is represented at the logical level in the same way as ordinary data, so that authorized users can apply the same relational language to its interrogation as they apply to the regular data." The data dictionary is held within the RDBMS; thus there is no need for offline volumes to tell you the structure of the database.

- Rule 5: Comprehensive data sublanguage rule.

  "A relational system may support several languages and various modes of terminal use (for example, the fill-in-the-blanks mode)." However, there must be at least one language whose statements are expressible, per some well-defined syntax, as character strings and that is comprehensive in supporting all the following items: Data Definition, View Definition, Data Manipulation (Interactive and by program), Integrity Constraints, Authorization. Every RDBMS should provide a language to allow the user to query the contents of the RDBMS and also manipulate the contents of the RDBMS.

- Rule 6: View updating rule.
  "All views that are theoretically updatable are also updatable by the system." Not only can the user modify data, but so can the RDBMS when the user is not logged in.

- Rule 7: High-level insert, update, and delete.
  "The capability of handling a base relation or a derived relation as a single operand applies not only to the retrieval of data but also to the insertion, update, and deletion of data." The user should be able to modify several tables by modifying the view to which they act as base tables.

- Rule 8: Physical data independence.
  "Application programs and terminal activities remain logically unimpaired whenever any changes are made in either storage representations or access methods." The user should not be aware of where or upon which media data files are stored.

- Rule 9: Logical data independence.
  "Application programs and terminal activities remain logically unimpaired when information-preserving changes of any kind that theoretically permit un-impairment are made to the base tables." User programs and the user should not be aware of any changes to the structure of the tables (such as the addition of extra columns).

- Rule 10: Integrity independence.
  "Integrity constraints specific to a particular relational database must be definable in the relational data sub-language and storable in the catalog, not in the application programs." If a column accepts only certain values, then it is the RDBMS that enforces these constraints and not the user program. This means that an invalid value can never be entered into this column; whereas if the constraints were enforced via programs, there is always a chance that a buggy program might allow incorrect values into the system.

- Rule 11: Distribution independence.

  "A relational DBMS has distribution independence." Existing applications should continue to operate successfully. The RDBMS may spread across more than one system and across several networks; however, to the end-user, the tables should appear no different from those that are local.

- Rule 12: Nonsubversion rule.

  "If a relational system has a low-level (single-record-at-a-time) language, that low level cannot be used to subvert or bypass the integrity rules and constraints expressed in the higher level relational language (multiple-records-at-a-time)."

MARKET EXAMPLE: SETTING UP A CLAIMS RDBMS

A claims RDBMS will have several considerations. For example, one part of the data dictionary will be the header file of all possible fields of the universal billing form for facility services.

- ❐ The data table will allow for available content from each possible field. The data table will allow "empty" to be recorded as "nothing."

- ❐ The entire content of a universal billing form could qualify as one database. Every component on the claim form can be related to the other data elements.

- ❐ For example, a diagnosis code of septicemia could be related to the revenue code for pharmacy. Septicemia is a systemic blood infection. It is a serious condition and can be life-threatening. A second table of diagnosis and revenue data would be compared to the claim data.

- ❐ It would be normal to have a diagnosis code of septicemia and have a high dollar amount of pharmaceutical charges due to expected treatment with intravenous antibiotics.

- ❐ If the dollar amount on the claim did not fit within the parameters of the revenue table, the claim would be denied or investigated further.

- ❐ This process is repeated in the second data dictionary file that could be populated by all the claims data from the HCFA 1500 form that represents the professional services provided to the patient. This would allow a simple comparison such as matching a facility fee with a professional fee for corroboration of a service.

This is a basic simplified application of the value in generating a database management system.

DATA MANAGEMENT OVERVIEW: IMPLICATIONS FOR PREVENTION, DETECTION, AND INVESTIGATION

Healthcare is a trillion-dollar market with billions of data elements moving throughout the healthcare continuum. Any attempt to audit and detect healthcare fraud is going to require an effective database management system. Incremental planning and definition will effectively utilize limited resources. Your data development team should include a series of industry experts. I recommend an operational industry expert for the subject under investigation, experienced investigators, an experienced auditor, a data analysis expert, and an information systems specialist. These roles will help define the type of information that is required to answer the questions presented.

With respect to anomaly detection, a system that is designed to mimic all normal procedures and outcomes should be structured to provide exception reports on any parameters that fall outside of that normal infrastructure. These irregular patterns should be analyzed and pursued. This route will lead toward an effective detection model.

■ REFERENCES

1. Codd, E. F., "Is Your DBMS Really Relational?" and "Does Your DBMS Run By the Rules?" *ComputerWorld*, October 14 and October 21, 1985.
2. Codd, E. F., *The Relational Model for Database Management, Version 2* (Reading, MA: Addison-Wesley, 1990).
3. Codd, E. F., "A Relational Model of Data for Large Shared Data Banks," *Communications of the ACM* 13, no. 6 (1970): 377–387.
4. Date, C. J., *The Database Relational Model: A Retrospective Review and Analysis: A Historical Account and Assessment of E. F. Codd's Contribution to the Field of Database Technology* (Reading, MA: Addison-Wesley, 2001).
5. Date, C. J., *An Introduction to Database Systems*, 5th ed. (Reading, MA: Addison-Wesley, 1990), pp. 389–393.

Normal Infrastructure

*Greed is a fat demon with a small mouth, and whatever you feed it is
never enough.*

—Janwillem van de Wetering

The preceding chapters discuss in detail members of the healthcare
continuum (HCC). The pipelines for the patient, the provider, the
payer, the plan sponsor/employer, and the vendor/supplier outline the
general framework of the various organizations and key operational features in
the execution of each player's business functions. Understanding the normal
infrastructure of each market player allows the opportunity to begin an audit
or investigation and the respective collection of data within each setting. An
essential component to the collection process is the interview of the individuals within these settings. Remember that these infrastructures are driven
by the people who work within them and lead them. A healthcare audit and
detection guidebook could not go without a discussion on the people behind
the process and those who are prone to the "fat demon" of greed.

NORMAL PROFILE OF A FRAUDSTER

This book portrays players within the HCC as both victims of fraud and possible sources of fraud. What does the normal occupational fraudster look like? The American Association of Certified Fraud Examiners has published an occupational fraud report (www.acfe.com) that provides insight into the typical general characteristics of those who commit occupational fraud:

- Male
- Intelligent
- Egotistical
- Inquisitive
- Risk taker
- Rule breaker
- Hard worker
- Under stress
- Greedy
- Financial need
- Disgruntled or a complainer
- Big spender
- Overwhelming desire for personal gain
- Pressured to perform
- Close relationship with vendors/suppliers

What Types of People or Entities Commit Fraud?

- Providers
- Insureds
- Individuals, domestic and foreign
- Approvers (employees) who pay claims to themselves or friends
- Rings—organized, established HCC players who create healthcare fraud schemes such as accident rings
- Nonproviders—nonmedical, nonrelated healthcare players who are able to create healthcare fraud

- Third-party administrators (TPAs)
- Payers, their agents, or their personnel
- Vendors and suppliers providing services within the healthcare industry
- Employers providing benefit coverage
- Personnel employed by providers, payers, employers, or various vendors
- Organized crime entities

What Is the Key Element of a Fraudster?

The key element of an individual who is most likely to be a career fraudster is a "lack of conscience." To provide a slightly different perspective, the diagnosis of antisocial personality disorder (APD) is presented. Individuals with APD have a general lack of concern for the law, rules of society, or rights of other people. They are at times associated with the term *sociopath*. It is estimated that this diagnosis is prevalent within 4 percent of the population. With 11,840,512 U.S. individuals and 257,553,015 individuals worldwide, that leaves us with about 269 million people with the perfect psychological profile to commit fraud.

Antisocial personality disorder should be considered when an individual possesses at least three of the following seven characteristics:

1. Failure to conform to social norms; unlawful behavior
2. Deceitfulness, manipulativeness, lack of regard for the truth
3. Impulsivity, failure to plan ahead
4. Irritability, aggressiveness
5. Reckless disregard for the safety of self or others; repeated violation of others; in parents, neglect or abuse of children
6. Consistent irresponsibility; lack of steady job or frequent changes
7. Lack of remorse after having hurt, mistreated, or stolen from another person

Individuals with APD tend to have experienced several predisposing events or histories. For example, the absence of parental discipline has been noted. The individual may have experienced extreme poverty or removal from the home. Predisposition can occur by being raised without parental figures from both sexes. With respect to discipline, inconsistent application and erratic application can be issues, as can being "rescued" each time the person is in trouble, resulting in a lack of negative consequences for bad behavior. Finally, maternal deprivation and lack of an appropriate "attachment" can also have an impact.

When interviewing a subject, how can one look for clues in a statement? The first involves noting outrageous logic, along the lines, for example, of this statement from Al Capone: "I am going to St. Petersburg, Florida, tomorrow; let the worthy citizens of Chicago get their liquor the best they can. I am sick of the job—it's a thankless one and full of grief. I have been spending the best years of my life as a public benefactor."

Here are other indicators to look for as well:

- Direct denial of an event, "I never did that," regardless of any incontrovertible evidence
- Statements that are inconsistent with known events
- Inconsistent emotional responses under similar circumstances within the individual's life, lack of an emotional response, or inconsistent emotional responses in comparison to social norms
- Series of failures due to lack of planning and consistent irresponsibility in various walks of life

ANOMALIES AND ABNORMAL PATTERNS

During my nursing school days, I asked my instructor if I could practice teaching by presenting an in-service to my peers. After several discussions, it was determined that I would do a class on reading EKGs. In preparation, I gathered materials, developed case studies to work on, and prepared notes for the actual presentation. I presented various anomalies such as Torsades de pointes, which is a heart rhythm that may cause a blackout or sudden death. Ventricular fibrillation is another deadly rhythm that can cause collapse and sudden cardiac death within minutes unless medical help is initiated immediately. The presentation ended by giving the class a series of EKG strips and asking them to interpret the results.

Toward the end of the class, a peer asked me a very good question: "What if you see an abnormal rhythm and do not know what it is?" A quick glance at the teacher told me I was on my own. My response was simple. All you have to remember is "what is normal"; everything else is abnormal. In addition, do not forget to look at the patient! If the patient is smiling and chatting away on the phone, the abnormal strip may just be movement or an "artifact." If the patient is blue and not breathing, then you know to call a code and ask questions later.

NORMAL INFRASTRUCTURE OVERVIEW: IMPLICATIONS FOR PREVENTION, DETECTION, AND INVESTIGATION

The first critical component is the understanding of normal infrastructure. The market is too fragmented, layered, and operationally, contractually, and legally segmented to keep track of everything that can break down or test each vulnerability. That is physically impossible. Therefore, the focus on understanding and monitoring data from an operations perspective for anomalies is a key aspect.

The second critical component is to understand what normal behavior is from a "people perspective." It is the "people" aspect that contributes to or initiates fraud. According to the ACFE research, similar attributes exist in individuals who cross the line. For example, the employee who is first to arrive at work, the last to leave, and the dedicated trooper who never takes vacation time is most likely the person you need to be vigilant of. This is not to say that an individual with a strong work ethic cannot exhibit these characteristics. The red flags are raised when an individual combines a protective behavior toward his or her work and a refusal to take absences from work. The concern by the perpetrator is that if he or she goes on vacation and someone else fills in, whatever activity the perpetrator is involved with may be found out during the absence.

In identifying what is normal in any particular process, it is easy to focus only on what is told. In gathering descriptions of certain procedures or explanations of various transactions, detection of abnormal activities will materialize. However, the next test is the concept of understanding what is *not* said or *not* told or described. How do you use an anomaly tracking system for the untold story? Chapter 10 introduces tracking the act of omission.

Normal Infrastructure and Anomaly Tracking Systems

Lying is done with words and also with silence.

—ADRIENNE RICH

Understanding normal infrastructure creates an opportunity for the untold story to unfold. Lying by omission can materialize in the data. This chapter provides examples of what abnormal looks like for each healthcare continuum (HCC) player.

THE PATIENT

The patient's role is that of recipient: He or she receives goods or services from other members of the HCC. The accounts receivable pipeline (ARP) demonstrates the typical flow of services and reimbursements (see Chapter 5). Recall that, from a reimbursement perspective, the type of patient varies. Patients include those receiving health insurance from private employers, public employers, their own independent purchases, or government programs such as Medicare, Medicaid, or a state program. Patients also

ealth insurance; of these patients, some have the
medical goods and services, and many do not.
ation (PHI) is normally used to facilitate healthcare
ient's various providers. PHI is also used in applying for
surance and evaluating disability benefits and workers'
benefits. Unfortunately, the usual pattern between patients—
ents—and payers is that of third parties. The patient typically does
nave a clear understanding of or direct financial accountability for the
payment of his or her providers' charges. This third-party relationship creates
market conflicts as well as vulnerabilities, increasing the chances that the patient
will become either a victim or a perpetrator of fraud.

Sample Patient Fraud Scenarios

- Most insurance companies reimburse the patient for healthcare expenses incurred while traveling abroad. In one example, an insured submitted fictitious foreign claims ($90,000) from a clinic in South America that indicated that the entire family was treated for injuries resulting from a car accident. A fictitious police report accompanied the medical claims. A telephone call to the clinic revealed that the insured and the dependents were never treated in that clinic.

- A family that qualifies for Medicaid "loans" its insurance card for a fee. Biometric cards implemented by some states are reducing this type of recipient fraud.

- A physician's employee steals prescription pads to write prescriptions for self-medication.

- Individuals with pain medication addictions go doctor shopping across state lines to avoid detection.

- Individuals accept cash for receipt of unnecessary services.

- Individuals obtain products and pharmaceuticals and resell them to other parties.

- Patients misrepresent personal or health information just to receive benefits.

- Patients may unknowingly receive services that are not legitimate; they may buy fake health insurance or sign nontraditional service contracts by providers for services that are not necessary.

Data Management Considerations

The critical consideration is developing a central source for all information accumulated on healthcare services. Currently few tools are offered that effectively organize and centrally locate a patient's health information from the provider, payer, vendor, and employer perspectives. This is significant in terms of preventing waste, fraud, and abuse. As electronic record-keeping software and similar tools improve in operability, the current clinical gap should narrow. Likewise, as pricing policies become more transparent and the patient plays an increasingly integral role in the finance of healthcare, the financial gap should also narrow.

The Untold Story

The patient, who is the primary driver of utilization in healthcare, is insulated from the payer, the provider, the employer, and the plan sponsor. The third-party system in essence does not allow a direct connection between the patient and the cost of the services he or she receives. Since the early 1940s and the continued development of employment-linked insurance, this connection between the cost of healthcare and direct financial accountability has continued to go down separate paths. In fact, health insurance is considered a cost of doing business. In addition, the premiums paid on behalf of employees are not considered income. (The implications of this model are discussed further in a later chapter.) Therefore the incentive of the patient for controlling costs is not part of the normal process of accountability. The market implications include stricter controls for the patient's PHI and a tighter alignment of cost accountability.

THE PROVIDER

Professional or facility-based providers are faced with segmented operational structures that prevent a fluid communication of all relevant patient information when providing ongoing services. The providers' role is often complicated by managing the relationship between their patients and the contractual arrangements that their patients may or may not have via their employers' carrier. In addition, providers are also subject to separate contractual arrangements that they may have with respective payers.

Most providers are moving forward with initiatives to adopt electronic health records. They will continue to face challenges in this arena. In particular, current offerings appear to be deficient in terms of front-end and back-end operating functions. For example, when a health information management department of a hospital receives a request for release of information, the labor involved in generating a production of a one-week hospital stay can take two to three hours. In addition, many current programs have limited options in terms of exporting content in a user-friendly format.

This market continues to struggle with reimbursement issues between the patient and the payer. Examples of provider facilities include professional offices, clinics, inpatient facilities, outpatient facilities, home health settings, nursing homes, and rehabilitation centers. The current market focus is on price transparency between the provider and the patient. However, this is just one small part of the story. The market is layered with multiple contracts and multiple financial arrangements. Unfortunately, this layered and segmented process increases the burden of administration costs and also creates opportunities for the ethically challenged.

Sample Provider Fraud Scenarios

- In Missouri, six co-defendants were sentenced for conspiring to defraud the United States through a system of kickbacks for patient referrals and the filing of false claims that resulted in overpayments from Medicare and Medicaid. The individuals sentenced included a licensed medical doctor, a registered nurse, a billing service owner, an employee who provided medical billing services, and two owners of several residential care facilities and home health agencies (HHAs). The six were ordered to pay respective restitution amounts totaling $526,000; four were sentenced to prison. One central aspect of the scheme involved the owner's referral of patients from its residential facilities to doctors in exchange for the doctors' certification that the patients were homebound and eligible for home health services. This arrangement allowed the doctors to bill Medicare and Medicaid for patient visits and the HHAs to bill Medicare and Medicaid for providing home health services.
- A sudden spike in Medicaid claim payment activity was noted with one dental practice. Payouts increased by $3.4 million, and the dentist's

very active practice removed 98 molars and performed 64 root canals—all on a single patient. (Please note that human anatomy dictates that a typical individual has 32 teeth.) An audit of the claims data noted the following:

- Thirty-three patients had 3,234 teeth removed, for an average of 98 teeth per patient.
- Forty-four patients had 3,152 teeth yanked—72 teeth per person.
- Sixteen patients had more than 1,000 root removals, which meant each patient had 64 removals.
- Thirty-three patients averaged 287 dental treatments apiece.

- Another case involved a well-known doctor on the West Coast, one who had his own popular radio show, *Medicine Man*, and promoted nontraditional medical regimens. His claims data analysis noted the following activity:
  - *Billing data:* A high percentage of claims were for complicated visits and bills that were generated while the doctor was traveling in Europe.
  - *Recent claim data:* Visits to chiropractors, acupuncturists, massage therapists, nutritionists, and personal trainers at a gym were billed under the doctor's tax ID number and under MD CPT visit codes. Clearly, this doctor was misrepresenting who was providing what service.
  - *Staff issues:* On staff was a recently immigrated, unlicensed physician who was paid $5 per hour. The doctor even continued to bill for a physician no longer associated with the clinic. At his trial, the doctor responded to his charges as follows: "I am just a caring doctor getting reluctant insurance companies to pay for alternative health treatments."

The provider as a victim can be noted in a variety of scenarios. An unfortunate growing trend is the planting of employees with the intent to steal inventory. A hospital in Texas experienced over a $3-million-dollar loss when its own pharmacist diverted and stole cancer medications to resell at a secondary wholesale market. A more complex victim role is that at a contractual level. Keep in mind that providers are insulated from contractual relationships between the payer and the employer-sponsored plan. This creates problems on the back end once a patient leaves the provider setting and issues are raised as to exactly what is covered by the insurance plan. The patient and the provider are often left sorting through any variances in expectations by both parties. This variance of unmet expectations is generating market discussion on the concept of price transparency. But what is price transparency and what does it really mean? This has yet to be answered in the marketplace.

Data Management Considerations

Security is a major issue in the management of PHI. Protective measures for ensuring system integrity as well as employee training on the minimum necessary disclosures should be routinely incorporated. Healthcare fraud schemes use false PHI or misuse real PHI. Providers have internal vulnerabilities as well as external. For example, if they outsource transcription, is it to a local U.S. facility or an overseas facility? If to an overseas facility, what protection is occurring during the transmission?

An anomaly detection program should look at internal and external issues. Fraudsters target providers to gain identity-type information, to steal patient data, to submit false claims, and to steal hospital inventory. It is important from the provider perspective to coordinate data management issues with other HCC members—patients, employees, payers. Providers also face economic structural fraud issues, in particular with contractual fee schedule arrangements. Providers should ensure that appropriate internal controls are in place to manage the terms of contractual relationships, in particular, those that involve both the exchange of PHI and any monetary transaction for goods and services.

The Untold Story

What is often not understood in healthcare is that a provider is insulated from contracts and transactions of services it provides within the HCC. A provider does not have access to the plan document that governs the monetary transaction between the insurance plan and an insured employer or between a self-insured employer and the third-party administrator (TPA) that is managing the employer's plan. For example, when a provider is approached for an audit by a payer, is it because the payer is gathering intelligence for its next contract negotiation? Is it because the payer has auditors who receive compensation based on what additional percentages they can reduce the bill by?

Likewise, the segmented marketplace, both clinically and financially, has served as a breeding ground for the ethically challenged. Providers who do participate in or initiate fraudulent schemes have two advantages. The first is that it is a high-volume market, which means lots of transactions for any party to decipher and avoid payment of a false claim. The second is the lack of transparency. This also provides the opportunity to avoid detection.

THE PAYER

The payer can be found in the marketplace in several roles, first, as a TPA that does not provide any risk programs (insurance coverage). The next is the TPA that does offer risk-based coverage programs. This payer provides insurance programs and serves as a TPA for self-insured employers or government-sponsored programs. This is followed by insurance companies and government TPA processors.

The same organization will also have business relationships in which it does not take the risk but acts in the role of TPA. The payers tend to contemporaneously manage three to four relationships. The first is their contractual arrangement with the employer. The second contractual arrangement is with the provider. The third would include any contractual arrangements with vendors. They have indirect relationships with beneficiaries. Typical flows of monetary transactions are between the employers and the TPA and back to the provider. Payers in essence administer the provisions of the benefit plan.

Payers utilize PHI throughout the claims adjudication process. They received PHI on the claim form itself and often will request additional PHI content from the medical record. Provisions for protecting PHI from a security and operational perspective are just as important as with providers who generate the information, for example, internal controls on how to handle and maintain information that is received and stored within their systems. Externally, TPAs have been known to outsource the scanning and OCR reading conversions (which convert the picture files of documents into files that can be word searched) to companies in other countries. As noted in the section above on providers, an important question to ask is what security controls are in place to protect the transmission of the information?

Sample Payer Fraud Scenarios

- A payer in Pennsylvania was fined and entered into a corporate integrity agreement (CIA) for allegations by providers relating to claims processing and coverage determinations. The providers claimed that the TPA failed to process or pay physicians' or other healthcare claims in a timely fashion, or at all; applied incorrect payments for appropriate claims submissions; inaccurately reported claims processing data to the state, including a failure to meet self-reporting requirements and impose self-assessment penalties as required under the managed care contract with the state; automatically changed CPT codes (current procedural terminology codes, used to explain the procedure provided); did not recognize modifiers (modifiers are additional codes that providers submit to explain the service provided); and did not reliably respond to appeals from patients, sometimes not responding at all or waiting over 6 to 12 months to do so.

- A TPA system offered transcription services to physicians for reporting disability status on beneficiaries. It was later found that the TPA altered the doctors' reports from the patients being disabled to *not* being disabled.

- Performance guarantee misrepresentations: On May 2, 1997, in the Northern District of California, a major payer agreed to pay $12 million to settle allegations that it filed false claims for payment under its contract with the government to process and pay Medicare claims. The agreement resolves claims that the San Francisco–based payer covered up claims processing errors discovered by Health Care Financing Administration auditors to obtain more favorable scores under an agency program for grading the Medicare carrier's claims processing capabilities. A *qui tam* suit was filed by former payer employees in the Medicare division in Chico, and these relators will receive 18 percent of the settlement amount. This false claims settlement follows a May 1996 criminal conviction of the payer for conspiracy and obstructing federal audits to evaluate the company's performance in the Medicare processing contract. The payer paid a criminal fine of $1.5 million when it entered its guilty plea. The payer ceased being a Medicare contractor in September 1996.

In the role of victim, payers are faced with the enormous task of processing over a trillion claims per year. At such a volume, they are constantly being hit with false claim submissions. On top of that, with the growing concern of the cost of insurance, emerging schemes such as selling fake insurance have gone up. Some of these perpetrators take the legitimate name of a well-known established carrier and change it just a bit, causing market confusion. For example, a perpetrator may take a name like United Health and change it to United Health Partners. Over a ten-year period, James Lee Graf of California collected over $42 million in premiums selling fake insurance before he was caught.

Data Management Considerations

Data management begins internally. What security measures are being utilized to receive, process, and maintain all PHI and its respective financial transactions? Second, what are the internal job functions and system infrastructures for audit and detection of healthcare fraud? In particular for payers is the level of training and ongoing education of their staff. The systems perspective is what edits are being utilized when claims are received. How often are these edits updated and *changed*? If a group of the ethically challenged is hitting the claims system, they are learning the system by following the patterns of denials. They will adjust based on what is accepted and what is rejected. Therefore, the operative word from a payer perspective is *change*.

From a contractual perspective, it is important to understand the type of provider and employer business that is being managed by the TPA. Does the payer have insurance programs as well as business from a self-funded plan? Controls for contractual provisions and the appropriated provisions of those terms need to be set in place and tested. This is followed by the process controls of financial and clinical transactions between the employer plan sponsor, the government plan sponsor, the provider, and any other vendors that are involved in the process.

The Untold Story

The core roots of health insurance have been long forgotten. The private-payer market launched its start from a hospital in Dallas. In 1929, Baylor

Hospital entered into a relationship with the local teachers to provide a regular employee deduction that went directly to the hospital as prepayment for any hospital services rendered. It was sponsored as a nonprofit, and because it was not part of the insurance community, the plan was not required to post monies into a reserve. This book will later discuss the evolution of Blue Cross and the development of the commercial carrier market. Specifically in this chapter, the evolution of the payer and the segmented contractual arrangements it has with employers independent of providers, as well as vendors, contributes to the market's insulation from understanding all the dynamics of a healthcare episode.

The Vendor/Other Parties

This group is the largest group and most diverse. It can include any other HCC player that is not a plan sponsor, payer, provider, or recipient. This group can range from billing services to ambulance services, durable medical equipment, case management support, and pharmaceuticals. The types of fraud range from healthcare false claim scenarios to economic structural frauds involving complex manipulations of fee schedules or contractual misrepresentations.

With respect to market standards on the management of PHI, this group also varies significantly. Groups such as support providers may be at par with industry standards. However, ancillary players such as equipment companies may not be as structured as they should be, at least not until market standards and compliance programs mandate internal controls for PHI. On the financial piece, they also tend to be insulated by other market players on both contractual and operational bases. For example, a patient in the hospital may receive dialysis services; however, those treating the patient are not employees of the hospital but a contracted service. This is a seamless unknown operational activity. On the financial side, this service can be billed by the contracting party or integrated into the patient's hospital bill. Regardless, it is a service that is not readily transparent to the patient or at times the payer.

Suppliers of products are inherently different. They do not interact directly with the patient but are part of the supply chain. This can include equipment offerings, pharmaceutical inventory, and product offerings. The biggest threat in this market is the introduction of counterfeit products and adulterated medications. *Adulterated*, for example, means taking a vial of Epogen and diluting it among ten different vials and introducing the drug back into the supply chain. The reduced potency is one obvious issue of concern, as are the often unsanitary conditions in which these drugs are prepared. This arena introduces the need for physical security in addition to the privacy securities of PHI.

Sample Vendor/Other Fraud Scenarios

- An ambulance company owner in Pennsylvania was sentenced to 15 months' imprisonment and ordered to pay $30,000 in restitution for mail fraud and failure to file a tax return. Because of a fraud conviction, the owner was previously excluded from Medicare and Medicaid. As a result, he used a "straw party" to start two ambulance companies and billed Medicare and Medicaid for transports that were not medically necessary.

- A pharmaceutical company that deliberately falsified price reports to the Texas Medicaid program for its products was successfully prosecuted and settled in court. Under terms of the agreement, Dey, Inc. will pay a total of $18.5 million, with more than $9 million going to the state. The remaining portion of the settlement will go to the federal government, which jointly funds the Texas Medicaid program and has reached its own settlement with the company.

- Dey, a subsidiary of German pharmaceutical giant Merck KGaA, manufactures and markets inhalant products that are generally prescribed for persons suffering from respiratory illnesses. Under Texas law, drug manufacturers are required to report the prices at which they sell their products to wholesalers and distributors. The Texas Medicaid program then uses this pricing information as a basis for calculating provider cost and reimburses Medicaid providers accordingly. The attorney general's Civil Medicaid Fraud Section found that Dey deliberately falsified its pricing reports for the benefit of its customers, which directly led to overpayments by the Texas Medicaid program.

- Many inappropriate transactions involve marketing of incontinence supplies. In one case, a supplier was found to have delivered adult diapers, which are not covered by Medicare, and improperly billed these items as expensive prosthetic devices called "female external urinary collection devices."

- Systematic abuse of the federal healthcare programs and of private-payer organizations by a third-party billing company is found in the recent case of Emergency Physician Billing Services, Inc. (EPBS). At the time of the investigation, EPBS provided coding, billing, and collections services for emergency physician groups in over 100 emergency departments in as many as 33 states. Based on allegations presented by a *qui tam* relator, the United States charged that EPBS and its principal owner, Dr. J. D. McKean, routinely billed federal and state healthcare programs for higher levels of treatment than were provided or supported by medical record documentation.

  EPBS was paid based on a percentage of revenues either billed or recovered, depending on the client. EPBS coders received a base pay with bonuses based on the number of charts processed and were required to process 40 emergency room medical charts per hour, or the equivalent of a chart every 90 seconds. By contrast, a competitor of EPBS requires 120 charts per day. The EPBS coders were able to meet these quotas by taking shortcuts and disregarding information in the chart. As the trial court noted, no coder at EPBS ever attended training or any other informational meeting regarding emergency department coding other than in-house EPBS training, and no coder ever contacted a physician with questions regarding a chart.

  After a trial in which the U.S. District Court for the Western District of Oklahoma found EPBS and Dr. McKean liable under the False Claims Act, the defendants agreed to pay $15.5 million to resolve their civil and administrative monetary liabilities. In addition, Dr. McKean agreed to be excluded from participation in federal healthcare programs for 15 years, and EPBS entered into a comprehensive CIA. Currently, the government is pursuing physician groups that benefited from EPBS's fraudulent practices.

Data Management Considerations

As an HCC player—provider, payer, employer, or patient—it is important to establish controls in the use of any vendor or supplier. This includes management of PHI and any respective financial transaction. The management of data should also separate activities that are involved in direct and indirect patient care. Currently the universal bill form does not include the identification of a billing agent. If a provider subcontracts with a dialysis team and submits fees for this service, the current environment does not allow for that disclosure. Price transparency is an issue just as in every other market component. However, in this group in particular the transparency of *who* is providing the service is also a market problem and contributes toward the difficulty in detecting waste, fraud, and abuse. The next few chapters discuss data mapping and data mining issues. With respect to vendors and suppliers, data analytics are extremely important while the market catches up on appropriate internal controls for the transactions of this group.

The Untold Story

The vendors and supplier are often insulated from various parties in the HCC. This places all parties in equally vulnerable positions. As a result, all parties should pay additional attention with respect to controls. As the electronic world evolves at a faster rate than do internal controls, compliance standards for PHI, and respective monetary reimbursement models, watch out for fraud schemes to outpace any efforts to date. The introduction of Medicare Part D for prescription medications is like winning the lottery for the ethically challenged.

It is unfortunately too easy to hit payer systems at a rate of 1 million claims per minute with the use of modern electronic technology. It is also more difficult to data mine just on one premise alone. Recall from Chapter 5 that the UB-92 form has numerous data elements on its claim form, exceeding 40 potential items. The claim forms for prescription medication do not even require a diagnosis code. In essence, no medical justification is required for either medications or supplies. The diagnosis code in healthcare is the *why* along with the CPT code; the procedure is the *what*. The codes communicate *what* we are doing and *why* we are doing something or providing care to the patient. This analysis or opportunity to data mine, detect, and investigate is diminished just by lack of information alone.

In recent discussions with professionals in the drug-diversion world of investigators, when the subject of communicating a diagnosis code for prescriptions was raised, two very different responses materialized: "This will only give payers one more excuse to not approve services," and "This will help separate prescription abuse and/or drugs being diverted." Both comments have substance and are reflective of the current state of our healthcare delivery system. It should not surprise you that the first comment came from a physician. The market is so stressed that the communication of why a provider is treating a patient is viewed as a threat. The second comment is from a payer who would like the ability to adjudicate the claim with all possible justification for something that should not be so difficult to communicate.

This raises an issue that is not often discussed, that of predatory payment practices—*predatory* in the sense that the payment systems use PHI not so much for testing the validity of a claim and its medical decision tree but for intelligence data that directly impacts their profit margin. Who ultimately wins in the insulated, segmented, fragmented battleground of provision and payment of healthcare services?

Organized Crime

Organized crime entities are the ultimate winners in this game. They have the luxury of having no regard for laws, compliance programs, reporting or requirements, quality controls, or patient safety standards. What matters to this group are things like getting illegitimate access to PHI, stealing inventory, and reintroducing inventory that has been stolen, counterfeited, or adulterated. Laws have no impact on this group. The intent is to steal. The list of fraudulent activities can go on and on, as can statements like these:

"I have a great idea for a quick high-profit scheme."

"It will require this type of resource, people, and systems."

"We can split the profits in the following manner."

"We do the following activities to avoid detection."

Fraudsters never include in their plans "We should get caught and prosecuted." Fraudsters do not go into high-risk, illegal businesses to get caught. They go into them to reap high monetary rewards.

Sample Organized Crime Fraud Scenarios

- A Russian resident hired runners in the United States to run to P.O. boxes set up to receive checks for false claims submissions. His specialty was to collect the Social Security numbers of deceased Russian immigrants. He did not even have to travel to the United States to steal from its government programs.

- Outpatient surgical clinics set up practices to recruit employees with benefit plans. They plant their employees in an employment setting. They recruit other employees, train them, and deliver them to the clinic to receive services that are not medically necessary. They pay the employees, the recruiter gets paid, and the provider charges high fees. This is known as the rent-a-patient scheme.

- A South Florida man was convicted for stealing large quantities of medications, including Epogen and other pharmaceuticals, and then reintroducing adulterated versions of the drugs into the supply chain. The market price for the high profits he received from his scheme were untimely deaths, medical complications, and confused providers who normally do not include in their assessments complications from counterfeit drugs.

Data Management Considerations

Data mapping, data mining, interoperable electronic operations, price transparency, and operational transparency add value to the delivery of healthcare services. They also put dents into organized crime. Transparency among legitimate players causes illegitimate players to stand out more.

The Untold Story

As the healthcare market struggles with controls among the HCC players, compliance programs, audits, price transparency, operational transparency, and use of technology, organized crime flourishes. Crime groups develop market opportunities in the areas in which the least number of controls exist. They profit in the areas in which little is required for reimbursement. As consumer-directed health plans roll out into the market with few or no tools, an evolution of schemes targeted directly at consumers will come into play.

Normal Infrastructure and Anomaly Tracking Systems Overview: Implications for Prevention, Detection, and Investigation

The market needs interoperability of electronic healthcare and financial records to fight the battle of rising organized crime activity in healthcare. A decrease in fraud cannot happen without it. Developing audit programs that focus on standards for normal business flow within each HCC player will contribute toward detecting any activity that falls outside the normal patterns. This includes operational activity, electronic activity, and contractual activity. Data-mapping this function is the next step toward developing effective controls. This topic is introduced in the next chapter.

CHAPTER 11

Components of the Data Mapping Process

Discovery consists of seeing what everybody has seen and thinking what nobody has thought.

—ALBERT SZENT-GYORGYI, HUNGARIAN BIOCHEMIST AND 1937
NOBEL PRIZE WINNER FOR MEDICINE

H ealthcare is a trillion-dollar industry. The amount of electronic claims data for just one region of Medicare claims can reach multiple terabytes of text-delineated content. This is a large amount of data to process and decipher. To tackle large quantities of data in any audit and investigation, the process begins with data mapping. A comprehensive and well-outlined data map serves as a solid foundation to see everything, often for the first time, and then think what no one has thought.

WHAT IS DATA MAPPING?

Data mapping involves the identification of all possible data elements for study. In order not to miss any critical elements, it is important to understand the movement and content of data elements. Movement of the data may help identify modifications of the data element that should be collected. In addition, understanding the content and meaning of the data element helps to ensure that any modification or transition status of a data element is collected as well. In this book, the data elements are derived from any component or series of components of the healthcare continuum (HCC). Further, these components are mapped out for the respective pipelines previously discussed: health information pipelines (HIPs), accounts receivable pipelines (ARPs), operational flow activity (OFA), service market activity (SMA), product market activity (PMA), and consumer market activity (CMA). The delineation and representation of the data involve a series of steps. Keep in mind that mapping protected health information (PHI) and creating a road map will help in discerning hidden data patterns that will make anomalies more readily apparent. In audit and fraud investigations, PHI is equivalent to money.

Data mapping begins by obtaining all relevant forms of PHI within each applicable HCC player. The type of information includes data that is communicated verbally, in hardcopy format, via facsimile, and electronically. During the OFA process, include all departmental data as well as the employees involved in those communications. The mapping process should identify internal versus external categories. The process involves differentiating between internal and external data elements and their communication modes. In mapping ARPs, include both direct and indirect financial implications. The identification of the PMAs and SMAs involved will determine if specific subject matter expertise is required for an in-depth understanding of the content of the clinical data. Ultimately, understanding the CMA pipeline will provide guidance on any recruitment aspect of the scheme if applicable.

Once the data elements to be mapped are identified, the appropriate warehouse for all forms of PHI needs to be defined and developed. Key considerations include size of data, the type of electronic data surveillance, the level of custom programming, and the analytics to be utilized. Each data element in the warehouse needs to be defined. This is expanded further by creating decision trees to map the data elements electronically. Next is the programming of algorithms. These algorithms are typically driven based on the theories of the investigation or the defined audit scope. For example, in the rent-a-patient fraud scheme, perpetrators recruit patients to have their surgeries on Saturdays and Sundays to avoid attention by taking sick days.

The theory would be the detection and review of all weekend surgeries. The screening algorithm would include separating all claims for surgeries that were conducted on a Saturday or Sunday. Note that in a retrospective investigation, updates to the warehouse and algorithms are driven by developing results within the data. In a proactive investigation, be prepared to update and add to each layer in this process as new evidence enters into the mix from external sources.

Remember, it is very important in the structure of your warehouse to measure all monetary issues. Have a plan early on to identify and measure proof of loss. This may be complicated in schemes in which the profit is not directly measured on the claim form itself.

The following is a sample flow checklist for data mapping:

- ☐ Flowchart HIP.
- ☐ Flowchart ARP.
- ☐ Flowchart OFA.
- ☐ Flowchart PMA.
- ☐ Flowchart SMA.
- ☐ Flowchart CMA.
- ☐ Create specs for data warehouse.
- ☐ Define each spec in the warehouse.
- ☐ Collect the contents of the UB-92 (professional fees) and HCFA 1500 (facility fees) data elements.
- ☐ Define the clinical specifications to be collected.
- ☐ Define the operational specifications to be collected.
- ☐ Define the contractual specifications to be collected.

Data mapping requires an understanding of the movement of information within each pipeline. Exhibit 11.1 walks through the hospital pipeline and the respective ARP.

Within this pipeline, obtain the hospital's organizational chart. Use it as a guide to ensure comprehensive understanding of the facility in addition to all of its operational components. Within this flow, obtain information on all computer and paper systems used, and determine what role vendor support systems provide. With respect to vendors, do they use an independent system

Provider/Facility Pipeline

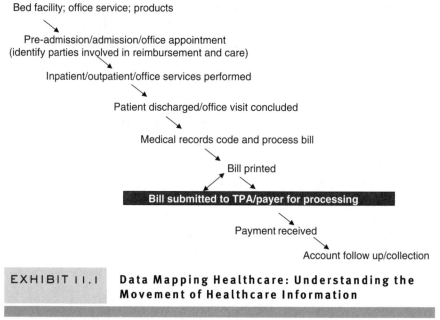

Bed facility; office service; products

Pre-admission/admission/office appointment
(identify parties involved in reimbursement and care)

Inpatient/outpatient/office services performed

Patient discharged/office visit concluded

Medical records code and process bill

Bill printed

Bill submitted to TPA/payer for processing

Payment received

Account follow up/collection

EXHIBIT 11.1   **Data Mapping Healthcare: Understanding the
Movement of Healthcare Information**

Source: Medical Business Associates, Inc. (www.mbanews.com).

or do they tap into the facility's systems to do their work? Perform the same analysis with any subcontracted services.

Exhibit 11.2 addresses the same issues within the payer's operational flows. The concept for providers will work in this environment. Again, obtain an organizational chart and follow through on obtaining information on all computer and paper systems, vendor support systems, offshore versus onshore operational activities, and any contracted services. Focus particularly on adjudication activity.

Review procedures for audits and investigations of claim activity. How many are actually conducted, and what are the results? How are systems and procedures tested to ensure eligibility of claimants? What controls are in place to ensure the benefits are calculated according to the plan document? How are deductions and co-insurance amounts verified? How does the claim system verify and determine maximum limits on claims submitted? How are checks processed and denied? Finally, if the contractual arrangement between the plan sponsor and the third-party administrator (TPA) calls for performance guarantees, how will these terms be audited within this

Payer Pipeline

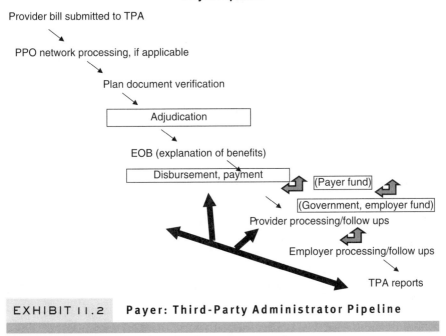

Provider bill submitted to TPA

PPO network processing, if applicable

Plan document verification

Adjudication

EOB (explanation of benefits)

Disbursement, payment

(Payer fund)

(Government, employer fund)

Provider processing/follow ups

Employer processing/follow ups

TPA reports

EXHIBIT 11.2   Payer: Third-Party Administrator Pipeline

Source: Medical Business Associates, Inc. (www.mbanews.com).

pipeline? Likewise, if a provider enters into an agreement with a TPA, what right-to-audit clauses have they agreed on to ensure that the terms for handling claims are being complied with? Exhibit 11.2 highlights the operational components that should be included in any audit and investigation.

Note that data mapping identifies which data segments are collected within each HCC player. The audit may include one, several, or all of the HCC players, depending on the audit scope or the investigation being conducted. By preparing your warehouse by market segment, the audit parameters can always be expanded.

Critical to the data mapping process is an understanding of the movement and location of PHI. The operational flow approach helps to minimize lost opportunities for data collection. As noted previously, data-map all sources of relevant PHI. This includes provisions for collecting verbal, hardcopy, and electronic forms of data among departments and employees, and internally and externally (vendors). Again, sample documents to collect may include organizational charts, computer systems, paper systems, vendor support, subcontracted services, and contractual arrangements. The checklist of activities includes setting up data definition for movement and location of PHI data (PHI data warehouse), obtaining contractual terms among the parties that impact use of PHI, and obtaining internal control procedures for the PHI currently in use. Finally, obtain a complete menu of items to collect, create, and map within the data warehouse for PHI information. This process is repeated during the HIP, ARP, OFA, PMA, SMA, and CMA processes.

Data Mapping Overview: Implications for Prevention, Detection, and Investigation

This chapter outlines the process for data mapping. Data mapping is the first step toward creating the organization and structure that will set the framework to derive intelligence from data. Healthcare is an industry that processes over a trillion dollars in claim activity annually. Organization and structure are required to successfully sift through large amounts of data and make sense of it all. They create the opportunity to see what everyone else is seeing and to analyze and process what no one else has thought of.

The next chapter progresses with the mining of the data that is collected. What we are often told is happening in reality may be far from the true story. Data mining takes the audit process to the next level. Data mapping plus data mining provides the tools to challenge what is being presented.

CHAPTER 12

Components of the Data Mining Process

How many legs does a dog have if you call the tail a leg? Four; calling a tail a leg doesn't make it a leg.

—ABRAHAM LINCOLN

WHAT IS DATA MINING?

The science of extracting information from large data sets or databases is known as *data mining*. It is a new discipline that has its roots in statistics, machine learning, data management and databases, pattern recognition, and artificial intelligence. This science derives intelligence from data sets and provides opportunities to create predictive modeling.

This concept can be applied in the context of this audit and investigative guidebook. What does data mining look like in the application of the pipeline audit models? First, the healthcare continuum (HCC) overview: What players are involved within the data sets? Second, in applying the health information pipeline (HIP) model, an HIP data mining question may include, "Within the set of clinical records, can we predict the likely patient outcome of a certain treatment regimen?" The accounts receivable pipeline (ARP) financial analysis of the treatment regimen can then help predict the most likely cost factors associated with that regimen.

This is followed by an operational flow activity (OFA) data mining question: "How much staffing is required to take care of patients receiving the treatment regimen?" Next, service market activity (SMA) and product market activity (PMA) data mining questions might be, "What products are required to take care of the treatment regimen?" and "What services are required to provide that treatment regimen?" Finally, a consumer market activity (CMA) data mining question might be, "What is the typical profile of the patient receiving that treatment regimen?"

The following is a sample of definitions noted for *data mining*:

- "Data Mining is often described as the data-driven extraction of information from large databases." (http://home.pacific.net.sg/~cecil/dmining.htm)

- Data mining, also known as knowledge discovery in databases (KDD), has been defined as "the nontrivial extraction of implicit, previously unknown, and potentially useful information from data." (W. Frawley, G. Piatetsky-Shapiro, and C. Matheus, "Knowledge Discovery in Databases: An Overview," *AI* [Fall 1992], pp. 213–228)

- "Data Mining is the process of extracting knowledge hidden from large volumes of raw data." (www.megaputer.com/dm/index.php)

Data Mining in Healthcare

Data mining is the extraction of hidden predictive information and hidden patterns of actual occurrences from large sets of multiple databases. The technology-based audit tool of data mining allows the opportunity to encapsulate data from a highly segmented and fragmented marketplace. It creates proactive decision-making tools from clinical (HIP), financial (ARP), operational (OFA), product (PMA), service (SMA), and consumer (CMA) perspectives. It gives HCC players the potential to collect and design comprehensive data warehouses through the appropriate mapping function. The data mining design of algorithms and decision trees impacts intelligence gathering on future trends, behaviors, and intelligence-based pipeline decisions. The retrospective analysis tools also help in the audit and detection to implement appropriate internal controls within all pipelines among all HCC players.

Components of the Data Mining Process within the HCC

Once the data map of a market player has been defined and then created, a segmented data mining process should be initiated. This may be followed by aggregating data among one or more market players. Once the movement has been identified, procedures should be structured to understand the content of the data collected. Note that the mining aspect involves creating decision trees and algorithms to process the data. Approaches will vary on proactive versus historical investigation. Identify early on data elements that will measure proof of loss. Design opportunities to analyze intelligence on both an individual and an aggregate analysis.

This process is then followed by understanding the content and location of personal health information (PHI) data. Obtain data definitions for items collected in the data warehouse. Define algorithms by verbal, hardcopy, and electronic, and among departments and employees. The algorithms are further defined by internal and external sources (vendors). In addition, decision trees should data-mine contractual terms by party and respective internal control procedures. Once these decision trees have been defined, data queries (data mine) should be set to test normal patterns of content, movement, and expectations of the PHI data contained within the warehouse.

Create reports for any item that does not fall within a normal pattern. Create a secondary warehouse of anomalies. Again, it is to understand the movement and location of HIP data and any respective pipeline data. Once the reports are generated, review the original data map and warehouse definitions for any adjustments. This process is repeated for each pipeline's (ARP, OFA, PMA, SMA, CMA) database.

Recall from Chapter 11 the data mapping checklist:

- ☐ Flowchart HIP.
- ☐ Flowchart ARP.
- ☐ Flowchart OFA.
- ☐ Flowchart PMA.
- ☐ Flowchart SMA.

- ❏ Flowchart CMA.
- ❏ Create specs for data warehouse.
- ❏ Define each spec in the warehouse.
- ❏ Collect the contents of the UB-92 and HCFA 1500 data elements.
- ❏ Define the clinical specifications to be collected.
- ❏ Define the operational specifications to be collected.
- ❏ Define the contractual specifications to be collected.

This is followed by the data mining checklist:

- ❏ Data-mine UB-92 and HCFA 1500 data elements.
- ❏ Data-mine certain operations (i.e., aggregation of precertification and customer service information and other payer information).
- ❏ Data-mine clinical records.
- ❏ Redefine clinical specifications.
- ❏ Data-mine HIP.
- ❏ Data-mine ARP.
- ❏ Data-mine OFA.
- ❏ Data-mine PMA.
- ❏ Data-mine SMA.
- ❏ Data-mine CMA.
- ❏ Create warehouse of anomalies.
- ❏ Create warehouse of predictive patterns.
- ❏ Repeat the process and redefine as applicable.

Exhibit 12.1 gives an overview of the historical development of the concept driving data mining tools.

DATA MINING OVERVIEW: IMPLICATIONS FOR PREVENTION, DETECTION, AND INVESTIGATION

Processing terabytes of claims data cannot be accomplished in a timely or intelligent manner without the tools of data mapping and data mining. How

Data Mining: Part I
Classical statistics: regression analysis,
standard deviations, cluster analysis, etc.
+
Study data and data relationships

↓

Data Mining: Part II
Artificial intelligence (AI): heuristics; human thought-like
processing; not available until the 1980s
+
Relational database management systems (RDBMS)

↓

Data Mining: Part III
Machine learning: 1980s–1990s
+
Statistics and artificial intelligence

↓

Data Mining
Adaptation of machine learning techniques to business
applications creates the study of data hidden patterns

EXHIBIT 12.1   Historical Progression of Data Mining

much is just 1 terabyte of data? According to Roy Williams's *Data Powers of Ten*, 1 terabyte is equivalent to 50,000 trees made into paper and printed, or all the x-ray films in a large technology-based hospital (www2.sims.berke ley.edu/research/projects/how-much-info/datapowers.html). How about 2 terabytes of data? Imagine an entire academic research library.

How can any one organization, let alone a small team of auditors, tackle such a large volume of data and derive intelligence from it? Without data mining, deriving useful intelligence simply could not be done in a high-volume, data-intense marketplace such as healthcare. A tail may as well be called a leg, in that case. Prevention, detection, and investigation would be severely compromised. The opportunities for falsehood via false claim activity would proliferate without these tools.

The next chapter summarizes the blending of data mapping and data mining.

CHAPTER 13

Components of the Data Mapping and Data Mining Process

Falsehood is easy, truth so difficult.

—GEORGE ELIOT

Truth is always difficult; falsehood is so easy to bury in healthcare. Otherwise we would not have the opportunity to fund a $24-million-per-hour industry dedicated to waste, fraud, and abuse. Blending the science of data mapping and data mining is critical toward developing a warehouse to derive intelligence; without these tools, it is almost impossible for those hunting for healthcare fraud to put a dent into the amount of money that is lost by the hour. Data mapping is discussed in Chapter 11 as a separate skill set because it is often overlooked or not well thought out. Data mining is then discussed in Chapter 12. The two concepts are developed independently of each other; however, a contemporaneous component does exist.

Consider the data mapping and mining process a long road trip. First, we need the appropriate automobile. This cannot be determined until after we know how many passengers (healthcare continuum players) are to be transported. We need a (data) map to route our trip. We need to be prepared for variations (anomalies) on the travel route that do not appear on the map.

Once we arrive at each destination, we take in the information from that stop and reevaluate the route. It is an ongoing process.

The critical elements of data mining and data mapping include all of the steps discussed in the previous two chapters. In addition, consider whether any illicit activities uncovered involve one party (singular action) or more than one party (collusion). Data mining and data mapping by individual market player support the identification of a singular issue. If collusion is at play— either by several of the same HCC players or by several types of HCC players— blend data mapping and data mining to identify plural issues. The aggregation of data warehouses by market players becomes critical in detecting these types of anomalies. Thus, understanding the movement and content by market player and by group promotes the effective study of hidden data patterns.

Establish segmentation and aggregation of the data by the industry sector type within the HCC—the patients, providers, payers, suppliers, and support vendors. Recognize organized crime as a constant illegitimate player in this process. This segmentation and aggregation should continue with noting the type of reimbursement model. Is this a prospective, concurrent, or retrospective fee and adjustment schedule? Again, this should be addressed by each pipeline within each legitimate and illegitimate player. Note the documentation tools within each pipeline within each player and the designated operational internal controls as well.

Data mapping and data mining require the definitions for the data elements, the collection of that data, the designs of the decision trees in which the data will be processed, and the ongoing surveillance of the data. Once a warehouse has been appropriately mapped and data mining activated, the ongoing opportunity is the surveillance aspect. This analysis is not a one-time event but an ongoing, evolving tool for efficiently obtaining that intelligence. Ensure that resources are incorporated into the ongoing management of the warehouse.

The work in this book takes us to the next level of analysis. The data integration provides the opportunity to develop profilers. Profilers provide the infrastructure to convert anomaly output data into intelligence. Anomaly tracking systems involve the process of movement and content of information. When the anomalies by HCC player are integrated into one organizational chart and one computer system (or warehouse), along with data from paper systems, vendor systems, and subcontracted systems, the knowledge derived becomes seamless. By integrating protected health information (PHI) and monetary transactions throughout the pipelines, all the factors impacting a healthcare episode become apparent. This is done through the integration of complex contractual arrangements, fee schedule arrangements, identification of third parties, data mapping of anomalies, identification of fraud schemes, identification of waste and abuse scenarios, and formulation of loss amounts.

Management of new information and the *learning* aspect of the mapping and mining will evolve if all respective health information pipeline (HIP) and PHI data definitions, data collection, data decision trees, and data monitoring become a fluid integrative process. The following is a sample response to intelligent data outputs:

1. Identify the anomaly output and study the hidden patterns of the anomaly.

2. Prepare a data analysis profiler and allow for output of the offense noted.

3. Document the sequence of events leading to the offense.

4. List the relevant data content listing.

5. Identify list of potential perpetrators.

6. Identify list of potential witnesses.

7. List relevant statements.

8. List corroborating evidence.

9. List material evidence.

10. Document proof of loss.

11. Provide graphic representations of data analysis and proof of loss determination.

In auditing and investigating healthcare fraud, sample analytical profilers for the above methodology may include medical errors, financial errors, fraud schemes, general audit, forensics, waste, and general system issues.

FORENSIC APPLICATION OF DATA MAPPING AND DATA MINING

The blend of the two methodologies creates a growing body of science referred to as *exploratory data analysis* (EDA). EDA in the healthcare environment can be broken down further. First, a review of forensics: The term *forensic* in essence represents "legal" or "related to courts" (from Latin, it means "before the forum"). This means that the information derived from the intelligence from EDA may be suitable for use in court. The science component can be broken down by any process or system that has an objective methodology that can be repeated by a third party utilizing a scientifically defined method. Therefore, with EDA, forensic science is the application of EDA scientific methodology to answer questions that may be of interest to the legal system or legal proceeding.

The scientific method embodies the techniques of mapping, mining, auditing, and investigating a query; acquiring new intelligence; and corroborating previous intelligence. It is a process that can be measured, observed, and repeated by a third party. This process is subject to principles of reasoning. In essence, the reasoning process includes deriving the same or similar conclusions from defined theories using a defined methodology. Two types of reasoning will be reviewed.

The first is *deductive reasoning*: A conclusion is discerned by the theory or premise of previously known facts. If the theory is correct, then the conclusion must be true. Inference is drawn from what one already knows. This is the value of data mining. EDA tools allow for deciphering data or anomalies via mining techniques, so that they become known. This allows for deductive reasoning. For example, take a set of known facts of a particular surgeon: Within the last 25 heart bypass surgeries, 100 percent of patients were discharged with total charges of $15,000. A premise or theory may be that the next 10 patients will be discharged with charges totaling $15,000.

The second type of reasoning is *inductive reasoning*: when the theory or premise of the issue is believed to support the conclusion. This may be noted in arguments that are based on analogy or generalization to a conclusion.

For example, take a data set for the same cardiac surgeon: Within the last 25 heart bypass surgeries, 100 percent of patients were discharged as deceased. A premise or theory may be that the patients were all deceased to begin with. Upon completion of an investigation, this was proven to be correct.

Therefore, EDA provides a scientific methodology of deriving intelligence from large volumes of data. EDA in healthcare and as described in this book is the statistical tools utilized in reviewing, communicating, and using data through the HCC and the respective pipelines. In forensic applications, we look at the data to define causality. In other words, the intelligence derived will help understand or define the relationship between cause and effect.

The following is a procedural list of this application:

EDA Methodology

1. Identify use data.
2. Determine data sets.
3. Data sets may include parties, entities, workflows, subject matter, and content communication.
4. List current propositions.
   - Propositions may include numbers, words, and images.
5. List assertions.
   - Assertions may be derived from observations or measurement of a variable.
6. List assumptions.
7. Identify sources of data: verbal, paper, electronic.
8. Identify tools associated: verbal, paper, electronic.
9. Identify data dictionary for each system involved.
10. Define headers, detail data, and current mapping of data elements.
11. Data mapping:
    - Map data elements.
    - Create data models in theory and instance.
    - Integrate data.
    - Perform data transformation.
    - Create data definitions and relationships.
    - Document data patterns.
    - Consolidate data.
12. Data mining:
    - Set up data classifications.
    - Set up rule association mining.
    - May involve statistics.
    - Information retrieval.
    - Machine learning.
    - Pattern recognition.

13. Steps 1–12 result in electronic medium exchange analysis (knowledge discovery in databases [KDD] to process patterns identified).

14. Pattern activity may be found by
    - Classification.
    - Association ruling mining—identification of related variables.
    - Clustering—partitioning of data into subgroups.

15. Data analysis involves the identification of the trends, patterns, problems, issues, and conclusions associated with prior propositions or identification of new propositions.

16. Clinical health and financial information:
    - Identify and understand its movement.
    - Identify and understand its content.
    - Identify and understand movement and content in terms of all types of transactions: verbal, paper, electronic.
    - Identify and understand respective systems and parties in movement and generation of content.

DATA MAPPING AND DATA MINING OVERVIEW: IMPLICATIONS FOR PREVENTION, DETECTION, AND INVESTIGATION

As mentioned in the previous chapter, we are working in an industry that takes us easily from terabytes (10^{12} bytes) of data to a pegabytes (10^{15} bytes) of data (which is about three years' worth of Earth Observing System [EOS] data from NASA). Two pegabytes of data is all the information contained in *all* U.S. academic research libraries. This is truly a needle in the haystack. Roy Williams in *Data Powers of Ten* gives further examples of descriptive quantities (www2.sims.berkeley.edu/research/projects/how–much–info/datapowers.html). An exabyte (10^{18} bytes) is equivalent to the total volume of information generated worldwide annually; volume terms such as zettabyte (10^{21} bytes) and yottabyte (10^{24} bytes) cannot even be visualized. The models and concepts presented in this book are effective in focusing efforts within large quantities of data. EDA tools provide the opportunity to analyze data that normally would take a lifetime, if not generations, to analyze.

The added emphasis on volume of data is to underscore the need for EDA tools to get through large amounts of data. In addition, if we map our warehouse, mine it, and derive intelligence from it, in the forensic world any conclusion drawn *needs* to be based on a defined scientific methodology or forensic standard in order for the process to be designated as conclusions drawn from a scientific methodology. The EDA process will provide effective prevention and detection tools. However, when the process enters into investigation, the intent is to eventually lead to a successful prosecution. The efforts of prosecution will not hold up for conclusions drawn that are not driven by forensically recognized scientific methodology.

The next chapter focuses on specific data analysis models in the application of EDA tools.

CHAPTER 14

Data Analysis Models

I'm a great believer in luck, and I find the harder I work, the more I have of it.

—Thomas Jefferson

The harder you work on the front end, the luckier you will be in materializing information that will generate productive results. In healthcare, it is a blend of luck generated from well-organized and structured audit and investigations. This chapter applies a sample series of data analysis models. These models are the results of output activity from data mining. In this book, we have discussed the healthcare continuum (HCC). In the data output world, we have a new continuum to monitor, understand, and use as a guide in audit and investigation of healthcare fraud. This is referred to as the *anomaly continuum*. View these models as potential frameworks for building data warehouses of information for analysis.

DETECTION MODEL

Exhibit 14.1 begins with the concept of detection. *Detection* is the discovery of clues within the data. This book is all about *finding the anomaly*. The model reflects taking segmented market pieces and blending them into one data

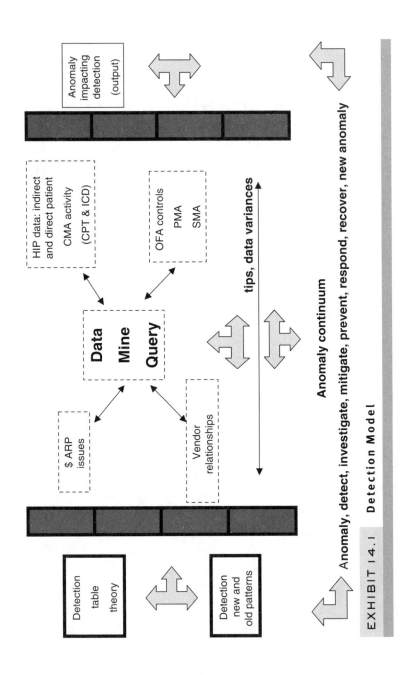

Anomaly impacting detection (output)

HIP data: indirect and direct patient CMA activity (CPT & ICD)

OFA controls PMA SMA

Data Mine Query

$ ARP issues

Vendor relationships

tips, data variances

Anomaly continuum

Anomaly, detect, investigate, mitigate, prevent, respond, recover, new anomaly

Detection table theory

Detection new and old patterns

EXHIBIT 14.1   Detection Model

source for seamless analysis. Any anomalies will be noted. These anomalies feed the detection table for future analysis. This output is then evaluated for either response or follow-up investigations.

The following sample case flow is an actual case with hypothetical names.

SAMPLE CASE: DR. HEALER

CASE HISTORY

Who: Dr. Healer, MD
What: Radio host for a program called *Medicine Man*; skilled healer with nontraditional practices
When: Growing practice over last five years
Why: ?
Where: Five walk-in clinic services

DATA SET

Billing data: High percentage of complicated visits; Dr. Healer generated bills while traveling in Europe.
Recent claim data: Visits to chiropractors, acupuncturists, massage therapists, nutritionists, and personal trainers at a gym billed under Dr. Healer's tax ID number and under MD CPT visit codes.
Staff issues: Dr. Foreign, staff physician, an unlicensed doctor, was on staff for $5 per hour; Dr. Gone continued to bill out of this clinic, although he no longer was associated with the clinic.

DR. HEALER STATEMENT

"I am just a caring doctor getting reluctant insurance companies to pay for alternative health treatments."

Pipeline Application

Health information pipeline (HIP) issues involved a higher-than-average complication rate. The physician evaluation management codes were statistically above average for the diagnoses being submitted as treated by the provider. The accounts receivable pipeline (ARP) issues noted a higher code rate submission in addition to an abnormally higher patient volume for just one doctor. The operational flow activity (OFA) issue involved the operational activities associated with the service market activity (SMA) being provided by the clinic.

Detection Model Application

If we follow the anomaly continuum from left to right, the above data set output would be noted as follows. First, in Exhibit 14.1, find the Detection table theory. Dr. Healer's high-volume activity responded to an edit function that tracks above-average practice growth rate without the addition of new staff on the claim form. The relational database that is illustrated between the two brick walls in Exhibit 14.1 contains the relevant data for analysis. The ARP box contains all the monetary activity.

The HIP contains the clinical services rendered. One of the anomaly outputs was the appearance of wellness services presented as illness-based services. The OFA activity noted basics such as the doctor providing services while he was traveling. Someone did provide the service at the clinic; however, this professional was not presented on the claim form. The vendor relationships involved included the personal trainer and nutritionist who were billing their services under Dr. Healer's ID.

INVESTIGATION MODEL

An *investigation* involves ascertaining whether various activities or statements are true. It is an investigation of inquiries. In the case of Dr. Healer, a statement or data set of "Dr. Foreign, staff physician, an unlicensed doctor, was on staff for $5 per hour" would create an opportunity for corroboration via appropriate evidence. Evidence to collect may include confirmation of license status, if any; educational training; clinic marketing materials; and payroll records.

The statement "High percentage of complicated visits; Dr. Healer generated bills while traveling in Europe" needs to be broken down as well. The breakdown activity is a subtle but very important point with investigations. An investigation is like an a la carte menu at a high-end restaurant. Each item and issue needs to be broken down into a singular form and investigated within that space. Then it is all pulled back together. This book places a great deal of emphasis on data aggregation because healthcare is such a fragmented and segmented marketplace. The models presented walk through the activity of aggregation. When it comes to investigations, the aggregation component is utilized. However, each data element needs to be investigated individually and then within the aggregation of data sets.

The above data set has two distinct pipeline issues and operational factors for consideration. The first part of the statement, "high percentage of complicated visits," represents an ARP issue; it is being driven by claims data analysis. The claim form has the CPT code (the procedure code that is telling us what is being done to the patient); in fact, it is submitted with the ICD code (the diagnosis code that is telling us why something is being done to the patient). When a provider such as a doctor and/or facility bills for a healthcare service, the normal expectation is that they always communicate the *what* and the *why*. This trend has carried over into the ordering of diagnostic tests such as laboratory tests or x-rays. Most facilities, in particular, require that the physician actually list the diagnosis on the prescription. Facilities have made this requirement not so much by regulatory mandates but because they will not be able to submit an invoice for services without it.

Currently a physician can write a prescription for a medication, the patient can redeem that prescription and get the drug, the patient can submit the claim for reimbursement, and the pharmacy can submit invoices with that prescription without the communication of any *whats* or *whys*. Dr. Healer was convicted because the analysis and investigation of his high percentage of complicated visits was, in fact, not very complicated and the patient may or may not have been treated by Dr. Healer. The patient could have been treated by the unlicensed physician. In some cases, the patient was just never seen. The patient could have received a massage as a doctor's visit. The investigation requires an analysis of the medical records, a review of the objective clinical data utilized or assessed by the doctor to make any medical determinations. The next chapter discusses in more detail how to analyze medical records and the impact of individual analysis as well as analysis in aggregate form.

The point of distinguishing the process of reimbursement among facilities, doctors, and prescriptions is this: If Dr. Healer truly had a high complicated patient population, mostly likely these patients would have been receiving some type of prescription regimen. The lack of a diagnosis requirement with prescriptions limits the detection and investigation discussed so far. This is a major vulnerability for all benefit programs that provide medication coverage. With respect to Dr. Healer, if medications could be profiled by diagnosis, several other opportunities would exist for analysis.

For example, is Dr. Healer also prescribing medications with no basis? If he uses an unlicensed doctor on his staff, presents wellness services as illness services, and sees himself as "a caring doctor getting reluctant insurance companies to pay for alternative health treatments," what other alternative treatments is he providing with prescribed medications? What if Dr. Healer was presented with Aunt Betty, who has no insurance? Would Dr. Healer get reluctant payers to pay for Aunt Betty's medication by billing the drug under his insured patient? What if Dr. Healer believed in nonformulary stress-management prescriptions? Would his concern for perceived depression or stress fuel a group of people dealing with addiction issues?

Next, let us look at the second part of the data set statement: ". . . while traveling in Europe." The investigation aspects in this statement go beyond the HCC. Within the HCC, an analysis of the appointment book, scheduling procedures, and the narrative notes within the patient records will identify the true author as well as the clinician actually involved with the patient. Further corroboration would involve interviews with staff and patients. Outside of the HCC, the investigation would involve subpoenas for credit card records or third-party sources such as hotels or travel agents to confirm the actual travel patterns and activities of Dr. Healer. This information would be pulled back into the HCC as items of actual clinical activity.

Exhibit 14.2 reflects the integration of this concept into the anomaly continuum. Note that this is just one part of the continuum. This chapter is progressing from one model concept to the next. However, a continuum is a series of continuous parts in which, at any point, two parts can generate activity in a third part or add another layer to an active component. For example, the focus on Dr. Healer has been on the false claim activity associated with the high percentage of complicated office visits. However, the investigation could easily detect a new and previously unknown anomaly. This would feed back through the entire anomaly continuum.

Investigation of fraud consists of the multitude of steps necessary to resolve allegations of fraud—interviewing witnesses, assembling evidence, writing reports, and dealing with prosecutors and the courts. The investigation of fraud, because it deals with the individual rights of others, must be conducted only with adequate cause of predication. *Predication* is when all of the evidence and circumstances of a case "would lead a reasonable, professionally trained, and prudent individual to believe a fraud has occurred, is occurring, and/or will occur" (www.acfe.com). Predication is the basis on which an

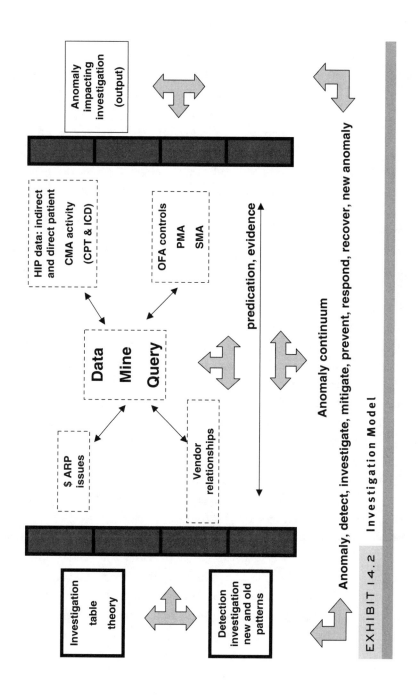

EXHIBIT 14.2 Investigation Model

179

examination is commenced. Fraud examinations should not be conducted without proper predication. *Fraud theory* is used to create a hypothesis, test it, and prove (either beyond a reasonable doubt or with the preponderance of evidence) that a fraud has been committed.

The Association of Certified Fraud Examiners (ACFE) provides several guidelines when conducting a fraud examination. The following steps (in the order of their occurrence) are used in the fraud theory approach. First, analyze the available data. This book is providing specifics within the HCC. Next, create a hypothesis. This hypothesis is inevitably the *worst-case scenario*—in furtherance of this hypothesis, fraud examiners know that each specific scheme has its own unique characteristics that constitute the "red-flags" of fraud. Follow this by testing the hypothesis; this involves creating a *what-if* scenario. Once this has been done, refine and amend the hypothesis. In testing the hypothesis, the examiner may find that all facts do not fit a particular scenario; if this is the case, the hypothesis must be revised and retested. If the known facts are tested with negative results, it could be that a fraud is not present or cannot be proven.

The ACFE also teaches an examination methodology. There are essentially three tools available to the fraud examiner in every fraud examination. The first is interviewing—the process of obtaining relevant information about the matter from those with knowledge of it. The second is supporting documents—the examiner must be skilled at examining financial statements, books, and records. The examiner must know the legal ramification of the evidence and how to maintain the chain of custody over documents. The third is observation—the examiner is often placed in a position where he or she must observe behavior, search for displays of wealth, and, in some instances, observe specific offenses.

The ACFE model can be incorporated throughout the audit and investigation guide within this text. This text provides the road map to understanding specific issues that are unique to this marketplace. With respect to the concept of *intent*, note that in fraud, intent *must* be shown. Intent is rarely self-evident, but rather must be demonstrated by showing a pattern of activity. Exploratory data analysis (EDA) provides the opportunity to prove intent through data mapping and data mining techniques.

Traditional means for proving intent include that the accused had no legitimate motive for the activities, repeatedly engaged in identical or similar activities of an apparent wrongful nature, made conflicting statements or made statements that he or she knew to be false, made an actual admission, or engaged in behaviors that impeded the investigation of the offense. Emerging means for intent are found in EDA activity. For example, in the case of Dr. Healer, he had to know that the bills submitted during his travels in Europe were false. Statistical analysis in addition to clinical analysis of the medical records by actual provider and travel records can provide a strong argument that the doctor had intent to misrepresent his claims. Another case example involves a doctor who had a statistical profile of 100 percent of his cases being discharged deceased. The clinical and statistical analysis conducted on claims and available records can generate the theory that "the patients were deceased" before surgery.

MITIGATION MODEL

The concept of *mitigation* builds on issues noted within detection and investigation along with the subsequent models to be discussed in this chapter. Mitigation is the act of reducing or making a certain set of circumstances less severe.

In the case of Dr. Healer, mitigation occurred in the prosecution of Dr. Healer. Dr. Healer was convicted of false claims and removed from the system as a licensed physician, thereby preventing further harm and loss. Other applicable issues were substandard care and medical unbelievability patterns. What made this case complicated was tracking down Dr. Healer's assets. Ultimately, Dr. Healer did receive a criminal conviction, civil lawsuits were initiated, and he ultimately lost his license.

Mitigation does not stop at the point of conviction of the perpetrator. The findings of this anomaly should be followed up with the third-party administrator's adjudication and edit procedures. It feeds our mitigation model in Exhibit 14.3 by adding the experience back into the system. Incorporating the pattern of this fraud into the model prevents or minimizes similar occurrences, helps find ongoing schemes elsewhere with other parties, and reduces the time it takes to discover these schemes. Mitigation feeds detection by reducing in the future the amount of time it takes to make a fraud known.

As previously mentioned, the ACFE reports that the average life span of a fraud is 18 months. Dr. Healer had a good lead time of five years. Therefore, what was happening during the adjudication of the Medicaid claims for this

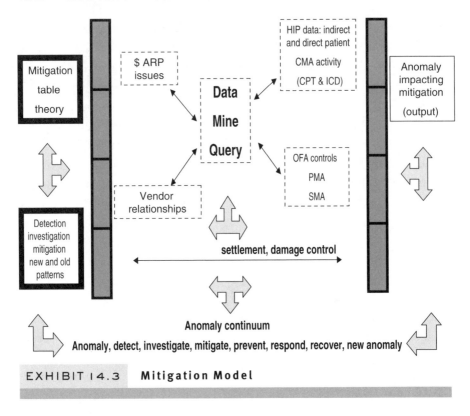

EXHIBIT 14.3   **Mitigation Model**

state? How was Dr. Healer able to stay below the radar screen? Upon evaluation and review, the next step would be establishing internal controls.

PREVENTION MODEL

The *prevention* model is about incorporating internal controls. For example, Dr. Healer had an unlicensed professional practicing medicine. He had vendors presenting wellness services as illness services. What controls can be placed in the management of HIP data that would prompt the claims adjustor to question claims that are similar to Dr. Healer's?

The following is an example of prevention with respect to a physician's license. Each facility or organization that employs a physician is supposed to have a credentialing process. This is the process to ensure that the individual hired to provide care actually has the appropriate credentials.

Mark Nepokroeff practiced medicine in Niagara County, New York, without having completed medical school. His diploma was a fake. However, New York gave him a medical license, and allowed him to perform IME exams and to treat workers' compensation claimants. The federal government had him doing disability eligibility exams for Social Security Disability and SSI. His punishment: four months in federal prison and $233,439 in restitution.

Nepokroeff's attitude toward the disabled was astonishing. He has stated, "There is no such thing as a totally disabled person," "Most people on workers' compensation just want a free vacation," and "Most people on workers' compensation are fraudulent." His response to hearing that one of his workers' compensation patients had jumped out of a top window of Erie County Medical Center was to laugh and say, "Well his problems are over."

Source: www.injuredworker.org/Insurance_fraud.htm.

In this case, the credentialing process failed to identify the lack of licensure by this physician. In addition, the statement, "Well his problems are over" reflects an individual who most likely gave clues as to his lack of medical training, either by the records he maintained on patients or his lack of clinical judgment in his communications with other licensed professionals. He most likely had patient complaints that should have resulted in some type of peer review. In other words, if he was not trained as a physician, someone should have seen it in his care of his patients.

In Exhibit 14.4, prevention model theory is added to the data collection and decision-making process. It is reconciled with previously collected detection, investigation, and mitigation data. The focus is on the HIP data edits. However, it is important to look at the ARP issues. If the third-party administrator (TPA) system missed the licensing issues and diagnosis issues, it has another opportunity to evaluate the fluctuations in monetary

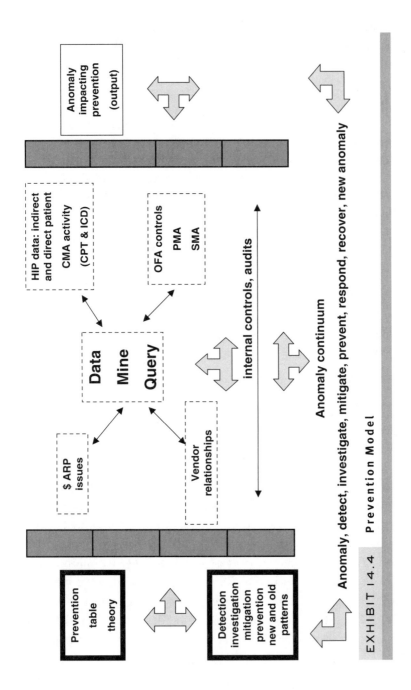

EXHIBIT 14.4 Prevention Model

transactions. This was true in Dr. Healer's case, where the practice activity, the volume, and complication rate only went up.

Prevention is about a complete review and audit of the adjudication procedures of the TPA. What about from a plan sponsor perspective? What internal controls should be in place and what accountability does the plan sponsor have? From the perspective of a private market self-insured employer plan, the market history still indicates that these types of plan sponsors have very few internal controls. As of this writing, the market still has self-insured sponsored employer benefit plans that have never been audited. In an environment in which benefits are such a high line cost of doing business, simply no excuse exists.

The first question for any self-insured employer is to internally evaluate what role is responsible for negotiating the contract. Next, what role receives the invoices and reports that communicate the expenditures by the TPA and the request for vendor fees? Third, how does the employer representative verify the accuracy of the vendor fees and the expenditures made on behalf of its employees? If double-digit increases are the market trend for employers, they need to get a handle on how their money is being spent. If not, they will continue to be vulnerable for funding waste, fraud, and abuse in healthcare. Note the discussion at the beginning of this book. Waste, fraud, and abuse are generated by all legitimate and illegitimate (organized crime activity) players within the HCC. Finally, can the employer corroborate every monetary transaction noted in the contract? Can the employer audit for any monetary transaction that is not itemized in the contract? If the answer is *no* to any of these questions, the employer is at a significant risk and is extremely vulnerable to uncontrolled cost management in addition to healthcare waste, fraud, and abuse.

The government-sponsored benefit plans have a head start on auditing. They audit their TPA vendors on a regular basis, and those audits and investigations have generated results. The concepts are no different from those of a private plan sponsored program. In fact, employers can learn from the government's audit and investigation activities. For example, if a TPA has been fined for misrepresenting performance guarantees as a government vendor to a Medicaid program, it is plausible for a self-insured private employer who is served by that same TPA to audit for similar issues.

The needs for all benefit plan sponsors are the same; however, the avenues are different. Government-sponsored plans have legislative mandates and rights for participation in their programs. These mandates address items that are contained within the claim form as well as other cost-type reporting activities. This is apart from any other regulatory requirement of the Employee Retirement Income Security Act (ERISA) for self-insured employers. With respect to healthcare fraud, it was only the recent updates to the Health Insurance Portability and Accountability Act of 1996 (HIPAA) legislations that took the definition of fraud in healthcare to a different level for private plans (Title XI, 42 U.S.C., Public Law 104-191).

HIPAA federalized the crime of healthcare fraud by making it illegal for anyone to knowingly and willfully

- Defraud any healthcare benefit program or obtain by means of false representations any money or property of a healthcare benefit program.
- Make false statements, which criminalize any false or fictitious statements in any matter involving a healthcare benefit program.
- Embezzle, convert, or steal any funds, property, or assets of a healthcare benefit program.
- Obstruct, delay, prevent, or mislead the investigation of federal healthcare offenses.

Note the statute's use of the phrase, *healthcare benefit plan*. It does not stipulate "government-sponsored benefit plan" or "privately sponsored employer benefit plan." The federal statutes cover "a healthcare benefit plan." With this in mind, take a look at the following cases:

PAYER CASE #1: CONVICTION

On May 2, 1997, in the Northern District of California, Blue Shield of California agreed to pay $12 million to settle allegations that it filed false claims for payment under its contract with the government to process and pay Medicare claims. The agreement resolves claims that the San Francisco–based Blue Shield covered up claims processing errors discovered by HCFA auditors in order to obtain more favorable scores under an agency program for grading the Medicare carrier's claims processing capabilities. A *qui tam* suit was filed by former Blue Shield employees in the Medicare division in Chico, and these relators will receive 18 percent of the settlement amount. This false claims settlement follows a May 1996 criminal conviction of Blue Shield for conspiracy and obstructing federal audits to evaluate the company's performance in the Medicare processing contract. Blue Shield paid a criminal fine of $1.5 million when it entered its guilty plea. Blue Shield ceased being a Medicare contractor in September 1996.

Source: U.S. Department of Justice, *Health Care Fraud Report, Fiscal Year 1997,* www.usdoj.gov/dag/pubdoc/health97.htm.

PAYER CASE #2: SETTLEMENT WITH ABSTRACT FROM THE CORPORATE INTEGRITY AGREEMENT (CIA)

"This Settlement Agreement ("Agreement") is entered into between the United States of America, acting through the United States Department of Justice and on behalf of the Office of Inspector General ("OIG-HHS") of the Department of Health and Human Services ("HHS") (collectively the "United States"); and AmeriChoice of Pennsylvania, Inc., formerly known as Healthcare Management Alternatives, Inc., collectively referred to throughout this Agreement as "ACPA." ACPA and the United States are hereafter referred to as "the Parties." The Agreement is agreed to and executed by the authorized representatives of the Parties.

II. PREAMBLE

A. ACPA is a for-profit corporation located at all relevant times within the Eastern District of Pennsylvania.

B. The United States contends that, from September 1995 through June 1998, ACPA submitted or caused to be submitted claims for payment to the Medicare Program ("Medicare"), Title XVIII of the Social Security Act, 42 U.S.C. §§ 1395-1395ggg, and/or the Medicaid Program ("Medicaid"), Title XIX of the Social Security Act, 42 U.S.C. §§ 1396-1396v.

C. The United States alleges *violations of the False Claims Act,* 31 U.S.C. §§ 3729-3733, by ACPA from September 1995

(Continued)

through June 1998, based on ACPA's *handling, processing and/or payment of claims submitted by providers (including its failure to process or pay claims in a timely fashion or at all)*, ACPA's **inaccurate reporting of claims processing data to the Commonwealth of Pennsylvania** (including its failure to meet self-reporting requirements and impose self-assessment penalties as required under the managed care contract with the Commonwealth of Pennsylvania) and ACPA's **coverage of home health services to qualified beneficiaries (including its failure to do so),** hereinafter referred to collectively as the "Covered Conduct."

D. ACPA does not admit the contentions of the United States as set forth in Paragraph C above.

E. In order to avoid the delay, uncertainty, inconvenience and expense of protracted litigation of these claims, the Parties reach a full and final settlement as set forth below..." (emphasis added).

Source: www.usdoj.gov/usao/pae/News/Pr/2005/jun/ACPA%20settlement%20FINAL.pdf.

PAYER CASE #3: CONVICTION

On July 16, 1998, BCBSIL pleaded guilty to Medicare fraud charges for the years 1985 through 1994 and agreed to pay $144 million in fines to the federal government, the largest penalty assessed against a Medicare claims processor for fraud. As a result of its fraudulent activities, BCBSIL received $1.29 million in undeserved bonuses.

Blue Cross/Blue Shield of Illinois paid a record $144 million to settle charges that the company had falsified claims and hid files from federal investigators. The company was also accused of turning off the phones to avoid taking calls from Medicare beneficiaries checking on the status of their claims.

Source: www.consumersunion.org/conv/pub/stateilstates/000608.html.

None of these cases represents privately sponsored employer benefit plans—thus the basis for why the audit and detection of healthcare fraud of government programs is one step ahead of privately held employer benefit programs. Yet these are the same entities that are serving the privately held benefit employer sponsored market. Civil litigation has been found among various provider entities and payers. However, most of these cases are settled under the condition of tight confidentiality clauses. As a result, the final issues and their resolution do not become part of the public domain.

A comprehensive data warehouse includes data intelligence of anomalies by sponsored programs. The privately held marketplace has a great deal to learn from the government-sponsored programs. The reverse is also true. Government-sponsored programs have a great deal to learn from how healthcare episodes are processed in the commercial environment. All of these attributes feed the concept of prevention. They also feed the concept of response. What have we learned from detection, investigation, mitigation, and prevention? The next model expands by incorporating market variables into the equation.

RESPONSE MODEL

This component of the anomaly continuum is about the *response* to the irregularity noted. The response can take the form of words or action. Let us review the following case, which involves a third-party billing company:

CASE: THIRD-PARTY BILLING

Emergency Physician Billing Services, Inc. (EPBS) provided coding, billing, and collections services for emergency physician groups in over 100 emergency departments in as many as 33 states. Based on allegations presented by a *qui tam* relator, the United States charged that EPBS and its principal owner, Dr. J. D. McKean, routinely billed federal and state healthcare programs for a higher level of treatment than was provided or supported by medical record documentation.

EPBS was paid based on a percentage of revenues either billed or recovered, depending on the client. EPBS coders received a base pay with bonuses based on the number of charts processed and were required to process 40 emergency room medical charts per hour, or the equivalent of a chart every 90 seconds. (By contrast, a competitor of EPBS requires 120 charts per day.) The EPBS coders were able to meet these quotas by taking short-cuts and disregarding information in the chart. No coder at EPBS ever attended training or any other informational meeting regarding emergency department coding other than in-house EPBS training and no coder ever contacted a physician with questions regarding a chart.

The defendants agreed to pay $15.5 million to resolve their civil and administrative monetary liabilities. In addition, Dr. McKean agreed to be excluded from participation in the federal healthcare programs for 15 years and EPBS entered into a comprehensive CIA. (See Lewis Morris, Assistant Inspector General for Legal Affairs, Testimony Before the House Committee on Commerce, Subcommittee on Oversight and Investigations, April 6, 2000, http://oig.hhs.gov/reading/testimony/2000/00406fin.htm.)

The market response from this action was clear from a criminal perspective. EPBS was pursued by the Department of Justice for false claim activity. However, the secondary market response was the generation of a compliance guidance by the Department of Health and Human Services. (See "Office of Inspector General's Compliance Program Guidance for Third-Party Medical Billing Companies," *Federal Register* 63(243), December 18, 1998, retrieved from http://oig.hhs.gov/fraud/docs/complianceguidance/nhsolicit.pdf.) In response to market activity within the HCC, the above-referenced compliance guidance was generated.

Several emerging issues of third-party medical billing companies were noted. First, third-party medical billing companies are increasingly providing crucial services to doctors that could greatly impact the stability of the Medicare Trust Fund and the cost of healthcare in this country. Second, healthcare professionals are consulting with billing companies to provide timely and accurate advice with regard to reimbursement matters, as well as overall business decision making. Finally, individual billing companies may support a variety of providers with different specialties. As a result, the following general components of an effective compliance program can be found within this document. They include the following list:

1. Implementing written policies, procedures, and standards of conduct
2. Designating a compliance officer and compliance committee
3. Conducting effective training education
4. Developing effective lines of communication
5. Enforcing standards through well-publicized disciplinary guidelines
6. Conducting internal monitoring and auditing
7. Responding promptly to detected offenses and developing corrective action

Within Exhibit 14.5, the category of Market response: industry standards, compliance, and legislation was added to reflect these attributes in the data mining process.

The goals of compliance by third-party medical billing companies include improved medical record documentation; improved collaboration, communication, and cooperation among healthcare providers and those processing and using protected health information (PHI); increased likelihood of identification and prevention of criminal and unethical conduct; and added assurance that the third-party billing company fulfills its legal duty and does not submit false or inaccurate claims to government or private payers. Audits for compliance now become a data element in this continuum.

The following case involves a prosecuted case of a pharmaceutical manufacturer.

CASE: PHARMACEUTICAL FRAUD

A pharmaceutical company that deliberately falsified price reports to the Texas Medicaid program for its products was successfully prosecuted and settled in court. Under terms of the agreement, Dey, Inc. will pay a total of $18,500,000, with more than $9 million going to the State. The remaining portion of the settlement will go to the federal government, which jointly funds the Texas Medicaid program and has reached its own settlement with the company.

Dey, a subsidiary of German pharmaceutical giant Merck KGaA, manufactures and markets inhalant products that are generally prescribed for persons suffering from respiratory illnesses. Under Texas law, drug manufacturers are required to report the prices at

(Continued)

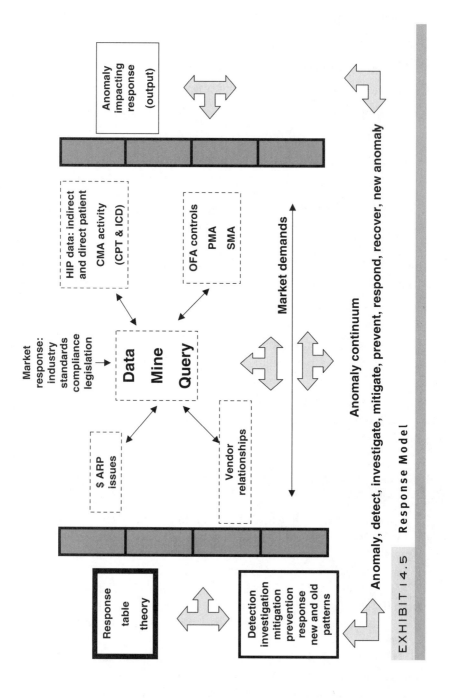

Anomaly impacting response (output)

HIP data: indirect and direct patient
CMA activity (CPT & ICD)

OFA controls
PMA
SMA

Market response: industry standards compliance legislation

Data Mine Query

$ ARP issues

Vendor relationships

Market demands

Anomaly continuum

Response table theory

Detection
investigation
mitigation
prevention
response
new and old patterns

Anomaly, detect, investigate, mitigate, prevent, respond, recover, new anomaly

EXHIBIT 14.5   Response Model

which they sell their products to wholesalers and distributors. The Texas Medicaid program then uses this pricing information as a basis for calculating provider cost and reimburses Medicaid providers accordingly. The attorney general's Civil Medicaid Fraud Section found that Dey deliberately falsified its pricing reports for the benefit of its customers, which directly led to overpayments by the Texas Medicaid program.

Source: Attorney General of Texas, Greg Abbott, "Attorney General Recovers $18.5 Million in Medicaid Fraud Case," www.oag.state.tx.us/oagnews/release.php?id=68.

This case is an example of another compliance guidance publication (see "OIG Compliance Program Guidance for Pharmaceutical Manufactures," *Federal Register* 68(86), May 5, 2003, retrieved from http://oig.hhs.gov/authorities/docs/03/050503FRCPGPharmac.pdf). The OIG notes that the components of an effective compliance program for pharmaceutical manufacturers should include several goals. First, manufacturers should ensure that they fulfill their legal duty to avoid submitting false or inaccurate pricing or rebate information to any federal healthcare program or engaging in illegal marketing activities. Second, they need to increase the likelihood of preventing, or at least identifying and correcting, unlawful and unethical behavior at an early stage. Finally, they need to minimize any financial loss to the government and any corresponding financial loss to the company.

The emerging issues within the pharmaceutical manufacture industry were noted in several areas. First, given the wide diversity within the pharmaceutical industry, there is no single best pharmaceutical manufacturer compliance program. Second, the pharmaceutical manufacturers are already subject to extensive regulatory requirements in addition to fraud- and abuse-related issues. However, it is expected that many pharmaceutical manufacturers have addressed their obligations through compliance programs. Again, this is another example of market response to identified problems within the healthcare market. These compliance requirements should feed the market industry response as a data element for future audits.

RECOVERY MODEL

Recovery is all about the act of regaining. It may include just the possibility of regaining something that was lost or taken. Recovery may also be seen in the form of restoration to a former or better state. Unfortunately, this is usually defined in terms of money, property, or some other type of physical asset. Attributes such as dignity, mobility, and life itself can never be replaced. In the arena of waste, fraud, and abuse, irreversible recovery in absolute terms may never materialize.

Exhibit 14.6 demonstrates the integration of the recovery process into the anomaly continuum.

Note the addition of one more data element entitled Litigation: criminal, civil, CIAs, and settlements. The determinations that are made from any of these activities should be included in the relational database activity. Known outcomes by a perpetrator can help at any component in this continuum. For example, under detection, the algorithms can be defined to look for other parties utilizing the same scheme.

Under investigation, the evidence that leads toward a successful prosecution can be used as a standard in future cases. With respect to mitigation, issues such as proof of loss or damage control can help create internal controls and other avenues to help avoid the same issue going into the future. Prevention incorporates new compliance initiatives. Response leads to updates and new policy initiatives. Finally, recovery, if any, sets forth opportunities for retribution, compensation, or contributions back to the injured parties.

The following is a series of cases that have been prosecuted. They represent players throughout the HCC.

SAMPLE CASE WITH RECOVERY OF CLAIMS SUBMITTED BY AN EXCLUDED PARTY

June 24, 2004: Wadley Ambulance Service (WAS), Oklahoma, agreed to pay $28,322 to resolve its liability under the CMP (civil monetary penalties) provisions applicable to false or fraudulent claims. The OIG alleged that WAS employed an individual that WAS knew or should have known had been excluded from participation in federal healthcare programs.

Source: U.S. Department of Health and Human Services, Office of Inspector General, "False and Fraudulent Claims, 2004," http://oig.hhs.gov/fraud/enforcement/administrative/cmp/cmpitems.html.

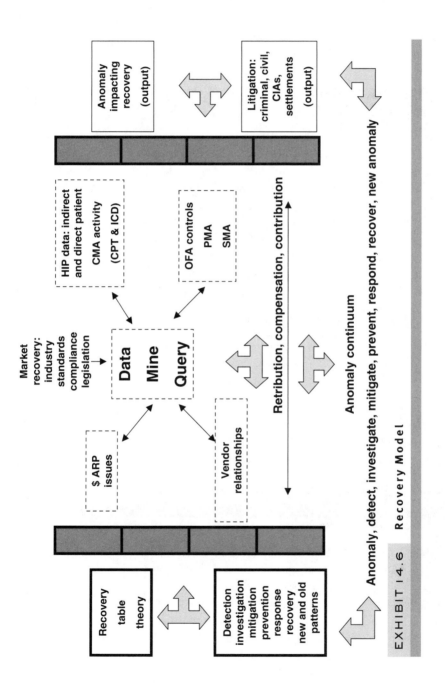

EXHIBIT 14.6 Recovery Model

This is an example of liability by firms that hire individuals who already have a prior record for false claim activity. If a party has been excluded from participation in a federal healthcare program, it is most likely because it has committed an offense that in essence resulted in expulsion.

SAMPLE CASE WITH RECOVERY FROM KICKBACKS AND PHYSICIAN SELF-REFERRAL

June 29, 2004: A New Jersey physician agreed to pay $500,000 and enter into a five-year integrity agreement to resolve his liability under the CMP provisions for violating the Stark Law and the Anti-Kickback Statute. The physician entered into two lease agreements with a home health agency/durable medical equipment supplier to which the physician referred federal healthcare program bene-ficiaries. The OIG alleged that neither lease was commercially reasonable and that both leases were shams to disguise kickbacks paid to the physician in exchange for referrals.

Source: U.S. Department of Health and Human Services, Office of Inspector General, "Kickback and Physician Self-Referral, 2004," http://oig.hhs.gov/fraud/enforcement/administrative/cmp/cmpitems.html.

The Stark laws do not want any physician to be influenced by financial incentives with third parties. The basis for this is that the physician may be influenced by compensation issues versus what is truly needed by the patient.

SAMPLE CASE WITH RECOVERY INVOLVING MANAGED CARE

December 31, 2001: Molina Medical Centers, a California Medicaid managed care plan, agreed to pay $600,000 to resolve its liability under the OIG's CMP provision applicable to any Medicaid managed care organization that misrepresents or falsifies informa-tion to an individual. The OIG alleged that the managed care plan sent misleading letters to its Medicaid enrollees in an effort to persuade the enrollees to continue to choose it as their Medicaid managed care plan. The OIG alleged that the letters appeared to be written and signed by the enrollees' primary care physicians even though they were actually written and signed by employees of the managed care plan.

Source: U.S. Department of Health and Human Services, Office of Inspector General, "Managed Care, 2001," http://oig.hhs.gov/fraud/enforcement/administrative/cmp/cmpitems.html.

SAMPLE CASE WITH RECOVERY INVOLVING OVERCHARGING BENEFICIARIES

July 28, 2003: A physician from Minneapolis, Minnesota, agreed to pay $53,400 to resolve his liability under the CMP provision applicable to violations of a provider's assignment agreement. By accepting assignment for all covered services, a participating provider agrees that he or she will not collect from a Medicare beneficiary more than the applicable deductible and co-insurance for covered services. The OIG alleged that the physician created a program whereby the physician's patients were asked to sign a yearly contract and pay a yearly fee for services that the physician characterized as "not covered" by Medicare. The OIG further alleged that because at least some of the services described in the contract were actually covered and reimbursable by Medicare, each contract presented to the Medicare patients constituted a request for payment other than the co-insurance and applicable deductible for covered services in violation of the terms of the physician's assignment agreement. In addition to payment of the settlement amount, the physician agreed not to request similar payments from beneficiaries in the future.

Source: U.S. Department of Health and Human Services, Office of Inspector General, "Overcharging Beneficiaries, 2003," http://oig.hhs.gov/fraud/enforcement/administrative/cmp/cmpitems.html.

This is a case of misrepresentation that is made by a physician to a patient. When a physician contracts with a government-sponsored program, he or she adopts the policies of that program. Very few self-insured employers have the opportunity to audit for this type of activity within their programs. This also includes premium-based employers. The issue typically is between the payers who have a contract with the particular provider. The private consumer has very little support in advocacy for this type of issue.

The following case is also a beneficiary issue. In the previous case, the physician misrepresented his contract with Medicare for cash. In this next case, the physician intimidated his patients for cash.

SAMPLE CASE INVOLVING INTIMIDATION

"An Indiana doctor was sentenced to 7 years incarceration, with 3 years suspended, for his scheme involving intimidating Medicaid beneficiaries. The doctor, who was previously found guilty during a 4-day jury trial, intimidated Medicaid recipients by telling them they would lose their benefits if they did not make cash payments."

Source: http://medicalcodingandbilling.blogspot.com/2005/03/oig-saves-american-taxpayers-money-by.html.

SAMPLE CASE WITH RECOVERY INVOLVING SELECT AGENTS AND TOXINS

July 26, 2004: Meridian Bioscience, Inc., Ohio, agreed to pay $50,000 to resolve its liability for an alleged violation of the Select Agent Program. The OIG alleged that Meridian possessed the select agent *C. immitis* from at least March 12, 2003 until March 4, 2004. The OIG alleged that during this time, Meridian failed to submit application materials, and failed to properly register with the Centers for Disease Control and Prevention.

Source: U.S. Department of Health and Human Services, Office of Inspector General, "Select Agents and Toxins, 2004," http://oig.hhs.gov/fraud/enforcement/administrative/cmp/cmpitems.html.

This group belongs to the HCC category of "other" or "vendor." The perpetrators in this case violated the regulations regarding the possession, use, and transfer of biological agents and toxins in Part 73 of Title 42 of the Code of Federal Regulations (the Select Agent Program).

SAMPLE CASE WITH RECOVERY INVOLVING PATIENT DUMPING

July 26, 2004: Redbud Community Hospital (Redbud), a small California hospital, agreed to pay $7,500 to resolve its liability for CMPs under the patient dumping statute. The OIG alleged that Redbud failed to provide an appropriate medical screening examination to a 47-year-old male who presented to its emergency department via ambulance after a bicycle accident. The patient was diagnosed and treated for a right clavicle fracture and was discharged. After being discharged, the patient allegedly experienced shortness of breath and was transported to another medical facility. At this medical facility, it was discovered that the patient had also suffered from a closed head injury, vertebral fracture, and an intra-abdominal blood clot. The patient was successfully treated at the second facility.

Source: http://oig.hhs.gov/fraud/enforcement/administrative/cmp/cmpitemspd.

This case represents a possible clinical breakdown by providers when treating patients with no insurance.

SAMPLE CASE WITH RECOVERY INVOLVING EMPLOYEE MISCONDUCT

In New Mexico, an Indian Health Service (IHS) contract employee was sentenced to three years' supervised release and ordered to pay $26,000 in restitution for embezzlement. The employee involved was supervising a construction project for IHS. He embezzled money in order to build an addition to his home.

Source: http://oig.hhs.gov/fraud/enforcement/criminal/04/0604.html.

IHS did not have the appropriate controls to prevent the employee theft. Employee misconduct is a vulnerability shared by all HCC players. In addition to internal controls, appropriate background checks should be conducted on employees hired. Particular screening should include employees who will have indirect and direct patient care involvement. Employees who will be handling PHI and any respective financial transactions should be screened as well.

SAMPLE CASE WITH RECOVERY INVOLVING MISUSE OF GRANT FUNDS

In South Carolina, a woman was ordered to pay $30,000 in restitution for embezzlement and theft. Working as the executive director of a rural health clinic that receives grant funds, the woman used a corporate credit card to make purchases for her own personal use. The fraudulent activity was discovered during an audit.

Source: U.S. Department of Health and Human Services, Office of Inspector General, "Misuse of Grant Funds, May 2004," http://oig.hhs.gov/fraud/enforcement/administrative/cmp/cmpitems.html.

Grant activity can fall under the "other" HCC category or that of a provider. This is similar in context to the employee misconduct. However, it involved research funds. Grant funds have their own specific regulatory requirements. The internal controls failed within the management of the grant.

SAMPLE CASE WITH RECOVERY INVOLVING TRANSPORTATION FRAUD

In Georgia, two individuals and an ambulance company were sentenced related to charges of providing medically unnecessary ambulance runs and for using nonlicensed personnel. One of the individuals was sentenced to 30 months in prison, and the other was sentenced to 21 months in prison. The company was ordered to pay a $650,000 fine. In addition, they were ordered to pay $959,000 in joint restitution.

Source: U.S. Department of Health and Human Services, Office of Inspector General, "Transportation Fraud, March 2004," http://oig.hhs.gov/fraud/ enforcement/criminal/04/0304.html.

This is another example of an HCC player falling into the vendor role. The investigation with transportation cases should include any parties such as providers who were in receipt of these patients. In some of these transportation cases, a provider did not exist at all. Some involved taxi rides to the mall and back. Note the following case.

SAMPLE CASE INVOLVING MEDICAID FRAUD

In Virginia, two operators of a cab service were sentenced to 27 months and 21 months in prison, respectively, for submitting claims to Medicaid for taxi services they did not provide. They were also ordered to pay $395,000 in joint restitution.

Source: U.S. Department of Health and Human Services, Office of Inspector General, "Medicaid Fraud, February 2004," http://oig.hhs.gov/fraud/ enforcement/criminal/04/0204.html.

SAMPLE CASE WITH RECOVERY INVOLVING PRESCRIPTION DRUG FRAUD

In Rhode Island, a pharmacist was sentenced to 37 months in prison for charges related to selling prescription drug samples to customers at his pharmacy. In addition, the pharmacist was ordered to forfeit $431,000 to the government and pay a $45,000 fine. Pharmaceutical representatives provided the drug samples to a physician who in turn diverted them to the pharmacy. In September 2004, the physician was sentenced to 10 years in prison for his involvement in this scheme and for administering diluted vaccines to immigrant patients.

Source: U.S. Department of Health and Human Services, Office of Inspector General, "Prescription Drug Fraud, November 2004," http://oig.hhs.gov/fraud/enforcement/criminal/04/1104.html.

Drug-related fraud schemes will be a target area for ongoing investigations. With the introduction of Medicare Part D prescription programs, expect a proliferation of activity. This activity will range from contractual manipulations of medication pricing to drug diversion, drug adulteration, and outright counterfeit activity.

SAMPLE CASE WITH RECOVERY INVOLVING DURABLE MEDICAL EQUIPMENT (DME)

An owner of a DME supply company was sentenced to 2 years' imprisonment and ordered to pay $273,000 in restitution and pay a $2,500 fine for mail fraud in connection with a Medicaid fraud scheme. The man submitted claims to Wisconsin's medical assistance program for DME that was never provided.

Source: U.S. Department of Health and Human Services, Office of Inspector General, "Durable Medical Equipment, January 2004," http://oig.hhs.gov/fraud/enforcement/criminal/04/0104.html.

This is an example of outright false claim activity—billing for products never received. A previous discussion noted the vulnerability with prescription medications and the lack of diagnosis information for claim submissions. The same could be said for durable medical equipment ordered by physicians for patients. The requirement or standard for including a diagnosis with any claims submission would provide a greater opportunity for detection just by the ability to data-mine equipment in comparison to diagnosis. The following involved durable medical equipment in which products were provided but misrepresented.

SAMPLE CASE INVOLVING MISREPRESENTATION

Many inappropriate transactions involve marketing of incontinence supplies. In one case, a supplier was found to have delivered adult diapers, which are not covered by Medicare Part D, and to have improperly billed these items as expensive prosthetic devices called "female external urinary collection devices."

Source: Federal Register 60(154), August 10, 1995, retrieved from http://oig.hhs.gov/fraud/docs/alertsandbulletins/081095.html.

SAMPLE CASE WITH RECOVERY INVOLVING
COLLUSIVE ACTIVITY

In Missouri, six co-defendants were sentenced for conspiring to defraud the United States through a system of kickbacks for patient referrals and the filing of false claims that resulted in overpayments from Medicare and Medicaid. The individuals sentenced included a licensed medical doctor, a registered nurse, a billing service owner, an employee who provided medical billing services, and two owners of several residential care facilities and HHAs. The six were ordered to pay respective restitution amounts totaling $526,000; and four were sentenced to prison. One central aspect of the scheme involved the owners' referral of patients from their residential facilities to doctors in exchange for doctors' certifying of the patients as homebound and eligible for their home health services. This arrangement allowed the doctors to bill Medicare and Medicaid for patient visits and the HHAs to bill Medicare and Medicaid for providing home health services.

Source: U.S. Department of Health and Human Services, Office of Inspector General, "Home Health Agencies, February 2003," http://oig.hhs.gov/fraud/enforcement/criminal/03/0203.html.

The previous scheme involved a series of HCC players. The application of evidence collection by the previously discussed pipelines by player will demonstrate anomalies in the claims data and patient record data, as well as operational records from payroll to inventory to scheduling of staff and patients. This is a complex structure in which intent and collusion were structured and planned.

DATA ANALYSIS MODEL OVERVIEW: IMPLICATIONS FOR PREVENTION, DETECTION, AND INVESTIGATION

Exhibit 14.7 highlights an overview of the models presented in this chapter. It is a visual representation of the referential analysis (Exhibits 14.1–14.6) that is required by market segment and as a whole. EDA provides the opportunity to conduct this referential analysis electronically. EDA addresses the

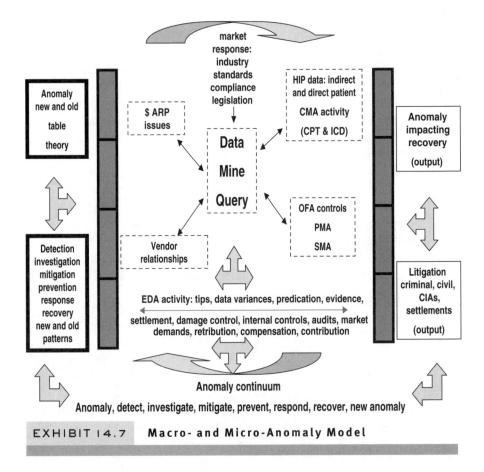

EXHIBIT 14.7   Macro- and Micro-Anomaly Model

management of high volume, segmented and fragmented operational structures, segmented and fragmented contractual arrangements, and complex clinical regimens. EDA provides the opportunity to find the needle in the haystack. This cannot be done without electronic data mapping and data mining tools. This cannot be done without understanding the operation dynamics of all parties. The historical development of each HCC player in terms of its financial structure is important in the prevention, detection, and investigation of healthcare waste, fraud, and abuse.

Historical discussion and understanding is required of the payer industry. How did the insurance industry evolve in its role of processing claims on behalf of government-sponsored programs? How did the private-payer market evolve in terms of pricing and market scope? What is the actual history behind the government-sponsored programs? With respect to providers, how has market price enhanced and compromised the delivery of healthcare services? What conflicts of interest exist in the provision of healthcare services?

Thus far, this book has provided guidelines for understanding and auditing the structure of healthcare. The next chapter focuses on tools that are effective for auditing the content of patient care.

CHAPTER 15

Clinical Content Data Analysis

Genius is one percent inspiration and ninety-nine percent perspiration.
—THOMAS ALVA EDISON

At some point in the process, a patient inevitably appears. It is very easy to lose focus of what healthcare is all about—the patient. As complex as the entire healthcare continuum (HCC) may be, it is important not to forget the patient's direct and indirect role within this HCC. The patient may initiate a service, or it may be initiated by one provider to another (for example, in ordering a consult). He or she may do so as a part of an employer-sponsored or a government-sponsored program. The plan sponsor records and uses the patient's protected health information (PHI), as does the provider that documents the results of the patient's care. In addition, the provider may receive a grant for research that eventually benefits a treatment regimen for a future patient. The provider documents the results of that research and its implications, including also whichever of the patient's PHI applies to the research program.

Transportation entities, such as ambulance companies or helicopter life support transfer services, require a patient in order to do their work, at least in theory. They, too, should have some type of patient record. What would the pharmaceutical industry be without the development of drugs to treat problems or develop cures for patients? Research studies have patient information as well as market response data that includes patient information.

Again, durable medical equipment suppliers need patients to use their products. Although their patient information may be limited to demographic information, it is information nonetheless. Even insurance companies and brokers need patients to whom to sell their "just in case you need healthcare services" insurance coverage. They typically have that screening health information tucked away. Direct patient care providers will and should have a clinical file of the patients they treat.

Data analysis of clinical information is compromised and complicated due to its qualitative characteristics and to the writing attributes of the author. How can one convert qualitative data into quantitative data? Believe it or not, it requires very little intelligence; just roll your sleeves up and prepare yourself for a lot of hard work. Thus, "Genius is one percent inspiration and ninety-nine percent perspiration." This conversion process occurs using the *SOAP content analysis tool*. Providers may be familiar with this acronym as a style of documenting patient care. In concept, they are correct. In application, as an audit and investigative tool, it changes in form and scope. This chapter discusses actual applications of the process, and later introduces a second tool, *narrative discourse analysis*. The focus of this tool is to evaluate the intent of the author.

What Is SOAP?

SOAP involves the abstraction of clinical information from patient records in a defined scope with specific procedures. SOAP is a ten-step clinical content data analysis tool that allows analytics of the content of the record. The following is the breakdown of SOAP:

- S—*Subjective:* patient information, or what the patient tells you. This may be documented as an actual quote or a paraphrased statement by the provider. At minimum, it should address the issue for which the patient sought treatment.

- O—*Objective:* patient data elements, or what the professional observes, measures, assesses, or analyzes from the assessments or diagnostics. At minimum, it should relate to the patient's statement.

- A—*Assessment:* a list of diagnoses and patient problems. At minimum, assessment includes the problem the narrative is addressing in its findings. The assessment should be associated with the patient's statements and the objective findings noted.

P—Plan: a list of all treatment protocols. At minimum, this includes the activities associated with the problem identified, the objective data collected, and the patient's statement.

The above information is collected and then an evaluation is based on the response to each of the above categories. The collection of data elements repeats itself. Any audit or investigation that at some point will generate a written report that could be utilized in litigation preparation and methodology should be in keeping with the concept of the standards for expert testimony. Note the following background information.

The U.S. Supreme Court's decisions in *Daubert v. Merrell Dow Pharmaceuticals, Inc.*, 509 U.S. 579 (1993), and *Kumho Tire v. Carmichael*, 526 U.S. 137 (1999), require that expert testimony meet the general tests of "reliability" and "relevancy." *Daubert* instructed trial judges to ensure "that an expert's testimony both rests on a reliable foundation and is relevant to the task at hand." The Court provides flexible guidelines for determining the admissibility of expert evidence, noting that scientific evidence must be "grounded in the methods and procedure of science." The expert must employ the same level of intellectual rigor as he or she would outside the courtroom when working in the relevant discipline. A 1977 Sixth Circuit Court decision notes that "the only question for the trial judge who must decide whether or not to allow the jury to consider a proffered expert's opinions is 'whether his knowledge of the subject matter is such that his opinion will most likely assist the tier of fact in arriving at the truth'" (*United States v. Barker*, 553 F.2d 1013, 1024 [6th Cir. 1977]). The SOAP methodology is being presented in this context.

THE SOAP METHODOLOGY

Step 1 is to obtain a set of clinical records. Analyze them to determine where the provider documents the elements of SOAP. For example, where does this provider typically document a patient's statement? Where does the provider document objective data such as physical assessments, diagnostic tests, and vital signs? Where does the provider communicate the patient's assessment and ongoing adjustments? Finally, where does this provider document its current and ongoing plan of care?

Step 2 in the process is to understand whether the provider uses any transitional documents. Does the provider document any aspect of patient care in documents not contained within the master medical record file? For example, the term *shadow chart* is associated with files that are kept separately within another department. These types of records are usually generated secondary to some type of operational issue. In one hospital audited, the staff kept shadow charts because they were unable to retrieve necessary records in a timely manner. A less altruistic provider was a dentist who kept two sets of records—one set of real records that contained what was actually done to the patients and a second so she could keep track of her communications with the payers.

Look at the document in Exhibit 15.1 and identify the elements of SOAP.

The very structure of this form does not promote the communication of patient statements, assessment, or plan of care. It is targeted to collect objective data only. The issue of content quality within hardcopy hand-written records is being carried over into electronic medical record formats. At times it becomes more difficult to discern within electronic records a complete picture of a patient's treatment regimen.

Step 3 identifies any known issue to be investigated or simply audited. It could range from measuring pain assessments to verification of whether services were actually provided. The process can be initiated generally just to test for the application of SOAP components.

SAMPLE CASE: HOSPITAL NARRATIVE

Exhibit 15.2 is a simple introduction in applying the concept to a hospital narrative.

Step 4 is to create your SOAP grid. A sample is provided in Exhibit 15.3.

Step 5 involves the application of the SOAP analysis to the narrative entry. The very first entry of 7/7/04 in Exhibit 15.2 is the only entry with a physical date. Based on reviewing flow and other documents in the record, we can make the assumption that the other entries in this actual sample were all written on 7/7/04. In addition, many authors may not use military time. Often, based on other documents within the medical record, assumptions can be made if the services are occurring during the day shift at the hospital.

IV Flow Sheet

Device	Gauge# _____
Date/Time of Insertion	
Nurse	
New Insertion	
Device	Date/ Time _____
Nurse	
Tubing Labeled/NurseCheck	
7-3 pm	_____
3-11 pm	_____
11-7 am	_____

Solutions	Time	By

Date	Time	Fluid level	Rate cc/hr	gtts/min	T	P	R	BP	CK Q HR	Secondary Sol thrpy	Action Comment	IN
	12:00 AM											
	1:00 AM											
	2:00 AM											
	3:00 AM											
	4:00 AM											
	5:00 AM											
	6:00 AM											
	7:00 AM											
											11 - 7 IV Shift	
	8:00 AM											
	9:00 AM											
	10:00 AM											
	11:00 AM											
	12:00 PM											
	1:00 PM											
	2:00 PM											
	3:00 PM											
											7- 3 IV Shift	
	4:00 PM											
	5:00 PM											
	6:00 PM											
	7:00 PM											
	8:00 PM											
	9:00 PM											
	10:00 PM											
	11:00 PM											
											3 - 11 IV Shift	

Key

Y   Intact
D   Drainage
C   Site Clear
R   Red
P   Pain
S   Swelling
I   Infiltrated
O   Occluded

Action

DC   Discontinue Rx
WC   Warm Compress
RS   IV Restart
TC   Tubing Change
DC   Dressing Change

Patient Name	Room #	Physician	Medical Record #

EXHIBIT 15.1   Illustration of a Nursing Record

EXHIBIT 15.2 Hospital Inpatient Narrative

7/7/04 2:30

Patient admitted to ASU Phase II. Recovery seat #19 per cart. Awake follow commands. Lungs clear bilateral. Respirations easy and unlabored. O2 saturation 98% on room air. Left flank with redness noted. Ice pack in place. Rates pain 8/10 at present. Attempting to void. Small amount noted in urinal. Cart (not legible). Urine slightly bloody. IVF infusing well. A. Jane RN

3P

Complains of pain 8/10 at present. Tolerated PO fluid and cracker without difficulty. Voided in bathroom. Urine blood tinged. Complains of burning with urination. Will continue to monitor. Discharge instructions reviewed with patient and family. All verbalized understanding. A. Jane RN

315P

Rates pain 6/10 at present. States "it feels a little better now." Voiding in bathroom. Urine pink in color. No clots noted. Will continue to monitor. A Jane RN

4P

Ambulated to bathroom. Voided. Complains of pain to L flank area. Rates pain 8 sharp. Received order for Norco 10/325mg to be given again. Medicated as ordered. VSS (vital signs stable) A. Jane RN

420P

States pain has decreased. Voided again. (not legible) colored urine. Rates pain 6/10. (not legible) Tolerated PO fluids without difficulty. Denies nausea. Ready for discharge home. Awaiting wheelchair. A. Jane RN

425P

Discharged home per wheelchair via attendant with family. A. Jane RN

SOAP ANALYSIS

		S	O	A	P
7/7/2004	2:30				
	3:00				
	3:15				
	4:00				
	4:20				
	4:25				
	TOTAL				

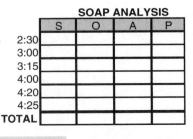

EXHIBIT 15.3 SOAP Grid for Inpatient Narrative

This lack of an A.M./P.M. designation occurred in the first entry of this example. Thus far we have had to make two assumptions. The goal in documenting patient care is to make all communications clear. They should require no other explanation from a secondary source.

Where are the elements of the patient statement? We have none. In the grid in Exhibit 15.3, under *S* at 2:30 P.M. we would place a "0" for not providing a patient statement.

7/7/04 2:30

Patient admitted to ASU Phase II. Recovery seat #19 per cart. Awake follow commands. Lungs clear bilateral. Respirations easy and unlabored. O2 saturation 98% on room air. Left flank with redness noted. Ice pack in place. Rates pain 8/10 at present. Attempting to void. Small amount noted in urinal. Cart (not legible). Urine slightly bloody. IVF infusing well. A. Jane RN

Now look for objective data. Remember, objective data is "what the professional observes, measures, assesses, or analyzes from the assessments or diagnostics." Some auditors may associate the term *objective* with items that do not include personal observations of the professional staff. It is any information that helps determine a diagnosis or an assessment of the patient.

7/7/04 2:30

Patient admitted to ASU Phase II. Recovery seat #19 per cart. **Awake follow commands. Lungs clear bilateral. Respirations easy and unlabored. O2 saturation 98% on room air. Left flank with redness noted.** Ice pack in place. **Rates pain 8/10 at present. At-tempting to void. Small amount noted in urinal.** Cart (not legible). **Urine slightly bloody.** IVF infusing well. A. Jane RN

The items in bold are designated as objective findings. Therefore, on the grid above under *O* at 2:30, an entry of "1" should be made. The next step is to locate the assessment in the narrative. The narrative entry should be evaluated for any determination of diagnosis or patient problems.

7/7/04 2:30

Patient admitted to ASU Phase II. Recovery seat #19 per cart. Awake follow commands. Lungs clear bilateral. Respirations easy and unlabored. O2 saturation 98% on room air. Left flank with redness noted. Ice pack in place. Rates pain 8/10 at present. Attempting to void. Small amount noted in urinal. Cart (not legible). Urine slightly bloody. IVF infusing well. A. Jane RN

Note that we have nothing to highlight. Therefore, under the 2:30 box for *A*, an entry of "0" should be made. Finally, for the plan of care, identify or list all treatment protocols.

7/7/04 2:30

Patient admitted to ASU Phase II. Recovery seat #19 per cart. Awake follow commands. Lungs clear bilateral. Respirations easy and unlabored. O2 saturation 98% on room air. Left flank with redness noted. **Ice pack in place.** Rates pain 8/10 at present. Attempting to void. Small amount noted in urinal. Cart (not legible). Urine slightly bloody. **IVF infusing well**. A. Jane RN

We have attributes to list under *P* at 2:30, so indicate a "1" for listing plan-related activity. During this process of taking qualitative information and converting it into quantitative data, do not focus on the quality of the statement. In the initial review, focus just on the determination whether the information exists. At this point, the SOAP chart in Exhibit 15.3 based on the analysis of the first entry should be updated to look like Exhibit 15.4.

The SOAP test continues with an analysis of the 3:00 P.M. entry. It begins with the patient statement. Note the items in bold. The *S* in the grid should be noted with a "1" for yes.

3P

Complains of pain 8/10 at present. Tolerated PO fluid and cracker without difficulty. Voided in bathroom. Urine blood tinged. **Complains of burning with urination.** Will continue to monitor. Discharge instructions reviewed with patient and family. All verbalized understanding. A. Jane RN

SOAP ANALYSIS

7/7/2004		S	O	A	P
	2:30	0	1	0	1
	3:00				
	3:15				
	4:00				
	4:20				
	4:25				
TOTAL					

EXHIBIT 15.4   **SOAP Update after 2:30 Reading**

Does the entry have objective data? Note the items in bold. The SOAP grid should have a "1" under *O* for data.

3P

Complains of pain 8/10 at present. **Tolerated PO fluid and cracker without difficulty. Voided in bathroom. Urine blood tinged.** Complains of burning with urination. Will continue to monitor. Discharge instructions reviewed with patient and family. All verbalized understanding. A. Jane RN

Does the entry below have an assessment? Note the lack of items in bold. The SOAP grid should have a "0" under *A* for no data.

3P

Complains of pain 8/10 at present. Tolerated PO fluid and cracker without difficulty. Voided in bathroom. Urine blood tinged. Complains of burning with urination. Will continue to monitor. Discharge instructions reviewed with patient and family. All verbalized understanding. A. Jane RN

Does the entry have a plan? Note the items in bold. The SOAP grid should have a "1" under the *P* for treatment activity.

3P

Complains of pain 8/10 at present. Tolerated PO fluid and cracker without difficulty. Voided in bathroom. Urine blood tinged. Complains of burning with urination. **Will continue to monitor. Discharge instructions reviewed with patient and family.** All verbalized understanding. A. Jane RN

The process is repeated for the next entry at 3:15 P.M., beginning with a patient statement. Note the items in bold and indicate a "1" under the *S* column for the 3:15 P.M. entry.

315P

Rates pain 6/10 at present. States "it feels a little better now." Voiding in bathroom. Urine pink in color. No clots noted. Will continue to monitor. A. Jane RN

Does the entry have objective data? Note the items in bold. The grid should indicate a "1" for data.

315P

Rates pain 6/10 at present. States "it feels a little better now." **Voiding in bathroom. Urine pink in color. No clots noted**. Will continue to monitor. A. Jane RN

Does the entry have an assessment or diagnosis? Note the lack of items in bold. The grid should indicate a "0" for no data.

315P

Rates pain 6/10 at present. States "it feels a little better now." Voiding in bathroom. Urine pink in color. No clots noted. Will continue to monitor. A. Jane RN

What are the findings for a plan of care? Note the items in bold. The grid should indicate a "1" for data.

315P

Rates pain 6/10 at present. States "it feels a little better now." Voiding in bathroom. Urine pink in color. No clots noted. **Will continue to monitor**. A. Jane RN

See Exhibit 15.5 for the grid updates.

The following is an analysis of the 4 P.M. entry. The designations have been noted for each category. This entry notes activity for *S*, *O*, and *P*, and nothing for *A*.

4P

Ambulated to bathroom. **(Objective)**

Voided. **(Objective)**

Complains of pain to L flank area. **(Subjective)**

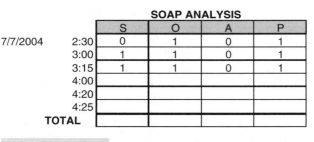

SOAP ANALYSIS

7/7/2004		S	O	A	P
	2:30	0	1	0	1
	3:00	1	1	0	1
	3:15	1	1	0	1
	4:00				
	4:20				
	4:25				
TOTAL					

EXHIBIT 15.5   SOAP Table Updates after Additional Readings

Rates pain 8 sharp. **(Subjective)**

Received order for Norco 10/325mg to be given again. **(Plan)**

Medicated as ordered. **(Plan)**

VSS (vital signs stable) **(Objective)**

A. Jane RN

The following is an analysis of the 4:20 P.M. entry. The designations have been noted for each category. This entry notes activity for *S, O, A,* and *P.*

420P

States pain has decreased. **(Subjective)**

Voided again. **(Objective)**

(not legible) colored urine. **(Objective)**

Rates pain 6/10. **(Subjective)**

Tolerated PO fluids without difficulty. **(Objective)**

Denies nausea. **(Objective)**

Ready for discharge home. **(Assessment)**

Awaiting wheelchair. **(Plan)**

A. Jane RN

The following is an analysis of the 4:25 P.M. entry. The designations have been noted for each category. This entry notes activity for *P* and not for *S, O,* or *A.*

425P

Discharged home per wheelchair via attendant with family. **(Plan)**

A. Jane RN

The chart in Exhibit 15.6 demonstrates Step 6 in this process: the hospital narrative entries provided in a qualitative form and converted into a quantitative form. Note this was only one page from a medical record. This conversion and subsequent conversions are part of Step 6 in the process. The process of applying this throughout an entire confinement can be time-consuming. Thus organization prior to initiating an audit on a series of records by a team of auditors requires planning. The steps in this process provide the opportunity for consistent data collection by auditor within one audit study. That is the focus in all the models presented in this book.

SOAP ANALYSIS

		S	O	A	P
7/7/2004	2:30	0	1	0	1
	3:00	1	1	0	1
	3:15	1	1	0	1
	4:00	1	1	0	1
	4:20	1	1	1	1
	4:25	0	0	0	1
TOTAL		4	5	1	6
%		67%	83%	17%	100%

EXHIBIT 15.6   **SOAP Update with Completion of Readings**

In this section of the narrative, what is understood is that some type of patient subjective statement is collected only 67 percent of the time. Objective data is collected 83 percent of the time. The SOAP findings show a significant weakness in documenting assessment only 17 percent of the time. Finally, we have 100 percent of plan activity noted; however, we do not know the basis for the activities.

This is how providers begin to create problems for themselves. Let us review a variety of possible interpretations. First, medical malpractice issues: How will this provider defend itself against medical negligence? How can Nurse Jane justify her treatment plan since she never associated it with any physician's order, relevant objective data, or the patient's complaint? Did she ever indicate that she reported any of the abnormal findings to the surgeon or primary care physician? What was the source of blood in the urine? What was the source of pain?

Next, a review of issues related to patient dumping: What if this patient did not have insurance? What if he or she did have insurance but was on a prospective payment schedule in which profit is tied to the provider's "efficiency" (that is, the use of fewer resources)? This patient clearly was discharged in pain with acute symptoms such as blood in the urine. Was this patient discharged without all of his or her medical issues being completely addressed?

Another perspective is predatory payment practices on the part of the payer. Let us consider that the commercial payer approved only one hospital day regardless of the reporting of active acute symptoms by the provider. This hospital discharges the patient secondary to denial of coverage by the carrier. Does the payer have contributory negligence for promoting patient dumping to increase its bottom line?

Under the issue of length of stay, clear documentation of the relevant SOAP data elements can help justify additional days within the hospital. The data elements in this narrative would make it difficult to justify the qualitative aspect and show justification for payment when the provider cannot identify, at minimum, the diagnosis being treated. Other issues that may be faced by the provider are substandard quality of care, insufficient justification for medical necessity, and patient safety issues. All are qualitative in nature. Note that this process is also effective in the reverse. It can prove medical necessity, extended length of stay, and the utilization for additional days of care.

The final perspective is from a prosecution or investigative perspective. The SOAP methodology allows the legal system a slightly different approach to handling clinical information, most typically when clinical experts are hired to evaluate or conduct a peer review of the treatment provided. Step 7 involves interrogatories, follow-up questions, and interviews. In preparation for an interview or a deposition statement, the analysis typically may involve a scenario like this:

"When I treat a patient with this problem, I typically would do the same. . . . "

"When I treat a patient with this problem, I typically would do the following . . . ; however, the treatment provided by this provider does not fall outside the standard of care."

The investigator will place the prosecutor in a completely different position by providing data that can lead to these types of questions.

"Is the standard of care ever met when a provider fails to obtain a patient's self-report (' patient complaint') or response to treatment, in particular when the patient verbalizes a complaint?"

"Would you be concerned about a provider who does not seek a patient complaint or status 33 percent of the time?"

"Is it a failure in the standard of care to fail to identify the patient assessment or operating diagnosis 83 percent of the time?"

This type of analysis takes away the focus on the clinical decision tree of a diagnosis treatment regimen and debate and moves it instead to a discussion on the actual behavior behind the care given to a patient. It can also provide a

SOAP ANALYSIS

		S	O	A	P	R	QA	SC	PS	A
7/7/2004	2:30	0	1	0	1	n	x			x
	3:00	1	1	0	1	n	x			x
	3:15	1	1	0	1	n	x			x
	4:00	1	1	0	1	n	x			x
	4:20	1	1	1	1	n	x	x		x
	4:25	0	0	0	1	n	x	x	x	x
TOTAL		4	5	1	6	6	6	2	1	6
%		67%	83%	17%	100%					

EXHIBIT 15.7   **SOAP Analysis Combined with Custom Indicators**

trend of behavior patterns by a provider when cases are profiled by that particular practice.

The emphasis has been to just focus on the content and meeting the minimum necessary components for documenting patient care. Step 8 contributes to the analysis by evaluating the substance of the narratives. These attributes can include quality assurance (QA), substandard care (SC), and patient safety (PC). In Exhibit 15.7, these are added to the SOAP grid for this inpatient narrative sample.

The provider's lack of cohesive communication creates a number of qualitative issues, as indicated in Exhibit 15.7. Quality issues are noted throughout the sample because the documentation never provides a clear picture of the assessment. When an assessment is finally noted—"ready to discharge"—no objective findings are noted to justify this assessment. That in turn raises the issue of substandard care. The actual discharge of the patient with active pain and bloody urine raises the issue of patient safety. All the factors, because of their deficiency, are noted in Exhibit 15.7 as *A* for "anomaly." An anomaly is simply a factor that is not normal and deserves further analysis.

Step 9 involves the concept of *relating*. Does the documentation relate to the other notations in the entry and the record itself? The basis for "related" is driven by the concept that in healthcare *normal* care includes obtaining a patient statement, obtaining data that correlates back to that statement, deriving an assessment based on the statement and objective findings, and initiating a plan of care that reflects the patient statement, the objective data, and the assessment findings.

The chart in Exhibit 15.7 has a column designated as *R*. This represents whether the statement met the minimum standard of relating from one component in SOAP to the next. For example, when the patient complains of pain, the rating information is very helpful, but the source of the pain is critical. Is it secondary to incision pain from surgery? Is it secondary to an adverse postoperative complication? At 4 P.M., the pain is noted as "sharp" and rated as an 8. The patient is medicated. At 4:20 P.M. prior to discharge the pain is reduced to a 6 on a scale of 1 to 10. Is the problem going away, or is the pain temporarily diminished, masking the issue at hand? We do not know, because of insufficient information. Again, these deficiencies create vulnerabilities for the provider and the patient. In this case, the complication would go undiagnosed. What is the source of the blood in the patient's urine? The same questions are raised with respect to patient safety when the patient is discharged in a condition that may not be stable.

Step 10 involves the preparation of an interim report and interim analysis and subsequent scope changes. The findings to this point should lead to a determination of other factors to assess and audit scope changes. For example, the audit may expand to all patients who were admitted for the same surgical procedure. It may focus on a sample of patients treated by Nurse Jane, or by the surgeon, or a random sample of outpatient versus inpatient surgical patients at this facility. Exhibit 15.8 represents a summary of this analysis. Factors *R*, *QA*, *SC*, *PS*, and *A* give rise to other factors that will require further audit and investigation. This may include additional internal control audits across the facility itself in addition to other patients to determine whether this is a typical pattern for that facility.

SOAP ANALYSIS

		S	O	A	P	R	QA	SC	PS	A	Other Factors
7/7/2004	2:30	0	1	0	1	n	x			x	?
	3:00	1	1	0	1	n	x			x	?
	3:15	1	1	0	1	n	x			x	?
	4:00	1	1	0	1	n	x			x	?
	4:20	1	1	1	1	n	x	x		x	?
	4:25	0	0	0	1	n	x	x	x	x	?
TOTAL		4	5	1	6	6	6	2	1	6	
%		67%	83%	17%	100%						

EXHIBIT 15.8   **SOAP Ongoing Analysis**

SOAP ANALYSIS

	S	O	A	P
9/13/1996				
8/6/1997				
4/1/1998				
6/3/1998				
8/4/1998				
TOTAL				

EXHIBIT 15.9   SOAP Grid for Physician Narrative

SAMPLE CASE: PHYSICIAN OFFICE NARRATIVE

The SOAP grid for a physician narrative should be prepared as shown in Exhibit 15.9.

The SOAP designations are noted within each entry. In addition, this case provides an illustration of other complex issues involved in the care of this patient. (See Exhibit 15.10.)

The records of the author of these narratives have a very qualitative aspect and style to them. In fact, a great deal of frustration is noted among the providers in terms of how to manage the care of this patient. This small sample of records may appear to be written by an emotionally removed clinical staff. However, important background information is that this patient has had unresolved medical issues from an injury that occurred in 1975.

In this sample, the provider does not have a defined diagnosis or it had not communicated an operating diagnosis. What is driving this patient's care? Is this patient terminal? Is his diagnosis still undetermined? The free form of narrative style writing often found in clinical records takes on the risk of incomplete communication of critical elements of patient care. As the market evolves into replacing handwritten with electronic records, we will gain in that the issue of illegibility of records will be resolved. However, the weaknesses that result from author styles of communication will be replaced with electronic "rules" that often will omit the record infrastructure

EXHIBIT 15.10   **Physician Narrative Sample**

09-13-96/ Worker, JOE

This patient has been seen now by Dr. Followup and reports that Dr. Followup did not find any definite cause for his bleeding. I believe I recently saw a copy of some of the Dr. Followup's reports and the question of esophageal varices was raised. **(OBJECTIVE DATA ONLY)**

08-6-97/ Worker, JOE

Patient returns, unbelievable recovery. When we saw this man in ICU after operation, I was absolutely convinced that he was going to expire. He had an abdominal abscess which basically encompassed his entire abdomen with his bowel being fixed posteriorly, obviously a very chronic abscess, obviously very extensive involving the abdomen, subcutaneous tissues on the right side out to the right thigh and on the left side out to the left inguinal area.

Surprising to everybody, he has survived. He comes in today and is quite cachexic, thin, abdomen is large. Incisional wound is open and is being treated with wet-to-dry dressings. b.i.d. The subcutaneous areas on the right and left side are closed. The skin is quite purple in this area.

On the left upper quadrant, the cavity doesn't seem to go far. On the right upper quadrant, it seems to go back almost to the diaphragm, by finger palpation.

To continue wet-to-dry dressings and advised to try and improve his appetite and nutrition as much as he can. (P) This is a patient who at one time was morbidly obese and now is cachexic. His entire family is morbidly obese.

Strange story. We'll see him again in 3 weeks (P). If he survives all this ultimately he will most likely require ventral hernia repair but one wouldn't want to consider that for a couple of years.
    (OBJECTIVE DATA AND PLAN DATA)

4-1-98/ Worker, JOE

Patient is basically stable. The abdominal wound is really about the same. There is this stellate scar in the lower abdomen which drains some. The nurses say that when they irrigate it, they get some blood. His weight is stable. He can be up and around. He is minimally active, but he can get around. His appetite is okay. He looks about his usual, which is like death warmed over. **(O)**

I doubt we are ever going to get past this point. We'll **see him again now in the couple of months (P),** but I think this is going to be a chronic stable condition. **(OBJECTIVE DATA AND PLAN DATA)**

6-3-98/ Worker, JOE

The patient returns. Has a scant amount of drainage **(O).** The hole in the mid abdomen is about the same, although it mostly has a squamous epithelium across it. There is apparently some tunnels that reach there **(O).** Basically, **just needs to be cleaned with peroxide daily (P).** He says he can get around okay **(S).** His son still helps him mostly, and he wants a letter that he can send to the Company to see if they will help pay for his son's help **(S).** I really do not think his present problems are related to his Company's injury in the first place, which apparently was in 1975. There was some discrepancy in that he says Dr. Surgery, who used to be in Smalltown, "took out his spleen." His recent CT scan and sonogram showed that the question of the mass in the left upper quadrant was, indeed, his spleen. Recent letter to his Company that says his injury of 24 years ago is not really related to his current problems today. **(SUBJECTVE, OBJECTIVE, AND PLAN DATA)**

8-4-98/ Worker, JOE

Patients returns. It has been a year since his surgery. He continues to be debilitated. His abdominal incision continues to drain a rather foul drainage, sometimes more, sometimes less. Home health nurses see him about 3x per week. Things basically have changed very little. He has actually gained a little weight, but some of that may be ascites. **(O)**

We've never had a clear understanding of what is going on here. He says he has the spleen out after the accident. His CT, sonograms, etc., show a large spleen, chronic calcification consistent with pancreatitis, little bit of dilatation of the biliary ducts, which has all been in the past. He doesn't seem to be unduly jaundiced. When we operated on him a year ago, we thought he was going to die, he had a total abdominal abscess with pus from the diaphragm to the pelvis. **(O)**

I am not quite sure we would want to do anything. He came very close to dying the last time we operated on him. His abdomen is totally frozen, there is no peritoneal cavity. The bowel is all totally frozen on itself although obviously in a non-obstructive pattern. **(O)**

In an effort to perhaps get a better view, I suggested we get an abdominal sonogram to see if we can see where these sinuses go **(P).** I am not sure we would want to do anything about it. It depends upon if the sonogram would show if one could simply get at a pocket to drain it, but a full laparotomy, I doubt, would be feasible **(P). (OBJECTIVE AND PLAN DATA)**

to ensure that the provider has the opportunity or is encouraged to communicate all the elements contained within the SOAP concept. (See Exhibit 15.11.)

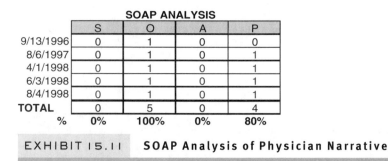

SOAP ANALYSIS

	S	O	A	P
9/13/1996	0	1	0	0
8/6/1997	0	1	0	1
4/1/1998	0	1	0	1
6/3/1998	0	1	0	1
8/4/1998	0	1	0	1
TOTAL	0	5	0	4
%	0%	100%	0%	80%

EXHIBIT 15.11   **SOAP Analysis of Physician Narrative**

ELECTRONIC RECORDS

The market is aggressively focused on incorporating electronic records throughout the HCC. Providers have had a more significant emphasis on this subject since they typically generate records at the time a patient initiates a service. However, records can be initiated elsewhere throughout the HCC. For example, an employer may generate healthcare records resulting from an employee-related injury.

An insurance company may generate healthcare records when evaluating a patient for insurance or disability coverage. Insurance companies have been known to offer transcription services to providers and now personal healthcare records for their insured. That aside, standards and compliance initiatives have been heavily focused within the provider market. However, the emphasis should be on developing compliance and standards for electronic health information contemporaneously throughout the HCC regardless of what role they have.

To date, a greater emphasis has been placed on the initiative, security issues, and infrastructure. Development of content standards has yet to be addressed with any sort of substance. Therefore, with respect to audits and investigations, the SOAP methodology provides a common ground and methodology to interpret a variety of styles and forms of clinical documentation. Exhibit 15.12 provides an overview of the SOAP methodology.

EXHIBIT 15.12   SOAP Methodology Overview

Step 1: Obtain a copy of the provider's standard set of medical records.

Step 2: Understand whether the provider uses any transitional documents.

Step 3: Identify any known issue to be investigated or simply audited.

Step 4: Create the SOAP grid for the audit.

Step 5: Apply SOAP analysis to each selected narrative entry.

Step 6: Initiate conversion of qualitative data into quantitative data.

Step 7: Determine appropriate interrogatories, follow-up questions, and interviews based on initial SOAP review.

Step 8: Determine substance attributes to rate the narratives and to fill in SOAP grid. These attributes can include quality assurance (QA), substandard care (SC), and patient safety (PC).

Step 9: Test the data for the concept of relating. Does the documentation relate to the other notations in the entry and the record itself?

Step 10: Prepare an interim report with analysis and subsequent required scope changes. Repeat this process with each audit scope change or update.

EXHIBIT 15.13   **Sample Electronic Medical Record Header File**

ADMISSION RECORD
Advanced Directive,Discharge,Date,Time,PT,AcctNo,FC,STARM,BD,
ATTENDINGPHYSICIAN,,PHYSICIANNED,RECNO,DateofAdm,
TIME,BYMEDSVC,TYPE,CAT,SOURCE,RELIGION /CHURCH,
SEX,MarSt,RACE,MEDIA,INIT,LastName,First Name,MI,
MaidenName, PrevAdmDate UnderWhatName STREETADDRESS,
CITY, STATE, ZIP, COUNTY,PHONENO,DateofBirth,
AGE, PLACEOFBIRTH, OCCUPATION, ALLERGIES, SOC SECNO,
EMPLOYER, STREETADDRESS, CITY, STATE, ZIP, PHONENO,
NEARESTRELATIVE, RELATIONSHIP, STREETADDRESS,
CITY, STATE, ZIP, PHONENO, EMERGENCYCONTACTNAME, RELATIONSHIP,
STREETADDRESS, CITY, STATE, ZIP, PHONENO, GUARANTORNAME,
RELATIONSHIP,STREETADDRESS,CITY,STATE,ZIP,GUARANTOREMPLOYER,
STREETADDRESS,CITY,STATE,ZIP,GUARANTOR,PHONENO,
PROVISIONALDIAGNOSIS, GUARANTOR, EMPLOYERPHONENO,
GUARANTOR, SOCSEC, ACCIDENT, DATE, EMPLOYERATTIMEOF ACCIDENT,
PRIONSINSTITUTIONLAST60DAYS, FROM, TO, PRIMARYCARRIER
SUBSCRIBER S NAME,, RELATN,GROUPPOLICYNO,SECONDARYCARRIER
SUBSCRIBERSNAME, RELATNGROUP, POLICY NOADDITIONALCARRIER
SUBSCRIBERSNAME, RELATN, GROUP, POLICYNO, ADDITIONAL CARRIER
SUBSCRIBERSNAME, RELATN, GROUP, POLCYNO, TIME, ALLERGIES,
CLINIC, X- RAY, LAB, PT, RT, TEMP, PULSE, PRESENTMEDICATIONS,
RESPNURSING, COMMENTSANDASSESSMENTS, PROCEDUREDONE
ANDRESULTSIFAPPLICABLE, BLOODPRESS, RT, LT, NURSE, SIGNATURE,
DISCHARGE INSTRUCTIONS, PHYSICIANSSIGNATURE, PLAB, OPCLINIC

Analysis Considerations with Electronic Records

In the electronic world, when records are requested, they may be provided in electronic format or a hardcopy version of the electronic file. The user needs to be prepared for both scenarios. If it is an electronic production, one file may contain what is referred to as a "header" file. Exhibit 15.13 shows a sample header file.

Note that the content associated with the header may be just a complete data dump with no discernable understanding of its content, as shown in Exhibit 15.14.

An electronic interoperable healthcare market opens the doors to tremendous opportunities in the area of waste, fraud, and abuse. Continued considerations of standards for security and infrastructure are evolving in the marketplace. The market does not move forward with respect to standards

EXHIBIT I5.I4   Data Dump of Clinical Content

NAME,SMITH,Jane,AGE/DOB,24/92580,RM/MR#SURG/24386ADMITTED,11705,DISCHARGED,120
5,DISCHARGE,SUMMARY,by,DISCHARGE,DIAGNOSIS,Left,ankle,fracture,dislocation,Fall,Right,ank
le,sprain,PROCEDURES,Left,distal,fibula,ORIF,with,syndesmosis,screw,placement.
,HISTORY,Please,see,H&P,for,further,details,HOSPITAL,COURSE,The,patient, was, admitted,
because,of,a,left,distal,fibular,fracture,with,syndesmosis,disruption,She,was, taken ,to, the,
OR, by, Dr., January18ᵗʰ, with, ORIF, with, Syndesmosis,screw,placement, The, patient tolerated, the,
procedure, well, but,continued,to,have,significant,post,op,pain,with,required,IV,medications.
She,also,had,significant,evaluation,and,work,with,physical,therapy,throughout,her,hospital stay,(14
words),The,patient,was,on,PCA,for,24,hours,past,her,hospitalization,), She,then,started responding,
o,the,Percocet,and,was,discharged,to,home,on,that,with,followup,with,Dr.,in,approximately one,
weeks,time,D/DT,3-5-05/4-18-05,MRH/sp,MsTHE,HOSPITAL,OF,COUNTY, NAME,SMITH,
Jane,AGE/DOB,24,RM/MR#IP,ADMITTED,Jan,7,2005,DISCHARGED HISTORY & PHYSICAL,
Doctor,Jane,is,a,24,year,old,white,female,who,fell,two,mornings,ago,and,sustained an, inversion,
injury,to,the,left,ankle, She,was,seen,in,the,E.R.,where,ankle,was,found,to,be,dislocated and, fracture,
The,ankle,was,apparently,relocated,The,films,were,apparently,reviewed,today,by,and,,
orthopedistAnd,Jane,was,informed,hat,she,would,need,surgery,for,the,ankle,is,scheduled,for,tomorrowHow
ever, she, has, had, pain, today, uncontrolled, with, medication, that,she ,is,on, She,also ,has,been,
unable,to,do,virtually, any, thing, except, lie,on,the, couch,per,her, mother,Therefore, she,is,being,a
dmitted,for,pain,control,prior,to,her,surgery PAST, MEDICAL, HISTORY, unremarkable,
PAST,SURGICAL, HISTORY, Appendectomy ,MEDS, Vicodin, for,the,last,couple, of,days,otherwise,
she,is,on,no,chronic,medications,ALLERGIES,NKDA,SOCIAL,HISTORY,She,lives,in,Mt.Prospect,Illinoi
s,and,works,cutting,hair,She,has,quit,smoking,She,uses,alcohol,rarely,She,engagedto,be,marriedFAMILY,
HISTORY,There,is,no,family,history,of,reactions,to,anesthesia,She,has,an,uncle,with,diabetes,There,is,sev
eral,family,members,with,cancer,including,breast,and,lung,cancer,she,has,a,grandmother,with,heart,disease
,**EXAM,**Jane,is,a,welleveloped,obese,white,female,in,no,apparent,distress,**VITAL,SIGNS,**B/P71,temp.99,
pulse,respirations,18,**HEENT,**TMs,are,clear,PERRLA,EOMI,Optic,fundi,reveal,normalvessels,and,sharp,d
iscs,Scleras,are,anicteric,and,conjunctivae,are,pink,Nasal,mucosa,is,mildly,erythematous,Oral,mucosa,is,m
oist,The,throat,is,clear,Dentition,is,in,good,repair,Neck,is,supple,without,lymphadenopathy,or,thyromegaly
,Carotid,upstrokes,are,symmetric,**LUNGS,c**lear,bilaterally,There,is,no,spine,or,c.v.a.,tenderness,**SMITH,
Jane.H&P,p2,HEART,** Rate, and,rhythm,are,regular;without,S3,S4,or,murmur,**ABDOMEN,
Bowel,**sounds,are,normal,The,abdomen, is,soft; without,tenderness masses,or,organomegaly,
EXTREMITIES, No, cyanosis,clubbing,or,edema, She,has,a,postop, Shoe,on,the,left, ankle, and,foot,
left,foot,neurovascularly,intact,with,2+,dorsalis,pedis,pulse,Deep,tendon,reflexes,are,symmetric,in,the,uppe
r,extremities, somewhat, dimished,in,the,right,lower, extremity, and, I, did, not, test,the, left,lower,
extremity, **ASSESSMENT, Left,ankle,dislocation/ fracture,with,difficult,to ,control, pain,PLAN,**
She,is,admitted,and,we'll,put her,on,a,PCA,overnight,We'll,keep,her NPO, after, midnight, in,preparation,
for,her,surgery,tomorrow,Wealso,obtain,an,X-ay,of,the,right,ankle,as this,was, not,evaluated, but,it,is,
quite,uncomfortable,and,ecchymotic**DD/DT,1-17/1-18-05, PG/cb,Doctor RADIOLOGY, REPORT,
NAME,SMITH,JaneDOB,9-251980, SEX, F, STATUS, ER/OP, REFERRING,MD,** EXMINATION
:Left, Ankle, Left, Lower, Leg, Post, Reduction, DATE, OF,EXAM 1152005, HISTORY, Fell,on,ice,
pain LEFT, ANKLE, AT,08:04, HOURS,Two,views, of,the,left,ankle,demonstrate,a, comminuted,
oblique,fracture,of,the,fibula,with,a,butterfly,fragment,displaced,mild,laterally, and, posteriorly, and,
oneshaft,width,dorsal,displacements,as,well,as,mild,lateral,angulation,of,the,main,distal,fracture,fragment,
There,is,also,a,dislocation,at,the,ankle,with,the,talus,displaced,relative,to,the,distal,fibula,and,what,appears,
to,be,a,fracture,fragment,arising,from,the,lateral,aspect,of,the,distal,tibia,There,is,also,a,small,fracture,of,th
e,posterior,malleolus,of,the,distal,fibula,SUMMARY:Dial,fibula,shaft,

---

regarding the content of the health information maintained. For example, the reimbursement market of healthcare made significant strides when it established the standard universal billing form. This standard form for submitting claims had a tremendous impact on efficiency.

The exploratory data analysis (EDA) opportunities continue to be measured in the value of gathering intelligence on healthcare expenditures and referential analysis of all the content within the claim form—for example, simple analyses of how many patients are being treated for a particular diagnosis. The universal billing form created this opportunity by forcing the market to submit the content of the bill in a consistent format among all providers. The standardization of the universal billing form along with sophisticated computer tools, has allowed for EDA opportunities of large volumes of data for waste, fraud, and abuse through comparative analysis from provider to provider and market to market. This opportunity to gather data intelligence can occur prior to actually reviewing and analyzing the medical records. Take Dr. Traveler as an example of EDA claims analysis (see Exhibit 15.15).

If medical records were even generated for Dr. Traveler, the profile of the content of the records would signal red flags. These types of providers

---

EXHIBIT 15.15   Dr. Traveler Case Profile

Case History:
Who: Dr. Traveler, MD
What: Cardiologist who specializes in home healthcare visits of the elderly population
When: Growing practice over last five years
Why: ?
Where: Home health visits

Data Set:
Billing data: High percentage of home health visits to Chicago area residents
Claim data set: On a blizzard day in 1999, in which 18 inches of snow shut down Chicago, Dr. Traveler billed for 31 home visits and 18 inpatient hospital and nursing home visits
Claim data set: Home health visits and treatment of 32 deceased patients
Claim data set: 70-hour workdays
Claim data set: Single day of claims generated 131 senior home visits
Claim data set: Single day of claims totaling 187 visits with the same ICD code for congestive heart failure
Claim data set: Single day of claims—70 patients had a single home address (the doctor's own)
Claim data set: Saw 380 patients over a three-day period
Business practice: Frequent provider of free health screening exams at senior citizen complexes and private nursing homes around the Chicagoland area

---

tend to show the following patterns within their medical records, if available at all:

- Statistically high improbable occurrence of diagnosis
- Patient statements that are communicated in provider terminology
- Patient statements that do not change, demonstrating no response to treatment
- Objective data that repeats itself from one narrative entry to the next
- Objective data that repeats itself from patient to patient
- Assessment data that does not change and is not variable from patient to patient
- Plan data that does not demonstrate any custom care and appears boilerplate from patient to patient
- Few or no supporting records such as diagnostic reports and laboratory tests

The case of Dr. Traveler presents sufficient predication to investigate based on the claims activity alone. The medical records analysis component in a case like this only further defines the scope and deceit of Dr. Traveler's activities. SOAP analysis can always be utilized to discern internal control activities such as drug diversion.

The case in Exhibit 15.16 uses the SOAP methodology to understand charging variances of a set of medications that were administered by a staff nurse. Statistically the SOAP content is complete. The score was 100%. However, the quality indicators tell another story. In this case, did the patient actually ever receive the medication? Predication is raised on the subject of drug diversion. The audit scope thus changes from auditing why over- and undercharges exist to investigating whether the drug is being diverted for personal use or illicit distribution and subsequent sale. (See Exhibit 15.17.)

NARRATIVE DISCOURSE ANALYSIS

Narrative discourse analysis is a methodology that analyzes a set or series of narrative communications. The process incrementally breaks down the communication of thoughts buried within words. It is a breakdown of speech and patterns. These patterns demonstrate trends of generic statements. Generic statements tend to be associated with untruthful statements

EXHIBIT 15.16   Case Example of Pain Reliever RN

Case History:

Who: Staff nurse on evening (3 P.M. to 11 P.M.) shift
What: High rate of overcharges on patient bills
When: Credits noted on evening (3 P.M. to 11 P.M.) and night (11 P.M. to 7 A.M.)
   shifts
Why: ?
Where: Unit 10 South

Sample Data Set: Patient Record

Jane Doe: 1/16/04 9 P.M.
"S" C/O Pain 8/10
"O" Percocet given 2 tabs 10 P.M.
"A" Pain secondary to surgery
"P" Give meds as ordered
   (Signed) Pain Reliever, RN

Jane Doe: 1/17/04 9 P.M.
"S" C/O pain 5/10
"O" Percocet given 2 tabs at 2 P.M. pain 8/10 medicated with relief
"A" Pain secondary to surgery
"P" Gave dose at 9 P.M.
   (Signed) On Call, RN

Data Sets: OPS Clinical Profile of Four Patients

Jane Doe: 1/18/04 8 P.M.
"S" C/O Pain 8/10
"O" Percocet given 2 tabs 10 P.M. VSS b/p 134/72 HR 86 RR 22
"A" Pain secondary to surgery
"P" Give meds as ordered
   (Signed) Pain Reliever, RN

Janis Doe: 1/18/04 9 P.M.
"S" C/O Pain 8/10
"O" Percocet given 2 tabs 10 P.M. VSS b/p 134/72 HR 86 RR 22
"A" Pain secondary to surgery
"P" Give meds as ordered
   (Signed) Pain Reliever, RN

John Doe: 1/18/04 10 P.M.
"S" C/O Pain 8/10

"O" Percocet given 2 tabs 10 P.M. VSS b/p 134/72 HR 86 RR 22
"A" Pain secondary to surgery
"P" Give meds as ordered
  (Signed) Pain Reliever, RN

Jake Doe: 1/18/04 11 P.M.
"S" C/O Pain 8/10
"O" Percocet given 2 tabs 10 P.M. VSS b/p 134/72 HR 86 RR 22
"A" Pain secondary to surgery
"P" Give meds as ordered
  (Signed) Pain Reliever, RN

---

or thoughts that are inhibited, whether by a conscious or unconscious choice. Specific statements tend to be associated with facts and thus tend to be truthful in nature. This section provides just an introduction to the concept and body of science. Imagine the classic example of "Do I look fat?" Any man who is asked this by his significant other will typically demonstrate patterns of generality that are not associated with specific description or communication. Exhibit 15.18 provides an overview of considerations to be applied.

Note that the conscious experience narrative is the investigator's tool for follow-up inquiries. This process allows for an evaluation of the truthfulness behind a statement. This tool is helpful when interviewing subjects, reading depositions, and reading a series of narrative medical record entries.

A narrative entry interpretation can be made in the historical text analysis form. For example, is the statement a generic or specific statement? The

SOAP ANALYSIS

	S	O	A	P	Time	Patient	Staff	QA	SC	PS	A
1/16/2004	1	1	1	1	9pm	JANE	PR	X	X	X	
1/17/2004	1	1	1	1	9pm	JANE	OC				
1/18/2004	1	1	1	1	8pm	JANE	PR	X	X	X	X
1/18/2004	1	1	1	1	9pm	JANIS	PR	X	X	X	X
1/18/2004	1	1	1	1	10pm	JOHN	PR	X	X	X	X
1/18/2004	1	1	1	1	11pm	JAKE	PR	X	X	X	X
TOTAL	6	6	6	6							
%	100%	100%	100%	100%							

QA—Quality of Care
SC—Substandard of Care
PS—Patient Safety
A—Anomaly

EXHIBIT 15.17   Pain Reliever RN SOAP Grid

EXHIBIT 15.18   **Narrative Discourse Methodology**

1. Ideal sample is a sample size of 3,000 words. How many words does the writing specimen have?
2. Count the number of sentences.
3. Dissect each sentence.
4. Find and identify all noun phrases in the text as to type of noun (singular, plural, uncountable, proper, and gerund).
5. Identify prominent grammatical features.
6. Identify the general use of verbs (past time, present time, general truth, etc.).
7. Identify the general format of the text (graphics, italics, layout).
8. Identify how definitions are expressed in the text.
9. Identify the types of nouns used in the definitions in the text (generic, specific).
10. Review the expressive and emotional characteristics of the writing.
11. Look for fluctuations in usage of pronouns (*I*, *me*, *he*, *you*, *him*, *it*, etc.). Note pronouns that replace nouns.
12. Identify all noun phrases as to type of noun. (See Exhibit 15.19, "Glossary of English Grammar Terms," for detailed definitions.)

    - *Singular:* one
    - *Plural:* more than one
    - *Uncountable:* substances, entities, or concepts that cannot be counted; do not have plural form
    - *Proper:* Specific word, person, place, thing, or organization
    - *Gerund:* a verb ending in -*ing* that functions as a noun

13. Identify the expressions and emotions in the narrative. What types of nouns are used? How do these describe the emotional mood of the sentences written? Moods could include the following:

    - Physiological arousal (heart-pounding)
    - Expressive behavior (quickened pace)
    - Conscious experience (reflective, act of justification, sense of moral correctness)

---

generic journal entry reflects what the author is expressing. A generic statement typically would include a conscious experience that is general in nature and has no specific event directly associated with it. Generic statements tend to be reflective and represent acts of justification. A generic statement circumvents the specific details with emotion versus communicating the details of an event. If the writer is being specific in the entry, he or she will provide details that document general truths. Generic statements without details should be marked for a follow-up interview of a subject.

The next aspect in the model is to evaluate what types of nouns are used. From these you can glean the emotional mood of the sentences written. Emotional moods can include physiological arousal, represented, for instance, by a heart-pounding statement. Another emotional mood is expressive behavior. Expressive behavior is communicating an attitude of mind by words and their meaning. The communication may move at a quickened pace, which accelerates or makes the image more alive with a story. The conscious experience provides insight into the individual's sense of moral correctness. Does the communication work hard at the justification of the story?

In reviewing the narrative, look to see if there is a pattern in writing. The final summary of the writing specimen should include the time in which the narrative was written. In addition, the findings of the narrative should indicate whether it is a general truth to a specific or a generic text entry. Document the frequent use of the definite (*the*) or indefinite (*a, an*) article. Note how proper nouns are used in comparison to other text. Also document the use of the gerund form. It is a significant feature of the general truth time frame.

Exhibit 15.19 shows key glossary terms that are used in narrative discourse analysis. The following case is an example of a narrative discourse with application of analysis.

CASE EXAMPLE OF NARRATIVE DISCOURSE: AL CAPONE

I am going to St. Petersburg, Florida, tomorrow; let the worthy citizens of Chicago get their liquor the best they can. I am sick of the job—it's a thankless one and full of grief. I have been spending the best years of my life as a public benefactor.

APPLICATION OF NARRATIVE DISCOURSE ANALYSIS

I am going to St. Petersburg, Florida, tomorrow; let the worthy citizens of Chicago get their liquor the best they can. *(20 words)*

This statement is a generic statement that uses nouns or noun phrases such as *citizens of Chicago* and *liquor*. It is a general statement rather than a specific one that represents a physiological response (heart-pounding).

I am sick of the job—it's a thankless one and full of grief. I have been spending the best years of my life as a public benefactor. *(28 words)*

EXHIBIT 15.19   **Glossary of English Grammar Terms**

Active voice

The subject of the verb performs the action (e.g., *The fugitives robbed the bank*).
See also **Passive voice**.

Adjective

A word that describes a noun or pronoun (e.g., *big, red, easy, French*).

Adverb

A word that modifies a verb, adjective, or another adverb (e.g., *slowly, quietly, well, often*). Many adverbs end in *-ly*.

Article

The indefinite articles are *a* and *an*. The definite article is *the*.

Auxiliary verb

A verb that is used with a main verb. *Be, do,* and *have* are auxiliary verbs. *Will, would, can, could, shall, should, may, might,* and *must* are modal auxiliary verbs. See also **Modal verb**.

Clause

A group of words containing a subject and its verb (e.g., It was late *when he arrived*).

Conjunction

A word used to connect words, phrases, and clauses (e.g., *and, but, if*).

Infinitive

The basic form of a verb, preceded by *to* (e.g., *to work, to eat*).

Interjection

An exclamation inserted into an utterance without grammatical connection (e.g., *oh!, ah!, ouch!, well!*).

Modal verb

An auxiliary verb that modifies the main verb and expresses possibility or probability. It is also called a modal auxiliary verb. The nine *modal auxiliary verbs* are *will, would, can, could, shall, should, may, might,* and *must*.

Noun

A word that names an object, concept, person, or place (e.g., *table, patience, teacher, America*). A **concrete noun** is something you can see or touch (e.g., *dog, car*). An **abstract noun** is something you cannot see or touch (e.g., *decision, happiness*). A **countable noun** is something that you can count (e.g., *bottle, song, dollar*). An **uncountable noun** is something you cannot count (e.g., *water, music, information*).

Object

In the active voice, a noun or its equivalent that receives the action of the verb. In the passive voice, a noun or its equivalent that performs the action of the verb.

Participle

The -*ing* and -*ed* forms of verbs. The -*ing* form is called the *present* participle. The -*ed* form is called the *past* participle.

Part of speech

One of the eight classes of words in English: noun, verb, adjective, adverb, pronoun, preposition, conjunction, interjection.

Passive voice

The subject receives the action of the verb (e.g., *The bank was robbed by the fugitives*). See also **Active voice**.

Phrase

A group of words that lacks a subject or a verb but that functions as a noun, verb, adjective, or adverb (e.g., *on the desk, the boy in blue jeans, confused by the report*).

Predicate

The part of a sentence that contains the verb and its modifiers. A predicate comments on or makes an assertion about the subject of the sentence. See also **Sentence; Subject**.

Preposition

A word that gives information about things like time, place, and direction (*at, to, in, over*). Prepositions usually come before a noun.

Pronoun

A word that replaces a noun (e.g., *I, me, you, he, him, it*).

Sentence

A group of words that express a thought. A sentence conveys a statement, question, exclamation, or command. A sentence contains or implies a subject and a predicate. In simple terms, a sentence must contain a verb and (usually) a subject. A sentence starts with a capital letter and ends with a full stop (.), question mark (?), or exclamation mark (!).

Subject

The part of the sentence that contains the main noun (or equivalent) about which something is said.

Tense

The form of a verb that shows when the action or state happens (past, present, or future). The name of a tense is not always a guide to when the action happens. The "present continuous tense," for example, can be used to talk about the present or the future.

Verb

A word that describes an action or state (e.g., *work, love, begin*).

This statement is a generic one that is quickly paced and explains that Capone is sick and tired. Describing himself as "a public benefactor" represents Capone's conscious experience; he offers no supporting statements.

CASE EXAMPLE OF A MEDICAL RECORD ENTRY

The following example applies narrative discourse analysis to a medical narrative entry.

HPI (history of present illness): Jane is a 24-year-old white female who fell two mornings ago and sustained an inversion injury to the left ankle. She was seen in the ER where the ankle was found to be dislocated and fractured. The ankle was apparently relocated. The films were apparently reviewed today by an orthopedist. Jane was informed that she would need surgery for the ankle. This is scheduled for tomorrow. However, she has had pain today, uncontrolled, with medication that she is on. She also has been unable to do virtually anything except lie on the couch per her mother. Therefore, she is being admitted for pain control prior to her surgery.

The above entry breaks down as follows:

- **HPI:** Jane is a 24-year-old white female who fell two mornings ago and sustained an inversion injury to the left ankle. **(22 words)**
- She was seen in the ER where the ankle *was found to be dislocated* and fractured. **(16 words)**
- The ankle was *apparently* relocated. **(5 words)**
- The films were *apparently* reviewed today by an orthopedist. **(9 words)**
- Jane was informed that she would need surgery for the ankle. **(11 words)**
- This is scheduled for tomorrow. **(5 words)**
- *However,* she has had pain today, *uncontrolled,* with medication that she is on. **(13 words)**
- She also has been unable to do virtually anything except lie on the couch per her mother. **(17 words)**

- Therefore, she is being admitted for pain control prior to her surgery. **(12 words)**

Here is another narrative entry by the same author with the word count broken down.

- **FAMILY HISTORY:** There is no family history of reactions to anesthesia. **(9 words)**
- She has an uncle with diabetes. **(6 words)**
- There are several family members with cancer, including breast and lung cancer. **(12 words)**
- She has a grandmother with heart disease. **(7 words)**

In the medical record entry case just presented, notice the use of certain unconditional words in the HPI section: *found to be*, *apparently*, and *however*. These terms demonstrate the writer's conscious experience. The author is searching for a possible explanation of the patient's status. The description of the treatment provided in the emergency room is generic and nonspecific. By comparing the HPI to the second set of entry items noted in the Family History, the number of words per sentence decreased. Specific statements are associated with fewer words per sentence. The Family History statements are associated with general truths. The structure is specific, not general, and does not show any strong set of emotions. In this type of analysis, these are considered more likely to be truthful statements versus sentences that are long and extensive and do not have specific details. Something has prompted the author to vary his or her style, tone, and format. The interview should place a greater focus on the first entry versus the second.

Clinical Content Analysis Overview: Implications for Prevention, Detection, and Investigation

The SOAP methodology tool analyzes clinical record content, including the exact words used and their meanings. The tool can be applied to content that is generated by handwritten notes or electronically generated reports. Some auditors and investigators have expressed concern that opportunities for detection will be lost in the electronic world. This could not be further from the truth.

Electronic content, if anything, creates a greater number of opportunities for detection because auditors can use data mining techniques in their examination of it. In addition, the audit logs within a computer system such as those tracking users and the electronic architecture of the computer systems create opportunities for tracking user behavior that did not exist before. A simple example is the notation of time. Between 60 and 80 percent of handwritten records make no notation of time. The understanding of when an actual event occurred is golden. Computer-generated records are formatted to record the time of entry regardless of whether the author remembers to do so. Finally, the methodology of SOAP and its ability to quantify qualitative data provide EDA opportunities to understand and prove intent.

The narrative discourse analysis provides an in-depth tool to analyze any statements of an individual to ascertain the substance behind spoken or written words. What are the true thoughts being communicated—directly or indirectly—by the author? Verbal communications may be consciously or subconsciously expressed. The SOAP methodology for clinical analysis combined with follow-up individual author analysis provides the auditor or investigator with a comprehensive set of tools.

The next chapter combines a series of concepts and tools presented in this book into actual profilers for various anomalies that are found within the HCC.

CHAPTER 16

Profilers

Always tell the truth. That way, you don't have to remember what you said.

—MARK TWAIN

P rofilers are the descriptions of behavioral characteristics and traits of data elements noted during a series of referential comparisons. Referential analysis is the comparison of a data element to a specified context. This chapter provides a series of profilers that can be used throughout the healthcare continuum (HCC). They help pull together the concepts and tools presented in this guidebook to a level of direct application. "Follow the money" in this chapter is equivalent to "follow the data." If the subject does not remember, the data, if processed correctly, will tell the story.

FRAUD AND PROFILERS

As this book has pointed out repeatedly, the primary motivating factor in fraud is the pursuit of money. However, fraud can be motivated by other factors. In the application of these profilers, other intentions will materialize. The first profiler is for fraud; see Exhibit 16.1.

Follow the money: What is the offense?

What type of patient?	What type of providers?	Who is funding the plan?	What type of payer?	Other parties?
insured	Hospital	Gov. plan	TPA	
employee	OPS	Premium-based payer	TPA/premium	
gov. employee	MD office	Self-funded employer		
uninsured with $	Nursing home			
uninsured w/o $	Other			

Who	*What*	*Why*	*Where*	*When*
Data and documents	Observations and interviews	Analytics: $ and operational	Analytics: $ and operational	SOAP: Patient information

Source	Predication	Fraud theory	Investigation and report

Anomaly Data Analysis Profiler

EXHIBIT 16.1 Fraud Profiler

EXHIBIT 16.2   340 B Program Abuse Case Sample

340 B Programs

- **Who:** *Federal Register*, 71(138), July 19, 2006, notices.
- **What:** Limitation on prices of drugs by covered entities.
- **When:** A manufacturer sells covered outpatient drugs to eligible entities. Such a manufacturer must sign a pharmaceutical pricing agreement with the Secretary of the U.S. Department of Health and Human Services in which the manufacturer agrees to charge a price for covered outpatient drugs that will not exceed an amount determined under a statutory formula.
- **Why:** Compliance requirements with Section 340B(a)(5).
- **Where:** Outpatient activity with 340 B program drugs.

340 B Part B

- **Who:** Covered entity
- **What:** Prohibits from reselling or otherwise transferring a discounted drug to a person who is not a patient of the entity
- **When:** Inventory management
- **Why:** 340 B program abuse
- **Where:** Medicaid and manufacturer issues

Case history: Dr. Margin purchased Cancer Drug X for his healthcare facility, Treatment ABC, located in Ohio under the 340 B program status. Sales reps were out in the marketplace and were told that they could get Cancer Drug X for $1,882.20 (50% below AWP pricing of $3,764.40). In addition, marketing advertisements were found by Dr. Margin offering to other in-state and out-of-state providers for 50% lower than wholesale prices. The 340 B program price for Dr. Margin at his Treatment ABC facility was $1,529.54. He was selling the drug to other facilities for a 23 percent markup. The manufacturer noted a 13 percent drop in wholesale activity. Treatment ABC facility is known for treating individuals with allergies and not cancer. Treatment ABC is a nonprofit with 44 nationwide association affiliates.

Exhibit 16.1 represents a graphic decision tree, a visual presentation of the logic discussed in this book. The following case discussion represents a potential 340 B program abuse. Note the data sets in Exhibit 16.2.

The audit work plan would involve the *W* reviews. For example, identify *who*. Identify all the parties involved in the transactions of the 340 B drug, from purchase to inventory to receipt by a patient. The *what* involves data mining for clues. Look for utilization review and inventory controls. Conduct a multipayer analysis of both private and public payer claims data.

Data-mine the clinical records. Profile the patients. Identify the manu-facturer involved and its files on sales and distribution activity. The audit plan should then identify the *when*. Look at both concurrent and retrospective activities. Is the 340 B product being marketed in any way? Evaluate the *why*. It is most likely for profit, but ensure that no other basis exists for the activity. Finally, *where* is this occurring? Create a flowchart of all the players. Conduct the appropriate pipeline audits. Include the entity, the third-party entities, the manufacturer, and the patient. Audit work plan includes the following:

- What data should be collected?
- What is the value to the perpetrator?
- What would be the offense?
- What makes this story complicated?
- What are the general data issues?
- HIP (health information pipeline).
- PHI or IIHI (protected health information and individual identifiable health information).
- HCC (healthcare continuum).
- OFA (operational flow assessments).
- PMA (product market activity).
- CMA (consumer market activity).

Exhibit 16.3 identifies the specific HCC players involved in this process. The 340 B discounted drugs are simply not getting to the intended population. A great deal of focus is placed on the pharmaceutical industry with respect to high costs. The malfeasance of this type of fraud scheme is that the discounted drug never gets to the disadvantaged population. The table also highlights a reference to Part A of the 340 B program. This involves tracking the appropriateness of rebates received by the provider. Issues of duplicity need to be tested within this program. Although the 340 B program has been in existence for a very long time, the number of successful prosecutions of this program is unclear. This area presents opportunities for audit and investigations of highly needed resources for our underserved patient population.

Drug Flow: Follow the $, PHI, Utilization, Inventory

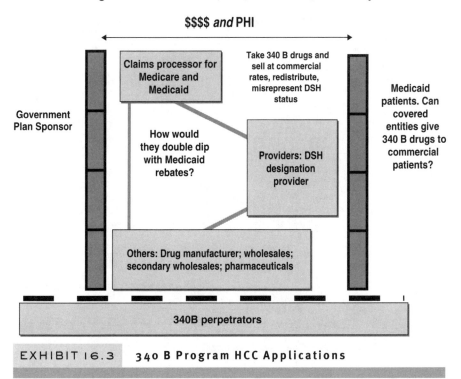

$$$$ and PHI

Claims processor for Medicare and Medicaid

Take 340 B drugs and sell at commercial rates, redistribute, misrepresent DSH status

Government Plan Sponsor

How would they double dip with Medicaid rebates?

Providers: DSH designation provider

Medicaid patients. Can covered entities give 340 B drugs to commercial patients?

Others: Drug manufacturer; wholesales; secondary wholesales; pharmaceuticals

340B perpetrators

EXHIBIT 16.3 340 B Program HCC Applications

Graphically Exhibit 16.1 should now look like Exhibit 16.4. Note this illustration is an audit and investigative guide. The profiler is a systematic methodology to collect and analyze evidence.

The fraudulent activity is clearly focused on profit. The intent is to steal from a government-sponsored program to provide discounted drugs. This model does exist in the marketplace. Effective investigations and prosecutions are needed to close the loop on this type of activity. The fraud profiler is the description of behavioral characteristics and traits of data elements that during the course of referential analysis patterns of material misrepresentation are noted in the data. Remember the elements of fraud:

- Misrepresentation of a material fact
- Knowledge of the falsity of the misrepresentation or ignorance of its truth
- Intent

Follow the money: What is the offense?   340 B program abuse: Drug diversion and trafficking

What type of patient?	What type of providers?	Who is funding the plan?	What type of payer?	Other parties?
insured	Hospital	Gov. Plan	TPA	Yes, third party clinics receiving 340 B drugs at commercial rates.
employee	OPS	Premium-based payer	TPA/premium	
gov. employee	MD office	Self-funded employer		Manufacturer providing 340 B drugs to DSH provider.
uninsured with $	Nursing home	Other		
uninsured w/o $	Other			

Who: Dr. Margin	What: Reselling 340 B drugs	Why: $	Where: Other clinics	When: Ongoing
Data and documents	Observations and interviews	Analytics: $ and operational	SOAP: Patient information	
Clinical files Inventory, purchase, and resale records	Patients, clinical staff, third party clinics, manufacturer representatives	Pipeline review: ARP, HIP, OFA, PMA, CMA	Test clinical content for any clinical analysis by Dr. Margin	

Source: note references	Predication: yes	Fraud theory: yes, see above	Investigations and report

Anomaly Data Analysis Profiler

EXHIBIT 16.4   Completed Fraud Profiler

Source: Medical Business Associates, Inc. (www.mbanews.com).

- A victim acting on the misrepresentation
- Damage to the victim

Referential analysis is applied in the fraud profiler by comparing the data sets listed in Exhibit 16.4 to a specified context (also noted in Exhibit 16.4). Doing so provides the opportunity to study the misrepresentation, the perpetrator's knowledge of the falsity, intent, victims acting on the misrepresentation, and the damage to the victim.

MEDICAL ERRORS AND PROFILERS

Why have a discussion on medical errors in a healthcare fraud audit and detection guidebook? Medical errors cost the market a significant amount of money. Evidence can look like a medical error when in fact it involves fraud. Medical errors fund waste and abuse activity. In addition, the process of auditing and detection applies. Often we can learn lessons from medical error issues that can be applied in the fraud environment. They provide a further understanding of the concept of normal versus not normal. A medical profiler is the process of clinical behavioral characteristics descriptors and traits of data elements including the fees associated with those clinical services noted during a series of referential comparisons. Referential analysis is the comparison of the specified clinical data element to a specified context within the applicable parties of the HCC.

To illustrate the application, we return to a paragraph that appeared in Chapter 15's discussion of narrative discourse analysis:

> HPI: Jane is a 24-year-old white female who fell two mornings ago and sustained an inversion injury to the left ankle. She was seen in the ER where the ankle was found to be dislocated and fractured. The ankle was **apparently** relocated. The films were **apparently reviewed today** by an orthopedist. Jane was informed that she would need surgery for the ankle. This is scheduled for tomorrow. However, she has had pain today, uncontrolled, with medication that she is on. She also has been unable to do virtually anything except lie on the couch per her mother. Therefore, she is being admitted for pain control prior to her surgery.

Take note of the discharge date and the multiple dates of dictation (see Exhibit 16.5). This dictation took place several months after the fact. This patient was admitted in the emergency room on a Saturday night. The ER doctor failed to diagnosis the multiple fractures or negligently sent the patient home without stabilizing the fracture. That aside, the radiograph was not read by the radiologist until after the fact, the reason being that at this small community hospital the radiologist came in only on certain days of the week. Simple attention to issues such as dates is important when trying to understand exactly what happened.

CASE: THE HOSPITAL OF MEMORIAL COUNTY

This case involved a series of misrepresentations and alterations in the record. This case is fraudulent in its misrepresentation. However, money was not the intent. Avoidance of liability was the intent. Was it that the doctor did not notice the fracture and now is medically negligent, or was this patient discharged for having no insurance? Is this a case of patient dumping? The SOAP test was applied to the records. In addition, the itemized charges were reviewed for any evidence of the ER doctor actually relocating the fractured ankle. If he did relocate the fractured ankle, it was done without pain medications or supplies.

EXHIBIT 16.5   Redacted Discharge Summary

NAME:	**SMITH, Jane**
AGE/DOB:	24/9-25-80
RM/MR#:	SURG/24386
ADMITTED:	1-17-05
DISCHARGED:	1-20-05

DISCHARGE SUMMARY

by Ms. Assistant

DISCHARGE DIAGNOSIS: **Left ankle fracture/dislocation**
Fall
Right ankle sprain

PROCEDURES: Left distal fibula ORIF with syndesmosis screw placement (8 words)

HISTORY: Please see H&P for further details. (6 words)

HOSPITAL COURSE:
The patient was admitted because of a left distal fibular fracture with syndesmosis disruption. (14 words)
She was taken to the OR by Dr. Surgery on January 18 with ORIF with syndesmosis screw placement. (18 words)
The patient tolerated the procedure well but continued to have significant post op pain with required IV medications. (18 words)
She also had significant evaluation and work with physical therapy throughout her hospital stay. (14 words)
The patient was on PCA for 24 hours past her hospitalization. (11 words)

Exhibit 16.6 is a redacted copy of the radiologist's report. Again, take notice that two separate reports are on the same page. This is not normal. Each procedure typically has its own report. This copy also has the number of words noted per sentence. Sentence word count is a step in the narrative discourse analysis that was discussed in Chapter 15. Take notice of the comparison reading. "Two views of the left tibia and fibula again demonstrate a comminuted fracture of the distal shaft of the fibula with improved alignment compared with the pre-reduction views" (28 words). Notice the phrase *improved alignment*.

Fractures are either aligned or not aligned. Again, recall the earlier statement that the itemized charges are not consistent with the statement by the radiologist. A later sentence notes, "There is mild lateral displacement of the talus at the ankle with associated widening of the medial mortis and persistent mild dorsal displacement of the main distal fracture fragment of the fibula." This sentence indicates that the fracture is not aligned. It is still displaced; most likely it was never aligned. For the nonclinical reader, this patient had two fractures within the ankle. This clinical picture would be associated with severe pain. Again, the pattern of writing, the clinical content, and comparison to the itemized charges points in the direction of liability avoidance. Once again, take notice and compare the date of the exam and the date of dictation. An ER visit with a fracture would normally have a formal reading on the same day.

Reviewing and analyzing itemized charges is important in any type of profiler. Many clinicians may alter records; however, very few are well versed in the concept of charge masters and exactly how they work. Blending of the two when manipulation of the records is taking place will only help identify the parties involved in the misrepresentation. The profiler should graphically look like Exhibit 16.7.

The application of the medical profiler in this case involved clinical behavioral characteristics descriptors of the ER admission and treatment. In addition, it involved the operational behavioral descriptors of the transcription process of records dictated by the medical staff. Finally, traits of data elements including the fees and lack of fees associated with those clinical services noted during a series of referential comparisons allowed a series of conclusions to be drawn. Referential analysis compared the clinical and financial comparison of the specified clinical data element to a specified context within the applicable parties of the HCC. In other words, the clinician kept using the word *apparently* within the HPI narrative note most likely because the services were not provided and the ER doctor did not treat the fracture properly.

EXHIBIT 16.6   Redacted Radiology Report

THE HOSPITAL OF MEMORIAL COUNTY
800 HOSPITAL STREET
MEMORIAL, IL 60000

RADIOLOGY REPORT
NAME: **SMITH, Jane**
DOB: **9-25-1980**   **SEX:**   **F**   **STATUS: ER/OP**

                             REFERRING MD: Dr. Family Practice

EXAMINATION: Left Ankle, Left Lower Leg Post-reduction. (6 words)
DATE OF EXAM: 1-15-2005

HISTORY: Fell on ice; pain. (4 words)

LEFT ANKLE AT 08:04 HOURS: Two views of the left ankle demonstrate a comminuted oblique fracture of the fibula with a butterfly fragment displaced mild laterally and posteriorly and one shaft width dorsal displacements as well as mild lateral angulation of the main distal fracture fragment. (41 words)

There is also a dislocation at the ankle with the talus displaced relative to the distal fibula and what appears to be a fracture fragment arising from the lateral aspect of the distal tibia. (34 words)

There is also a small fracture of the posterior malleolus of the distal fibula. (14 words)

SUMMARY: Distal fibular shaft fractures and distal tibial fractures with dislocation at the ankle as above. (15 words)

HISTORY: Status post-reduction of fractured dislocation of the left ankle. (9 words)

LEFT LOWER LEG AT 09:17HOURS: Comparison is 1-15-2005 at 08:04hours.
Two views of the left tibia and fibula again demonstrate a comminuted fracture of the distal shaft of the fibula with improved alignment compared with the pre-reduction views. (28 words)

Again noted is a fracture of the posterior malleolus of the distal tibia. (13 words)

There is mild lateral displacement of the talus at the ankle with associated widening of the medial mortis and persistent mild dorsal displacement of the main distal fracture fragment of the fibula. (32 words)

SUMMARY: Improved alignment status post-reduction of left ankle fracture dislocation. (9 words)

Dr. Radiology
Skp
DD: January 19, 2005
DT: January 19, 2005

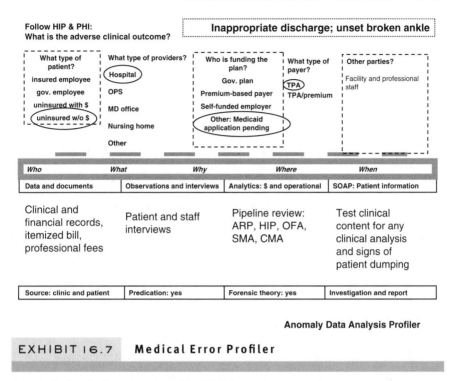

| Follow HIP & PHI: What is the adverse clinical outcome? | Inappropriate discharge; unset broken ankle |

What type of patient?	What type of providers?	Who is funding the plan?	What type of payer?	Other parties?
insured employee	Hospital	Gov. plan	TPA	Facility and professional staff
gov. employee	OPS	Premium-based payer	TPA/premium	
uninsured with $	MD office	Self-funded employer		
uninsured w/o $	Nursing home	Other: Medicaid application pending		
	Other			

Who	What	Why	Where	When
Data and documents	Observations and interviews	Analytics: $ and operational	SOAP: Patient information	
Clinical and financial records, itemized bill, professional fees	Patient and staff interviews	Pipeline review: ARP, HIP, OFA, SMA, CMA	Test clinical content for any clinical analysis and signs of patient dumping	

| Source: clinic and patient | Predication: yes | Forensic theory: yes | Investigation and report |

Anomaly Data Analysis Profiler

EXHIBIT 16.7   Medical Error Profiler

Source: Medical Business Associates, Inc. (MBA) (www.mbanews.com).

FINANCIAL ERRORS AND PROFILERS

Finance involves several components. The first is the world of managing revenues. It includes anything that will impact the amount of money paid, how it is processed, and the parties involved with the transaction. Finance affects all legitimate and illegitimate HCC players. Second, finance involves resources such as research grants, capital loans and expenditures, resource expenditures, credit lines, reserve allocations, and cost reports. In healthcare, financial cost reports can help a hospital receive a disproportionate share reimbursement from Medicare. Finally, finance is also the science of managing money.

This science requires the understanding of errors. Simply put, an error is a deviation from the correctness of a transaction. When it is referred to as an error, it is a mistake. This concept is consistent with a previous discussion in understanding what is *normal* within a set of financial transactions. Anything else is *abnormal* and should be evaluated for audit with a potential progression for investigation. Financial profilers target the descriptive behavioral characteristics of money matters. The traits of the data elements are noted when transactions, in particular contractual terms, and monetary amounts are processed through exploratory data analysis (EDA) referential activity. Money matters typically include clinical content or operational issues during the referential analysis.

Recall the case of Pain Reliever RN in Chapter 15. The data sets were noted within Exhibit 15.16 of that chapter. The focus was on evaluating the SOAP content after financial credit and debit activity did not make sense when compared to the medical records. This example is a continuation of credit and debit activity of charges at a hospital. Exhibit 16.8 was generated based on audits that were conducted to verify whether documentation existed in the medical records. As a result of the audit, certain adjustments were made to the financial records to submit a bill that reflected the service rendered to the patient. The table in Exhibit 16.8 has a series of credits and debits. The service code numbers were redacted.

This list notes two positive hits. Currently, Caspofungin Acet 5mg/ml is a popular drug target for thieves, who reintroduce it into the secondary wholesale market. The typical scenario involves a hospital employee or an individual who has access to the hospital's inventory for diversion of the medication.

Two bills currently residing in committee in both the U.S. House (H.R. 2345) and U.S. Senate (S. 1978) would ensure documentation of all movement of medications. Introduced in 2005, Timothy Fagan's Law is named after a 16-year-old liver transplant patient who received several painful injections of Epogen at home by his mother as a post-transplant regimen. Mom was told of the counterfeit alert and investigated the vials at home. She noted the counterfeit signs of the medication. Exhibit 16.9 represents the market flow. The gray market is the critical arena for counterfeit medications and the introduction of adulterated drugs. In the case of Timothy Fagan, the Epogen vials appeared to have changed hands at least 22 times before they were reintroduced into the regional wholesaler market.

Many questions remain as to how such a market standard has evolved and why the need for the secondary wholesale market (noted as the gray market) even exists. In the case of financial errors, traditional legitimate providers tend not to be prepared for organized crime infiltration into their

EXHIBIT 16.8   Drug Diversion Test

Item Description	Number of times adjusted	Quantity adjusted	Charges adjusted
D5W-UNDERFILL INJ 50ML	295	−293	($32,152.46)
HEP-FLUSH-SYR 10U\ML 5ML	205	−146	($5,839.00)
D5W-UNDERFILL INJ 100ML	182	−188	($20,030.16)
TACROLIMUS (FK506) 1MG CAP	117	−145	($1,616.48)
NORMAL SALINE (100)	93	−89	($9,824.26)
NS 0.9% 1L INJ	91	−38	($5,149.75)
D5W INJ 250ML	83	−1368	($7,021.55)
TACROLIMUS# 1MG SUSP	79	−193	($3,232.44)
CASPOFUNGIN ACET 5MG\ML	77	77	$189,031.74
FAMOTIDINE 20MG\2ML INJ	72	−47	($3,810.79)
ACETAMINOPHEN 325MG TAB*	65	−72	($295.61)
NS 0.9% INJ 500ML	65	−37	($4,089.59)
HEP-FLUSH-SYR 100 U\ML 5ML	63	−74	($3,067.67)
CEFAZOLIN 1GM\D5W 50ML DPX	60	−82	($7,311.46)
DOCUSATE@ 100MG CAP	58	−42	($310.73)
SENNA\DOCUSATE NA TAB	57	−54	($320.57)
HEPARIN-CPJT 5000U\0.5ML	56	−181	($2,490.09)
METOPROLOL* 25MG TAB	55	−71	($409.88)
ONDANSETRON 2MG\ML 2ML INJ	53	−81	($2,610.90)
LANSOPRAZOLE SOLUTAB 30MG	51	−41	($410.85)
MYCOPHENOLATE 250MG SUS	50	−44	($1,043.54)
NYSTATIN* 500TU\5ML SUS	49	−14	($319.11)
LORAZEPAM 2MG\ML INJ 1ML	49	−44	($2,157.09)
PANTOPRAZOLE 40MG TAB*	47	−43	($257.37)
VANCOMYCIN 1GM INJ	46	−40	($2,246.28)
Totals :	2118	−3350	$73,014.11

organizations to perpetuate such activities. The purpose of the financial error profiler is to identify financial variances; in this example, it is the credits and debits of hospital charges. The behavioral characteristics should then be processed by the internal control profiler. The behavioral characteristics associated with Caspofungin, an expensive antifungal, should be reviewed internally for theft at the facility (diversion). It is a high-dollar medication and therefore subject to theft for illicit profit.

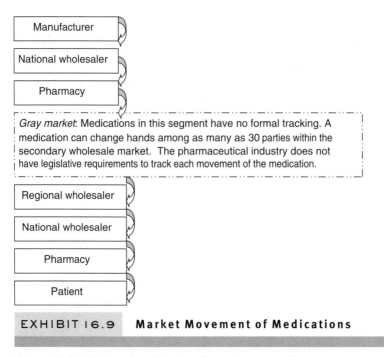

EXHIBIT 16.9   **Market Movement of Medications**

Source: Medical Business Associates, Inc. (www.mbanews.com).

The other medication that hit the alert status is Lorazepam. Lorazepam does not have a high-dollar value for the secondary wholesale market, but it does have high dollar value for illicit use (street use). The follow-up investigation of this drug will most likely target either resale distribution or personal use similar to the case study of Pain Reliever RN. Exhibit 16.10 demonstrates the application of a financial profiler. Again, conceptually the methodology of a profiler is similar to other profilers presented. The scientific methodology is to study the behavior patterns of the data elements noted in the chart.

Financial variances tend to lead toward a secondary issue. Other issues that result from financial variances may include system controls, incorrect application of contractual terms, failure to update charge masters, failure by the payer to update CPT and ICD codes within their adjudication systems, and failure by the employer to update beneficiary information. The potential issues are extensive, and they exist throughout the HCC.

Follow HIP and PHI and $:
What is the adverse $ outcome?

Medication credits > debits

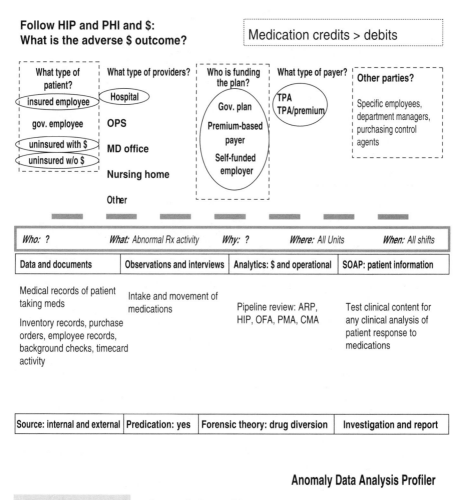

What type of patient?	What type of providers?	Who is funding the plan?	What type of payer?	Other parties?
insured employee	Hospital	Gov. plan	TPA	Specific employees, department managers, purchasing control agents
gov. employee	OPS	Premium-based payer	TPA/premium	
uninsured with $	MD office	Self-funded employer		
uninsured w/o $	Nursing home			
	Other			

Who: ?	What: Abnormal Rx activity	Why: ?	Where: All Units	When: All shifts

Data and documents	Observations and interviews	Analytics: $ and operational	SOAP: patient information
Medical records of patient taking meds	Intake and movement of medications	Pipeline review: ARP, HIP, OFA, PMA, CMA	Test clinical content for any clinical analysis of patient response to medications
Inventory records, purchase orders, employee records, background checks, timecard activity			

Source: internal and external	Predication: yes	Forensic theory: drug diversion	Investigation and report

Anomaly Data Analysis Profiler

EXHIBIT 16.10   Financial Profiler

Source: Medical Business Associates, Inc. (www.mbanews.com).

INTERNAL AUDIT AND PROFILERS

According to the Institute of Internal Auditors, internal auditing is an independent, objective assurance and consulting activity designed to add value and improve an organization's operations. It helps an organization accomplish its objectives by bringing a systematic, disciplined approach to evaluate and improve the effectiveness of risk management, control, and governance processes (www.theiia.org).

The internal audit profiler is about the descriptive behaviors throughout the operational flow activity of that entity. In this case, the focus is narrowed to two particular medications with two very different illicit purposes. The overview of the profiler for internal controls on this subject may begin with

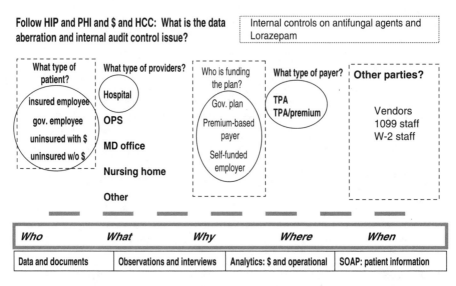

Follow HIP and PHI and $ and HCC: What is the data aberration and internal audit control issue?

Internal controls on antifungal agents and Lorazepam

What type of patient?	What type of providers?	Who is funding the plan?	What type of payer?	Other parties?
insured employee	Hospital	Gov. plan	TPA	Vendors
gov. employee	OPS	Premium-based payer	TPA/premium	1099 staff
uninsured with $	MD office	Self-funded employer		W-2 staff
uninsured w/o $	Nursing home			
	Other			

Who	*What*	*Why*	*Where*	*When*
Data and documents	Observations and interviews	Analytics: $ and operational	SOAP: patient information	
All documents associated with the OFA activities	All roles identified in the OFA	Detailed system and people OFA pipeline audit of all drug movements, purchase orders, inventory control, patient management control	Test patient records; use medical records	
Source: financial data	Predication: yes for $ variance	Audit theory: diversion	Investigation and report	

Anomaly Data Analysis Profiler

EXHIBIT 16.11   **Internal Audit Profiler**

Source: Medical Business Associates, Inc. (www.mbanews.com).

the components of Exhibit 16.11. The profiler checklist can be summarized as follows:

- ☐ What is the issue?
- ☐ What is the type of patient?
- ☐ What is the type of provider?
- ☐ Who is funding the plan?
- ☐ What is the type of payer?
- ☐ Are there any other parties involved?
- ☐ Who, what, where, when, and how?
- ☐ What data and documents should be collected?
- ☐ What observations and interviews should be initiated?
- ☐ What analytics are appropriate for the issue presented?
- ☐ What operational components are involved?
- ☐ What are the associated financial transactions?
- ☐ What type of clinical analysis should be initiated (SOAP)?
- ☐ What are your sources of information?
- ☐ Do you have predication?
- ☐ What is your audit theory, and do you have sufficient evidence?
- ☐ Have you organized the information of your investigation into a report?

This audit project would feed a previously discussed pipeline. Since we are discussing an issue within a provider setting, it would be appropriate to include in the audit plan a review of the operational breakpoints in the hospital. Controls should be tested at every point within the facility. Keep in mind that it should include all areas—those that indirectly or directly impact patient care.

Exhibit 16.12 provides a sample flow of issues to include in such an audit. In this case, we are discussing the role of two medications. The auditor needs to flowchart all of the possible movements of these two medications. An audit of the hospital charges can also evaluate whether anomalies are occurring in a particular patient area. This would imply a focused audit of an individual

Health Information Pipeline (HIP) and Accounts Receivable Pipeline (ARP) and Operational Flow Activity (OFA)

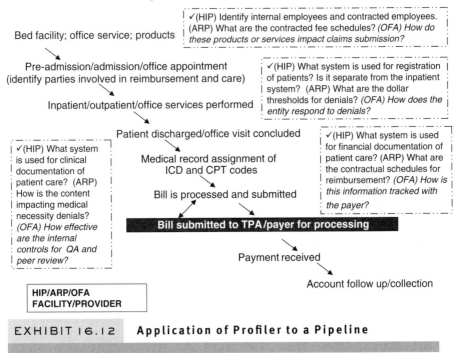

Bed facility; office service; products

✓(HIP) Identify internal employees and contracted employees. (ARP) What are the contracted fee schedules? *(OFA) How do these products or services impact claims submission?*

Pre-admission/admission/office appointment (identify parties involved in reimbursement and care)

✓(HIP) What system is used for registration of patients? Is it separate from the inpatient system? (ARP) What are the dollar thresholds for denials? *(OFA) How does the entity respond to denials?*

Inpatient/outpatient/office services performed

Patient discharged/office visit concluded

✓(HIP) What system is used for clinical documentation of patient care? (ARP) How is the content impacting medical necessity denials? *(OFA) How effective are the internal controls for QA and peer review?*

Medical record assignment of ICD and CPT codes

Bill is processed and submitted

✓(HIP) What system is used for financial documentation of patient care? (ARP) What are the contractual schedules for reimbursement? *(OFA) How is this information tracked with the payer?*

Bill submitted to TPA/payer for processing

Payment received

Account follow up/collection

HIP/ARP/OFA
FACILITY/PROVIDER

EXHIBIT 16.12   **Application of Profiler to a Pipeline**

Source: Medical Business Associates, Inc. (www.mbanews.com).

associated with a unit. If the anomalies are noted equally in all patient areas, the focus is going to be on the activities that support those units. This would tend to be back-end support services, such as central supply or the main pharmacy or perhaps satellite pharmacies that at times are located throughout a facility.

RECOVERY AND PROFILERS

Recovery profilers are the descriptions of behavioral characteristics and traits of data elements representing all the parties that have been noted during a series of referential comparisons. Referential analysis is the comparison of a data element to a specified context. In the recovery model, the specified context is what monies are left or available to compensate for the fraud and the damages that resulted from the perpetrator's activities. An analysis is required of the possible sources.

The first step is to obtain a comprehensive asset profile of all parties identified. For the provider, the likelihood of utilizing any physical supplies that are found and recovered would represent a high risk because it is not known how they were stored. If an employee was involved in the theft, the provider may actually recover from its crime policy. The most likely source would be through the distribution of assets seized by the perpetrators. The unfortunate reality of fraud, though, is that once the asset is stolen, it is gone. A high expectation for recovery is not very promising. Damage control often involves preventing the activity from happening again. Having the perpetrators prosecuted and wearing the color orange for a long time will help prevent other victims.

Exhibit 16.13 represents how this topic would be approached utilizing the recovery profiler.

ANOMALY AND PROFILERS

This is a general activity for ongoing data surveillance in which no known issue exists. View the overall EDA activity within this concept as general review of any exception activities, regardless of how minor they may appear to be. Trend the exceptions that are similar in scope. Apply the profiler checklist. Determine whether any of the exceptions impact any financial activity. Also this process should incorporate tracking of employee complaints as well as the patient complaints. One approach to evaluating a complaint is to pull the respective pipeline associated with it.

A recent example is a complaint from a beneficiary. The beneficiary stated that the pharmacy sometimes sent his spouse's prescription in the beneficiary's name; other times the pharmacy sent it in the spouse's name. This prompted the following audit protocol:

- ☐ Why would both parties be charged for the medication when only one delivery was made?
- ☐ What is the implication of a pharmacy ever dispensing a medication to a party without having a prescription?
- ☐ How much is the benefit plan actually paying for this set of medications?
- ☐ What internal control issues exist that the benefit plan manager cannot verify what was charged back to the benefit plan?

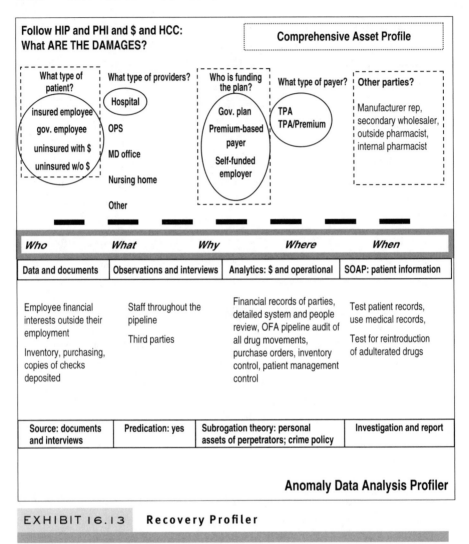

EXHIBIT 16.13   Recovery Profiler

Source: Medical Business Associates, Inc. (www.mbanews.com).

☐ The beneficiary does not have to worry about paying for the medications because they are charged directly to the plan.

Look at complaints as low-hanging fruit. They tie back to an operational issue or perhaps a breakdown somewhere in the system. At minimum, this infrastructure, just by the very last check item, is not utilizing the beneficiary as a frontline defense for identification of a possible false claim. Every organization should be doing some level of EDA activity. This should not be a function that is outsourced at 100 percent. In addition, an audit of the process should be conducted by a third party that has no conflict with the entities involved.

FRAUD AWARENESS AND PROFILERS

Healthcare is in a state of crisis, with plentiful opportunities for those who like to lie, cheat, and steal. However, very few organizations include as part of their defense educating the front line. How does an employee or beneficiary know to look at a consent form and realize that it is a contract for excessive payment of services? How do we help the uninsured not buy fake insurance? How do we help small business owners learn not to buy fake insurance on behalf of their employees? View the profiler process as an opportunity to understand the current level of awareness and education programs that should be provided. The following is a sample checklist of activity that can be initiated:

- ☐ Review process of hiring company employees with respect to health benefits.
- ☐ Collect information distributed to employees on health benefits/ current fraud hotlines/applicable data on its use.
- ☐ Review internal resources or communications such as employee newsletters.
- ☐ Obtain internal and external resources available to employees.
- ☐ Generate survey/review with company internal audit.
- ☐ Collect findings.
- ☐ Analyze findings.
- ☐ Follow up by making future awareness program suggestions.

Education is very much needed. For instance, 10 percent of drugs are estimated to be counterfeit. What can employees do to protect themselves? What are the signs? How can they protect themselves from medical identity theft? Beneficiary cards need the same level of protection as credit cards. The adverse outcome of a stolen benefit card includes not only fraudulently spent benefit dollars but also a false record of diagnosis and treatment that does not pertain to the legitimate cardholder. That creates as much damage, if not more, as credit identity theft. Employee and beneficiary education will pay significant dividends.

Profiler Overview: Implications for Prevention, Detection, and Investigation

Healthcare waste, fraud, and abuse are pervasive. The only advantage of this fragmented, multilayered industry is that fraudsters have to be very good at lying. Mark Twain could not have said it better: "Always tell the truth. That way, you don't have to remember what you said."

This book covers a lot of ground with respect to healthcare episodes and their transactions. Imagine the expertise and training it would require of a fraudster to appreciate the implication of one action throughout the entire HCC. Imagine the expertise of appreciating HIPs, ARPs, OFAs, PMAs, SMAs, and CMA behavior. The pipeline tools, combined with the profiler methodology with EDA integrated in the process to manage high-volume data, are the ultimate tools to ferret out any abnormal behavior.

CHAPTER 17

Market Implications

The great enemy of the truth is very often not the lie—deliberate, contrived and dishonest—but the myth—persistent, persuasive, and unrealistic.

—JOHN F. KENNEDY

This guidebook is written in a format that will help you navigate through the complex, multifragmented, multisegmented healthcare market. Healthcare is so convoluted that a road map is required just to understand all the parties involved, let alone what was done and for how much. What does all of this really mean?

THE MYTH

The term *fragmented* is used throughout this book in discussions about the healthcare continuum (HCC). *Fragmented* in this context describes a disorganized process that exists in or functions through separate parts. The process is not unified. The audit tools described in this book focus on finding all the pieces so that they can be integrated for the most appropriate type of audit or investigation. The integration also allows for effective detection.

Segmented is about taking these individual fragments and dividing them up further. In reimbursement, we divide up constantly by cost shifting the price of healthcare, excluding services and excluding preexisting conditions. In healthcare, we see various HCC players attempting to further segment various parts in the provision of healthcare services. I often hear something like this from consumers: "Our insurance just dropped four major hospitals in our area. My number-one complaint with what's wrong in healthcare is that I cannot choose where to go or what doctor to see." Cost shifting can occur by segmenting choices: Patients are directed to lower-cost providers with fewer service offerings; the system controls their choices and access.

What does this look like to a consumer? Take a recent visit to my family dentist. My son had to get a tooth pulled. The dentist informed me that he could not do it because the insurance company now considers tooth pulling a specialty procedure; to receive insurance coverage, we had to go to a specialized dental surgeon. Where is the common sense? As a consumer, I was frustrated because I have a family dentist whom I trust and who is competent to pull the tooth. The second dentist, the surgical specialist, required one office visit for an anesthesia assessment and then a second appointment for the removal of the tooth. Thus, my son having his tooth out required a total of three office visits and three fees.

When wearing my healthcare-expert hat, I clearly understood the payer reimbursement decision tree driving the medical decision-making process. I knew that if the dentist decided the type of anesthesia on the same day he pulled the tooth, he would not have been reimbursed for the decision-making process. But when wearing my "mom" hat, I was very agitated: My son lost three days of school instead of one; he experienced needless extra days of anxiety, which required my calming him down; and I was hit with three expenses that should have been combined into one. As an employer, I know that the three visits will go toward my utilization rating and eventually impact my insurance rates.

Academically I can see the pink elephant in the room: What the market has created is a perverse blending of clinical case management and financial case management without disclosure. Case management is a body of science that discusses the healthcare management of an individual patient. Two very distinct functions need to be separated. The first is managing the patient clinically; the second is managing the patient financially. Clinical case management is about the science of health; it should be based on the actual observations, assessments, diagnostics, and treatments of the wellness and disease state of the patient. Financial case management is the science of money matters—the financial portfolio of the patient's financial resources regardless of whether they are personal or through some type of employer-linked insurance or government-sponsored program.

In my optimal world, while the market resolves its issues, a patient should receive a care plan that looks like the following:

CLINICAL CASE MANAGEMENT

- "Based on our findings, it appears that you have the following issues: ..."
- "We believe the best treatment option includes ..."
- "The treatment regimen should be provided within this time frame ..."
- "The following is a list of resources for alternative treatment plans ..."

FINANCIAL CASE MANAGEMENT

- "The following is an analysis of your financial health resources: ..."
- "Your employer-linked insurance program has these provisions: ..."
- "Your government-linked benefits have these provisions: ..."
- "Your personal resources include ..."

OVERVIEW

The patient then determines which aspects of the clinical plan should be blended with the financial plan. Currently this is done in a vacuum without the patient's knowledge. It is driven by the segmented market of utilization review, payer approvals, and available clinical resources. *This is a critical failure of the current system and an injustice to the patient.*

Part of the market confusion among all parties from the patient to the provider to the payer and the employer is that when it appears that the patient is being managed clinically, the criteria are really an application of a financial analysis of benefit coverage. If this were not true, how could the market ever generate self-contradictory statements such as the following from a payer? "Services denied due to lack of medical necessity; however, please note that this does not mean that the services ordered by your provider were not medically necessary."

The case management concept needs to be separated into the two disciplines described. We have a duty to the patient and all parties to communicate what the clinical plan is versus the financial plan. Otherwise, this persistent myth will merely contribute toward the problems that exist in healthcare today. Perhaps Thomas Edison understood the concept when he stated, "The doctor of the future will give no medicine, but will interest his patients in the care of the human frame, in diet, and in the cause and prevention of disease." This cannot occur without full disclosure of what is happening financially. The sad reality is that the market is losing a lot of professionals who pride themselves in the art of patient care.

We have a new generation of healthcare professionals who must be financial analysts in addition to providers of patient care. The devil is never in the choices we make in life, but in their consequences. I can assure you that I know of no consumer who on his or her deathbed would want to wonder, "Is this the best clinical or financial advice?" The standard of care will never actually be as blatant as "Hey, this is what we can do based on what your benefit plan will let us do." However, in reality, that is what is happening in the marketplace.

"Persistent"

Future factors that will contribute to the convoluted mix of problems plaguing the healthcare system include concepts such as *medical necessity* and *medical unbelievability* (the latter is a new term introduced in 2007 by Medicare). How are these new concepts for cost control measured? How are they defined? Why would a provider ever prescribe a regimen that is not medically necessary? Imagine the confusion of the average consumer reading the explanation of benefits noted above: "Services denied due to lack of medical necessity; however, please note that this does not mean that the services ordered by your provider were not medically necessary."

That leads us to the concept of consumer-directed health plans. How is a consumer, without the training of a healthcare auditor, reimbursement analyst, healthcare professional, or claims analyst, ever supposed to self-advocate? Exactly what are we putting the consumer in control of? Are consumer-directed health plans another type of cost shifting that does nothing to address the real issues?

"PERSUASIVE"

This book also spends time reviewing reimbursement models. The incentive for profit by one HCC player is often in direct conflict with another player. To fully appreciate the complexities of healthcare reimbursement systems, we need to return to our healthcare reimbursement history timetable.

In 1927, on the eve of the Great Depression, Baylor Hospital in Dallas entered into an agreement with the local teachers' union. The agreement involved an employee deduction per paycheck paid in advance to the hospital. In turn, the hospital offered hospital-based care for these teachers and their families. This deduction was determined using a community-based rating model. Eventually, an organization known as Blue Cross emerged and started to provide the same type of program. Note, however, that a model known as *prepaid practice groups* (PGPs) already existed. Prior to this time period, private insurance did not exist for healthcare services. Health insurance offerings were avoided because appropriate premium rates were too difficult to predict, unlike rates for insurance upon the death of an individual. Private insurance plans started to appear in the late 1930s. These plans, however, were driven by risk-based models. They focused on the experience of the group. Blue Cross now had competition and was losing its customer base because of the new private-payer offerings. Blue Cross shifted toward a modified adjusted community rate plan, eventually abandoning it completely and joining the private-payer market risk model plans. Eventually Blue Shield emerged to serve coverage for professional services.

This introduction illustrates one of the very first critical "cost shifting" market movements. What does *cost shifting* mean? It is when the cost of certain activities is shifted to another party. The question is, to whom? At every point in the HCC, the question of "how does one profit?" is important to understand. Private payers profited by removing high-risk individuals from their plans. Private payers were growing at a rapid rate, because during World War II a wage hold was put into place. Employers started to realize that benefit plans could be seen as a non-wage form of compensation. The tax code encouraged employers to view benefit plans as a cost of doing business, and employees never had to claim their benefits as income.

The benefit plan offering generated a significant amount of cash in the healthcare system. During the 1940s and going forward, teaching hospitals were also recipients of large amounts of cash infusion by the government's investment in research and technology. The flow of cash from both areas generated a significant offering of healthcare diagnostics and treatment options. By 1946, the healthcare market had increased cash flow for hospital coverage. This resulted in increased utilization of hospital services. The amounts of insurance payments and premium programs went up. Hospitals expanded because of the available cash. The market had a significant buildup of resources. The amount of technology was growing at an accelerated rate. This fueled additional use and sale of insurance. The gap between the haves and have-nots exploded.

From 1930 to 1965, there was the first big cost shift, the shift of high-risk individuals to uninsured status. Who were these people? They were the elderly, the unemployed, the self-employed, the retired, and the disabled. With the aggressive advancements in healthcare, the disproportionate offerings between the haves and the have-nots became obvious.

The political arena debated the concept of compulsory insurance or a nationalized health plan. Instead, in 1965 Medicare was born to serve the have-nots. Medicare takes a *social insurance* approach, and its members are referred to as *beneficiaries*. Medicaid was also established; it is managed at the state level. Medicaid, however, uses a *welfare approach*, and its members are referred to as *recipients*. The market at the time believed that employer-linked insurance would eventually serve as a form of nationalized health insurance. Medicare Part A was created to pay hospital services, and Medicare Part B was created to serve the professional component. To devise a nationalized healthcare program was not necessary. The market, it was thought, would take care of itself.

''UNREALISTIC''

In the 1960s, the market experienced increased inflation and increased healthcare expenditures. On August 15, 1971, price controls were put into place. During the 1970s, the healthcare market continued to see increased prices, increased expenditures, decreased access, and increased premiums.

The employer-linked health programs could never serve as universal coverage because the incentive for profit eliminates high-risk individuals. What do these market conflicts look like?

- *Payer*, during the act of denying a service, increases its profit margin. The market movement for payers starts as shifting high-risk individuals out of the plan. This is a people shift. The second is a price shift. This may look like the "usual and customary" concept. The third is a service shift. This may look like not paying for preexisting conditions.

- *Provider*, during the act of prescribing and ordering a service, increases its profit margin. The shifts in this marketplace occur between "fee schedules" and prepayment fixed and prospective plans. The fee schedule type of payment tends to result in excessive treatment. The other shift is in the form of prospective payments, such as diagnosis-related groups and capitation. This is a predetermined amount. This tends to result in treatment being withheld. As private payers and vendors pass their costs on to the hospitals, the hospitals in turn go back to the government-sponsored programs for additional cost adjustments. In particular, charity write-offs and disproportionate share contributions increase toward the hospital.

- *Vendors*, when providing a service, increase their profit margins. This group follows the provider market, and at times the provider absorbs the loss when vendors do not adjust their prices to reflect payer activity.

- *Employers and plan sponsors*, when decreasing plan coverage, increase their business margins. Remember, healthcare plans are a cost of doing business. From the employer perspective, hiring an older employee or an employee with a chronic condition becomes a major liability. Employers respond to the payer offerings by changing their benefits plans, increasing employee contributions, mandating that employees participate in wellness activities before accessing certain healthcare services, and requiring employees' financial participation.

We have created a market of insulation. Consumer independence cannot exist in this marketplace. The patient is insulated from monetary decisions and clinical decisions. The provider is insulated from the payer and employer contractual arrangements. The employer is insulated from the payer and the provider contractual arrangements. All parties that use vendor support roles are typically insulated from the other parties' contractual arrangements. In healthcare, fraud, audits, and internal controls are about getting past this insulation. It is one of the barriers toward effective tools for prevention, detection, and investigation.

Terminology shifts have occurred in response to all of this activity. Physicians are categorized as *providers* and *producers*. Patients are *customers*. Medical services are noted as *profit* or *revenue centers*. Excessive income is now *profit*. Cost shifting is occurring among all HCC players. Mandating employer coverage will continue to generate cost-shifting behaviors.

This model is not seen in any other country. One consequence, a full discussion of which lies outside the scope of this book, concerns today's global economy. U.S. employers, if mandated to continue the goal from the 1960s to fill the gap of the uninsured, will be compromised when competing against non-U.S. companies, which do not have this growing overhead expenditure. The cycle of unwanted consequences will continue.

MARKET OVERVIEW: IMPLICATIONS FOR PREVENTION, DETECTION, AND INVESTIGATION

"The great enemy of the truth is very often not the lie—deliberate, contrived and dishonest—but the myth—persistent, persuasive, and unrealistic." If the U.S. market is going to make a serious dent in healthcare expenditures, it will involve a discussion that employer-linked healthcare is not working and is detrimental to U.S. employers in a global economy. The market is currently discussing the concept of price transparency. Unfortunately, it is mostly limited to the insulation between the patient and the provider. Price transparency is truly about removing all insulation. Any mandates imposed on the provider should also be imposed on the relationship between the payer and the employer and all parties identified within the HCC.

It is interesting to read articles written from the payer perspective that blame cost shifting on the government programs. The private-payer market existed prior to the implementation of Medicare. Its birth was driven by the people shift of noncovered, high-risk individuals by the private sector. In an attempt to control prices, Medicare placed price caps. These price caps drove the shifting of costs back to the private-payer market. The private-payer market shifted back to the employer market. The employer market shifted back to its employees. The question now is: to whom does the employee or the patient shift back? The implication for prevention, detection, and investigation is to stay on top of the current shift and incentives for profit. Without these opportunities, waste, fraud, and abuse will continue.

On a final note, who wins in all of this havoc? Earlier chapters discuss the increased activities of organized crime entities. Remember, regardless of laws, compliance requirements, and other market-imposed mandates, rules do not exist in the organized crime world. The legitimate players may avoid price transparency and other initiatives, such as making healthcare an all-electronic environment, and pursue goals of "interoperability" because it will expose the profit margin activity. However, in the mix of confusion and insulation, it is the organized crime entities that have the greatest number of opportunities to perpetuate schemes and go undetected.

Earlier in this book, reference was made to studies by the Association of Certified Fraud Examiners that the average life of a fraud scheme is 18 months. However, in healthcare, criminals can perpetuate their schemes for decades without detection. This can occur because we are insulated, fragmented, and segmented. We have price conflicts and profit incentive conflicts that directly oppose each other. All of this can occur within the execution of every healthcare episode. In terms of volume, we are talking about a trillion-dollar market. This trillion-dollar market has many "masters" driving politics. These include all the members within the HCC and their respective lobbyists advocating for their positions. The positions that are most often advocated, unfortunately, directly conflict with how one HCC player profits or controls costs in comparison with another player.

Conclusions

If your actions inspire others to dream more, learn more, do more, and become more, you are a leader.

— JOHN QUINCY ADAMS

MICROMANAGEMENT PERSPECTIVE

My personal goal in writing this guidebook is to provide interim evolving tools that will move with the market. The key is to identify the truth. As ancient Roman historian Livy notes, "The truth is often eclipsed but never extinguished." This audit guidebook is about seeing the truth among a set of events. In preparing for the final chapters of this book and pulling myself out of the box of details that went into writing it, I sent out a simple survey question: "If you could pick one thing wrong (a gut response) with the healthcare system from your experiences, regardless whether as a professional, patient, employee, employer, or observer, what would that be?" A variety of individuals received this question, including stay-at-home parents, lawyers, accountants, programmers, auditors, writers, researchers, and healthcare professionals. View their statements as symptoms of problems discussed throughout this book. Their responses define fragmentation, segmentation, and market conflicts. Their responses speak for themselves:

As a Healthcare Professional/Employee/Observer:

"Oh, and in addition to the compensation issue by payers driving down Dr. Quality are the gatekeeper receptionists that make it difficult to get your questions answered."

"My first take is the shift from the doctor as professional care giver and counselor to a piece worker on an assembly line. We can have all the technology in the world, but if business takes the patient and turns him or her into a commodity to be moved down the process line, then neither the doctor nor the patient will be satisfied with the result."

"We have more and more technology and yet medical errors continue to increase. Why? Because of the constant move to 'outsource' the profession. History is taken by a clerk; we have pharmacist 'assistants' whose training consists of learning how to run the drive-up window; blood work is being processed by someone whose last job was 'fry master'; the medical profession is no longer a profession. Can a country legislate care? I fear anything the government touches; however, strict licensing and education requirements should help. Increase medical grant and scholarship money so that doctors aren't on the verge of bankruptcy when they get out of med school. Stop the industrialization of medicine, which to me is the biggest concern."

"The first thing I thought of was . . . insurance companies are running the show. They tell the medical professionals what they are able to order for their patients, how long a person should be sick, and how much they will pay. Wow—what will it be like in the future?"

"I've seen services held with HMO insurance plans. Providing 'too many services' could mean the physician's monthly payment from the insurance company would decrease his or her monthly earning potential. I previously worked for a fertility practice that accepted an HMO plan. Initially it was a fee-for-service contract. Unnecessary blood tests were being ordered in excess. Once that contract went to a capitation plan, those patients received less-than-par care. Their charts were flagged a specific color in order to alert the staff. HMO patients were then only able to attempt treatments every other month as a means to keep costs down (although it was explained much differently to the patients). Medications were dispensed through the office to the

HMO patients, and they were put on very conservative doses. Monitoring became minimal. However, patients who were 'self-pay' or who had insurance coverage for these services were many times taken to a more aggressive treatment, sometimes unnecessarily. I've seen a lower quality of care with patients who had PPO plans as well. Physicians who contracted with some of these plans would be reimbursed less than the cost of the test to the physician (i.e., a blood test is sent to a reference laboratory . . . the lab charges the physician $30, but the insurance company will only reimburse the physician $18). The physicians could actually lose money. Some practices will only accept a certain amount of patients from a specific type of insurance or plan. A patient finds a physician (through their insurance carrier) in their area and on staff at a desired hospital. When they attempt to schedule an appointment, they are told that the physician is no longer taking new patients (from that plan). Some patients end up having to see any physician who will give them an appointment. Sometimes this means a less experienced physician (or let's be honest . . . one that maybe sucks). Physicians with lucrative practices don't have to deal with these insurance plans if they choose not to. Sometimes patients with HMO/PPO plans have to wait longer for an appointment than those without them."

"That what kind of insurance you have—how much and what company you are insured with—has a large determination on what kind of care you receive. It would be nice if there were more patient advocate people who knew how the healthcare system worked to help you through the ins and outs of the system—and how you would get access to these advocate-type people."

"No question about it, patient education is lacking."

"Pricing for health insurance shouldn't be pooled and assessed, but should be determined by the health of the individuals being covered. Every other type of insurance is based on inherent factors specific to the insured (i.e., car—type, age, condition, number of claims, driver history, etc.)."

"Recently, my biggest frustration in my field is the rush to get patients through the office, the surgical center, etc., as quickly as possible. This disallows for good solid education of the patient. It also hinders them from seeking further information if needed because the patient does feel rushed by the staff. They sense it. If we do not slow down to gather all the information that we need to care for the patient adequately and answer the patient's questions adequately by listening to what they are saying, not only verbally but also nonverbally, mistakes are more likely to occur. Mistakes mean lawsuits. Lawsuits mean more money being spent by physicians, insurance companies, other providers such as hospitals, drug companies, etc. All of this has a snowball effect on the rest of the community: bankruptcy, loss of jobs, physicians leaving the area, etc."

As an Employer:

"I know as an employer that I am funding the profits of many third parties such as the insurance company, and paying for waste in the system, and paying for those who short change the process by not paying their fair share."

"My gut response tells me that doctors are not motivated to spend more time with their patients. They don't listen and they don't diagnose, generally, unless you find a good one. It's easy to find someone to write you a prescription but hard to find someone who is a good diagnostician."

"No clear understanding of the billing. No standardization health insurance versus doctors' offices."

"I think there's a need for continuous, accurate, high-quality *scientifically based* education, beginning with toddlers, to foster development of positive attitudes and practices of the populace toward preventative healthcare practices, along with safety and personal responsibility for maintenance of good health. This must be coupled with medical tort reform."

"I do not trust the healthcare system if a loved one is in the hospital. I feel the need to be there to oversee everything, that is, to be the patient advocate."

"My first gut response is the variance of quality of care one receives depending on the type of health insurance one carries and/or with those in a higher vs. lower income bracket."

"First, the obvious thing that comes to mind is cost. I can give you feedback as a person who was involved in a company closing and left with the decision on what to do for healthcare. The unemployed person is faced with the dilemma of COBRA, which for a husband and wife is about $1,100 per month. How would you pay $1,100 per month for insurance when your unemployment pay just about covers that? Do you go without insurance? That would be disastrous. The second issue that comes to mind is the prices that are charged by physicians/facilities for procedures. I understand that there are huge liability insurances that each of these need to carry, but when the balance of the charges are expected to be paid by the patient, that adds an additional burden to their already stressful situation of being ill."

"It is the constant increase in the cost of all services."

As a Patient:

"When my husband was in between jobs, my pediatrician encouraged us to put the kids on 'KidCare.' Then we discovered that the whole family could be on the plan as well. I was thrilled that my kids were still able to see their pediatrician. Then I found out much later that she didn't accept KidCare, but just saw my kids as a courtesy. My choices on the KidCare plan would not have been very good. Luckily none of us ever got really sick, and didn't really require a lot of medical care. My daughter needed to be evaluated for ADD while we had KidCare. We had only a few choices, and ended up going to a specialty doctor in our area. My son, who is in Kindergarten, was in the early childhood education program (ECE) for three years through the school district. He had an individual education program (IEP), which I finally agreed to sign off on prior to Kindergarten. Now that he will be going into first grade this fall, I think he would benefit from further evaluation since he was starting to show signs of struggling. In order for me to get the ball rolling, I felt my best strategy was to get an independent evaluation. A friend who is very active with this insisted that I see 'the guru' of the (auditory processing) field. It took months to get an appointment. She will not bill your insurance, because she doesn't have to and she is in demand. At the time of your appointment, you need to pay her $500. You can submit this bill yourself to the insurance company, and hope they will pay something. If you were in a low-income bracket, and/or with an insurance plan that would not cover a service such as this, you may not be able to get the same quality of care as someone who does have the financial means and/or insurance coverage."

"I guess my opinion is just from a patient point of view. Does insurance fit in here? I think it is just *so-oo-oo* hard to deal with insurance companies and all their forms and restrictions."

"Knowing what is covered by your insurance. The books are unclear and when you call you can't trust the person answering the questions at the insurance company. Often they tell you that something is covered, or not covered, by your insurance policy and then they are wrong. If they tell you that it is covered and then the doctor's bill is submitted and it wasn't really supposed to be covered, you receive a big doctor's bill."

"Speaking from my own personal experience as a person receiving a positive diagnosis for a life-threatening disease, I feel the system makes it very difficult for an individual to get the proper doctor for treatment. I had to become my own advocate and call every possible doctor recommended to me via friends, acquaintances, and business associates. Often it took me several attempts before I would get a call back. Then, typically, I had to wait three weeks before I could even get in to see the doctor. While all this was going on, my already insanely scared self became even more nuts as my time kept ticking away."

"My concern is the inherent ability of the insurance companies to control not only the quality of the care obtained, but the availability of same. I think the greatest threat to this country at this time is the question of availability of proper healthcare . . . and no one seems to be doing anything about it."

"As a patient, the wait time is too long—1 1/2 hours to see a doctor is a bit much. I had this experience only yesterday. Second, don't advertise your expertise if you lack the ability to provide information."

"In this day and age of sharing of information, why do patients have to fill out similar forms with every referral to every physician, including information that can increase the risk of identity theft (SSN and DOB)? For example, I had major surgery on my neck a few years back, and the process required me to go to many doctors and have multiple MRIs and CT scans, etc. Almost every time I had to complete a form about my allergies, among other questions. Why isn't this simple information shared and accessible in a secured manner from my primary care records?"

"From a patient/consumer perspective, it is the cost factor. As a professional, I am concerned about access and quality of care."

"I think it would be the indifference to the patient as a living, breathing, feeling, and most importantly *thinking* human being who is not inferior just because they don't have medical training. I hate that doctors will dismiss a mother's assessment of her child's health, or push aside a daughter who is the primary caretaker and can give important information on the patient, and most importantly try to override a person's concerns or hesitation about a treatment. The examples are numerous whether in a doctor's office for a checkup or follow-up or in the hospital. Doctors and other medical personnel do not see the patient as a person, only as a disease or a number."

"The large numbers of uninsured or underinsured Americans; I'm sure the causes are more complex than some believe, but the result is unconscionable."

"The fact that the HMO/PPO puts the patient and doctor in an adversarial role; doctors are given an incentive to cut corners and deny care."

"Insurance . . . eligibility. . . payment, nonpayment . . . the whole mess of who has insurance . . . who remains uninsured . . . How does it really work and does the hospital really get reimbursed? . . . Get the drift?"

"There is never a face or a person that you can converse with regarding a coverage issue. My insurance company has not paid medical bills from a visit at the Emergency Room in September of 2006. I have on numerous times attempted to discuss the situation with a representative and can never get anyone who is accountable or responsible enough to make a decision let alone provide me any basis."

"In my opinion, the problem with the system is the disconnect between the patient and the provider because of the insurance buffer. In other words, there is no true free market in healthcare. The consumer (patient) has no input because he or she does not pay directly to the provider. The payment is through a third party (insurance). Imagine how things would be if third parties paid for all of the goods and services we use on a daily basis—gasoline, food, clothing, etc."

The diagnosis is a Tower of Babel. This list of comments reflects an overall lack of trust in the system and the process. Each one of these comments can be traced back to a pipeline within this book.

MACROMANAGEMENT PERSPECTIVE

Imagine indeed what would happen if third parties were utilized for the payment of goods and services. In my travels, I stopped at my local grocery store. I asked the general manager whether, if I did not have the money to pay, he would still let me leave with my groceries. He looked around first, leaned over, and quietly told me, "Ah, well, no." I followed up with, "What if I decided to leave the grocery store with my basket of items because I had no money to pay regardless? Then what?" Again, the quiet look around, with "Ah, well, I would have to call *the authorities*."

Obviously we could not pursue that routine at my local warehouse store. They have major precertification at the door. One cannot even walk into the warehouse without a membership card. They even have tiered cards for special members who have greater access levels based on status. They have such a high opinion of their customers that they provide a checkpoint at the exit door to review the items in your cart in comparison to your receipt, just in case a few extra items slipped in. Imagine the media fodder with that type of checkpoint at your local hospital.

A similar attempt at my local high-end retail store resulted only in a raised eyebrow glare with a gradual movement of the hand below the counter as I suggested that I would keep the merchandise without payment. What is the point? What other commercial industry exists in which we expect employees to provide a service without compensation or at a loss? What other industry exists in which the consumer expects to receive services without payment?

What would happen in the marketplace if our educational system depended on an employer-link-based system for its budget? Imagine a plan sponsor contracting with a TPA education center that supplied certain educational subjects based on the risk level. Students who had preexisting academic deficiencies would be denied coverage for any supplemental educational instruction. Individuals who were deemed cognitively defective would be cast away because they might use too many resources. I asked my 16-year-old how she would feel if she was told that she did not meet the grade mark and therefore could no longer receive an education. Her response: "Well, that would not be fair. Why should I not have the same chance as everyone else to get a good education? Why should my life be limited over someone else?" The same questions could be and often are applied to healthcare. Why should my life be limited over someone else when it comes to access and preservation of my personal health?

Overview of Prevention, Detection, and Investigation

Providing logical solutions to complex problems is a novel concept that deserves our constant effort. It requires the political honesty and transparency that the market is fighting like the plague. Waste, fraud, and abuse in the healthcare market are unlike that in any other industry. How many consumers do you know who walk into a used car dealership with their guard up? How many walk into the emergency room with a loved one with their guard up? When fraud, waste, or abuse occurs in healthcare, the damage goes beyond the financial theft and greed. It becomes a personal assault on an individual, physically and emotionally.

The previously discussed healthcare continuum (HCC) is noted in Exhibit 18.1. Potential contracts are demonstrated in this exhibit. A healthcare episode moving through this continuum can be easily impacted by up to nine contractual obligations. That is nine incentives for profit, nine different business operations, nine opportunities for manipulation, and nine layers of insulation. Of course, the final player, organized crime, is waiting below to tap into any one of these routes to perpetuate a scheme.

If I were to pick one thing to change, it would be to make all the dotted line arrows transparent. I believe that path would create an environment in which a healthcare episode could become a unified process. This would require interoperability throughout the HCC. The high-volume market would require its operation to be purely in electronic form to effectively process the data. In turn, this would allow for effective audit, detection, and investigation specifically for healthcare fraud, waste, and abuse, and it would make it easier

Health Care Continuum (HCC): Follow the $ and PHI

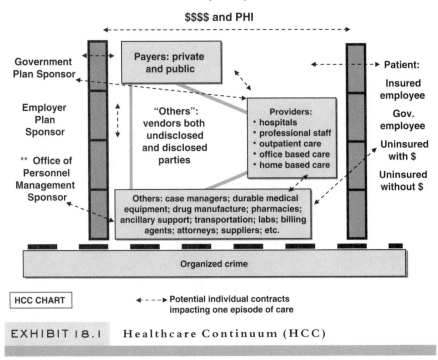

EXHIBIT 18.1   Healthcare Continuum (HCC)

Source: Medical Business Associates, Inc. (www.mbanews.com).

to ferret out escalating organized crime activity. How much more of healthcare can we split into fractions, financially, clinically, and now anatomically?

My change would require an act of Congress. However, whose lobby efforts would win? Each player in the HCC has its own political agenda. The HCC players are focused and functioning at a microscopic level. A macro perspective requires the acknowledgment that certain market-specific activities have an adverse affect on other components. Will the private payers give up their profits? Will employers tolerate weakening status in a global economy by being the providers of nationalized insurance when their international counterparts do not have this burden? Will the government continued to subsidize the outcast of high-risk individuals and excluded body parts? Will the Hippocratic Oath taken by the medical profession be lost in the new world of medicine and new terminology? Will the consumer tolerate the ambiguity or direct neglect of a loved one?

The Department of Health, Education, and Welfare (HEW) officially came into existence on April 11, 1953, during President Eisenhower's administration. In 1979, the Department of Education Organization Act provided for a separate Department of Education. On May 4, 1980, HEW became the Department of Health and Human Services (HHS). HEW developments after this time period included the following:

1980: Federal funding is provided to states for foster care and adoption assistance.

1981: AIDS is identified.

1984: National Organ Transplantation Act signed into law. HIV is identified by PHS and French scientists.

1985: Blood test to detect HIV is licensed.

1988: JOBS program is created, along with federal support for child care. McKinney Act is passed to provide healthcare to the homeless.

1989: Agency for Health Care Policy and Research (now the Agency for Healthcare Research and Quality) is created.

1990: Human Genome Project is established. Nutrition Labeling and Education Act is passed, authorizing food labels. The Ryan White Comprehensive AIDS Resource Emergency (CARE) Act begins providing support for people with AIDS.

1993: Vaccines for Children Program is established, providing free immunizations to all children in low-income families.

1995: Social Security Administration becomes an independent agency.

1996: Welfare reform is enacted under the Personal Responsibility and Work Opportunity Reconciliation Act. Health Insurance Portability and Accountability Act (HIPAA) is enacted.

1997: State Children's Health Insurance Program (SCHIP) is created, enabling states to extend health coverage to more uninsured children.

1999: Ticket to Work and Work Incentives Improvement Act of 1999 is signed, making it possible for millions of Americans with disabilities to join the workforce without fear of losing their Medicaid and Medicare coverage. The act also modernizes the employment services system for people with disabilities. Initiative on combating bioterrorism is launched.

2000: Human genome sequencing is published.

2001: Centers for Medicare and Medicaid is created, replacing the Health Care Financing Administration. HHS responds to the nation's first bioterrorism attack, a delivery of anthrax through the mail.

2002: Office of Public Health Emergency Preparedness is created to coordinate efforts against bioterrorism and other emergency health threats.

2003: Medicare Prescription Drug Improvement and Modernization Act of 2003 is enacted, the most significant expansion of Medicare since its enactment, including a prescription drug benefit.

At the top of the HHS website is the statement, "improving the health and well-being of America." The above items are doing just that. By comparison, the U.S. Department of Education evolved during the same time period as the healthcare market. Modern education was impacted by the same political issues—the Great Depression, World War II, and other socioeconomic issues. The Department of Education's mission statement is "to ensure equal access to education and to promote educational excellence throughout the nation." It has a focus on access; healthcare does not.

The advancement of education occurred as a social issue. The advancement of healthcare with respect to access occurred as a commercial market and as a private employer offering. The social advancement of healthcare evolved in the form of technology and research. Although the Department of Health, Education, and Welfare was created in 1953, historically the social aspect was on the improvement of health, welfare, and funding research. It was not on the financing of healthcare delivery. Education, from its inception, included funding and access as key components. Unlike healthcare, the public and private entities for education are separated. In healthcare, the public and private entities are intermingled.

My final question is this: What is the most effective route to controlling waste, fraud, and abuse while we ensure equal access to healthcare and promote clinical excellence throughout the nation? Until that question can be answered, I hope this guidebook assists you in deciphering the Tower of Babel that we have created in our market.

Index